FROM HOME TO HOME

:~

FROM HOME TO HOME

AUTUMN WANDERINGS IN THE NORTH-WEST, 1881–1884

A.S. (Alexander Staveley) Hill

VICTORIA · VANCOUVER · CALGARY

Heritage House Publishing Company Ltd.
#108 – 17665 66A Avenue
Surrey, BC V3S 2A7
www.heritagehouse.ca

Heritage House Publishing Company Ltd.
PO Box 468
Custer, WA
98240-0468

Library and Archives Canada Cataloguing in Publication
Hill, Alexander Staveley, 1825–1905.
     From home to home: autumn wanderings in the North-West, 1881-1884 / by A.S. Hill. — 1st Heritage House ed.

ISBN 978-1-894974-56-1
     1. Hill, Alexander Staveley, 1825-1905—Travel—Northwest, Canadian.
2. Northwest, Canadian—Description and travel. 3. Northwest, Canadian—
Social life and customs. I. Title.

FC3205.2.H54 2008   917.1204'2   C2008-905395-8

Library of Congress Control Number: 2008930360

Proofread by Alexandra Wilson
Cover design Stacey Noyes/LuzForm Design
Cover photo Glenbow Archives NA-234-9

Printed in Canada

Heritage House acknowledges the financial support for its publishing program from the Government of Canada through the Book Publishing Industry Development Program (BPIDP), Canada Council for the Arts, and the province of British Columbia through the British Columbia Arts Council and the Book Publishing Tax Credit.

The Canada Council | Le Conseil des Arts
for the Arts | du Canada

BRITISH COLUMBIA
ARTS COUNCIL
Supported by the Province of British Columbia

This book has been produced on 100% post-consumer paper, processed chlorine free and printed with vegetable-based inks.

CONTENTS

:~

Chapter I

~

From Home to Home—from my old home of Oxley Manor in Stafford-shire to the new Oxley in the foothills of the Rocky Mountains—it seemed at first a long step, a great migration; but distance really lies in the completeness of the separation, and this completeness of separation each year diminishes or destroys.

Few things bring more completely before the mind the progress of travel than to compare the narratives of vacation tours. In my earlier days Serjeant Allen's *Sportsman in Ireland* seemed to have sufficiently limited the capabilities of a long vacation to days spent in exploring and enjoy-ing our Western coasts. Some years later, Serjeant Talfourd's *Vacation Rambles* showed that a busy lawyer might then arrive at experiences of Swiss heights and German tables d'hôte. Later still, Mr. Kinglake's *Eothen* showed that advancing opportunities of transit had brought within reach the historic charms of Palestine and the sands of the desert, and if I now have in the following narrative of these long vacations illustrated the en-croachment of my professional holiday into lands even more distant than those explored by my learned predecessors, I have still left open to the enjoyer of whatever of long vacations may be left to us by enterprising Home Secretaries journeys to which M. Jules Verne may contribute the itinerary, and a long vacation may carry round the world some lawyer whose view of travel is rather comprehensive than microscopic. My tale is of some things that have been told, but also of much in which the trail of any preceding traveller was but faintly marked, if traceable at all. It is of a land of which the new life is but just breaking for mankind, a land of many hopes and much promise; a land where if the toil of life be boldly faced, its responsibilities manfully taken up, and its duties faithfully discharged, the search after the new home will, I doubt not, be found amply to reward even those who turn at first with the deepest regret from the old one left behind, indeed, but in no way deserted or forgotten. But we must not talk of that which is left behind; nowhere more than in the North-West is the bidding of the Master fraught with deep meaning, that he who has put his hand to the plough may not look back. Our ploughman has a long furrow before him; let him stick to it, it will lengthen every season, and will bring with its increasing length an increased source of wealth and comfort.

When I first made up my mind to spend a long vacation in Canada, I was anxious to rub up my memory as to its historical incidents; to learn of its cities and towns, what there was to see in them; of its country, what of its physical conformation, its flora and fauna; of its government, what of its powers, and the respective merits of its public parties, and the weight and influence they carried in their Dominion Parliament—to hear from those who had lately visited Canada, what I should be able to see with the most pleasure to myself, and chiefly, above all, how I could see and learn the truth of this wonderful North-West that had so long lain hidden from the world, and of the capabilities of which we then began to hear so much.

I found, however, that even with the kindest and best informed of friends there was considerable difficulty in obtaining answers to these questions. I have endeavoured therefore to put together in the following pages, as accompanying the narrative of my journeyings, information without which a visit to the country would lose much of its enjoyment. Many of those who may pick up this book have perhaps known long ago much that they may here find of these details; it is not for them that this part has been written, but they, perhaps even more than others, will appreciate the personal details of the scenes which I describe in the incidents of the autumns of 1881, 1882, 1883, and 1884.

The country which we speak of now as the Dominion of Canada, embraces all that part of America lying to the north of the United States, and bounded by the Atlantic, Pacific, and Arctic Oceans, with the exception of

Alaska. From East to West, from Belle Isle to Vancouver, from the 53rd to the 141st meridian, it is about 3,400 miles; and in latitude, from its most southerly point to the Arctic Ocean, from the 49th parallel at its least southerly boundary, or from the 44th at the most southerly promontory of its peninsula on Lake Erie, to the 70th parallel it is about 2,000 miles. The superficial area of Canada is about three and a half millions of square miles. It is a country of larger extent than the whole of Europe, and one of its landlocked seas, Hudson Bay, equals in extent half the Mediterranean, while the vestibule of its eastern frontier—the Gulf of St. Lawrence—covers a larger area by far than the historic Euxine.

It is, however, only of late years that we have been accustomed to speak of this great space on the earth's surface as Canada. That which till lately we designated by this name was the eastern part of the Dominion, including therein what are now the provinces of Quebec, Ontario, New Brunswick, Nova Scotia, and Prince Edward Island; but more especially it was to the two first of these provinces that we usually referred when we spoke of Canada. One of the old historians somewhat picturesquely describes the discovery of America in these words. "Christopher Colon did first light upon this land in the year 1492," and most people remember how that more than a year of years ago, on the Midsummer day of 1497, Sebastian Cabot, sailing in search of new countries under a patent of our Henry VII, "did first light upon" Newfoundland, and named that which is still the capital of the island after the Saint on whose feast day he then first sighted its southeastern shores. But it is scarcely necessary to go back further than the year 1534, when Jacques Cartier, whose statue adorns alike the squares of his native town of St. Malo and of Montreal, sailing under a commission from the French king, entered the Gulf of St. Lawrence through the Straits of Belle Isle, and taking a southwesterly course discovered the mainland of Canada, which he claimed for France by erecting a wooden cross with the inscription "Vive le Roy de France." In the year following, 1535, Cartier sailed up the St. Lawrence as far as the Isle of Orleans, which from the abundance of its wild grapes he christened "Isle of Bacchus," and crossing the basin anchored on the 14th of September in the St. Croix, as he called the smaller river, which here runs into the St. Lawrence, and which is now called St. Charles, opposite the Indian village of Stadacona, the site of the present city of Quebec. The magnificent rock "Cape Diamond," at whose foot the river flows, facing the bold cliff of Point Levis on its southern bank, forming as it were the gateway of a new land, could not fail to attract the attention of the adventurers and excite their enthusiasm. Entering into friendly relations with the Indian chief, Donaconna, Cartier laid up his 10 large ships in the St. Croix, and having been told by the Indians of a larger town up the river, he took his boats up through St. Peter's Lake, as this wide reach of the river is called, to Hochelaga, and explored the higher waters as far as the rapids above mentioned, which seemed to bar the further passage of vessels from the sea. The close of the year brought, however, before the explorers the reverse side of the medal. Winter set in with a rigour which the Frenchmen could scarcely have anticipated. Frost and scurvy did their work. Singing of penitential psalms, and vows and promises of pilgrimages availed not, and at last there was not one man left who could go into the hold to draw water for the others; Indian medicines, however, helped when all their devotions seemed of scant service, and on April 18th the ice gave way, and the French captain, taking with him the Indian chief, sailed back for France. Cartier's account of the fertility of the soil and the value of the products of the country may be read with much interest by anyone who will turn to the pages of Hackluyt. He failed, however, to discover any precious metals, the buried treasure which was considered the only thing which could give a real value to distant lands, and the absence of which caused the older Spaniards to pun on the native name, by saying the country was truly a Canada, "Aca nada"—here is nothing. An explorer who could not find in his new land the precious metals might possibly make a good pilot, but was not deemed to deserve the support of his Government, and so Jacques Cartier had to serve in that lower capacity in the expedition sent out under Mons. de Roberval in 1540, under a commission as Viceroy, to discover a North-West passage to the East Indies. Poor De Roberval frequently returned to France for new recruits, and met at last the fate of many a bold adventurer and servant of his country. He sailed from France on a fresh expedition in 1549, but of his fate the depths of the ocean or of the wild forest keep still the secret, and no tidings of him ever reached his country or those whom lie left behind.

During the 50 years that followed, the few settlers that were left dragged on a disregarded existence. At length Henry IV of France appointed the Marquis de la Roche Lieutenant General of Canada. He sailed from France in 1598, first attempting a settlement in the island of Sables. He then cruised for some time off the coast of Nova Scotia, returned home in disgrace and died of grief.

At length that which Royal Commissions had failed to bring about was accomplished by the enterprise of trade. Pont Grave, an experienced captain of St. Malo, who had distinguished himself by making several profitable fur voyages to Tadoussac, where the Saguenai runs into the St. Lawrence, engaged as his associate Mons. Chauvin, a naval officer, who obtained from Henry IV in 1600 a commission under which, forming themselves into a company, they carried out some very successful voyages, obtaining a great many excellent furs from the Indians in return for what we should probably in the present day designate as some very rubbishy articles de Paris.

After the death of Chauvin in 1603, a company of merchants was formed at Rouen, under the presidency of the commander De Chaste, Governor of Dieppe, and a large number of ships sailed under Pont Grave, associated with whom was a naval officer of great enterprise and ability, whose history and exploits form so interesting a part of early Canadian history.

Samuel Champlain had been attached to the court of Henri IV, and obtaining permission from him to join the Dieppe company, sailed with his comrades on March 15th, 1603, and they moored in the St. Lawrence on May 24th. The captain took his boats up as far as Sault St. Louis, and proceeded to examine its shores and the country lying to the south of the great river. He returned to France, and published in 1603 an account of his travels under the title of 'Des Sauvages, ou Voyage de Samuel Champlain,' and revisiting Canada he made further explorations, and passing southwards gave his name to the beautiful lake with which it has ever since, and ever will be associated. He at first took up Tadoussac, at the mouth of the Saguenai, as a trading station, but subsequently selected the far more commanding site at the mouth of the St. Charles, and there he laid the foundation of a city to which, keeping to the Indian word, which indicated the narrowing of the river, he gave the name of Quebec, and designated it capital of New France. Champlain wrote very clear accounts of his journeys, especially his attempt in passing up the river of the Outa-ouais to discover the North-West passage by striking upon the bay which Hudson had just discovered. In his second expedition up that river he turned off to the western shore of Lake Hudson and then south to Lake Ontario, where he made an alliance with the Hurons, and assisted them in their attacks upon the Iroquois, an alliance which New France had much cause afterwards to deplore. A complete edition of Champlain's Voyage was published in Paris in the year 1640.

It was during Champlain's governorship that Quebec, in 1629, first surrendered to the English under David Kirk; it was ceded again to France, however, by the treaty in the year following, and remained under French rule for another 30 years.

The long series of troubles between the French and the Indians began, as I have said, by the alliance that was made by Champlain with the Hurons and the Algonquins against the Iroquois. These Algonquins, whose descendants are well known to us as the Crees, and who at that time possessed the whole tract of country on the north shores of the St. Lawrence, from the Saguenai to the Lake Nipissing, had given refuge and assistance to the Hurons, known perhaps more correctly as the Tiormoritatis or Adirondacks. These bands had been driven from their territory on the west shore of Lake Huron by the five nations, consisting of the Mohawks, the Senecas, or Tsonnontouans, the Onnontagues, the Oneidas, and the Cayugas. These five tribes, afterwards joined by the Tuscaroras, became famous in American history as "The Six Nations," and were classed by the French under the common name of Iroquois. They violently resented the assistance given by the French to their enemies, the Algonquins and the Hurons. Many were the attacks made by them on the French colonists, and even to this day the marks of their tomahawks may be seen on the stairs of the Ursuline convent at Quebec. During the whole of that century the colonists were never free from alarms, and were frequently in hazard of total extermination; the province of New France had become almost as much a missionary station as a commercial settlement, a very general zeal for the Christian instruction of Indians was excited throughout the old country, and many individuals of rank and property devoted their lives and fortunes to the cause, and the great missionary body of the

Society of Jesus, the inner circle of the Catholic religion, were the leaders of, and finally took the direction of, this undertaking. In considering the work of the Jesuits it may indeed be questioned whether their contentions with the Governors and their want of toleration of other religions were not to some extent instrumental in preventing the advance of the colony; but the great piety, the high intellectual powers, the undaunted zeal, the unceasing perseverance, the entire forgetfulness of self, the patient endurance of hardship and heroic suffering, terminating often in death amidst the most excruciating tortures, raised among the wildest savages who prized above all things the ability to endure pain unmoved, a reverential respect for the Christians, and for the Christian God.

The history of the Jesuits has been well told by Mr. Parkman in his extracts from the volumes of reports which they regularly transmitted to their parent bodies in Paris and in Rome. Of the extreme accuracy with which these reports were made out, I may give an interesting illustration.

When I was at Quebec in the autumn of 1883 I had driven over to the house of my friend Mr. Dobell to see the beauties of the neighbourhood of Quebec, and wandering with him through his grounds, down the hill toward his big timber wharves and booms on the St. Lawrence at Silleri, I saw the monument which he and the village had erected to Masse, one of the earliest Jesuit missionaries, who died in 1646. My host told me an interesting history of the foundation of this mission and of the thriving Huron colony which the Jesuits had gathered round them at this place, and which continued to thrive till, after the death of Masse, the Iroquois came down from the lakes and massacred every one of them, and the whole colony was wiped out.

A few years ago two Jesuits came over from Paris, and brought with them from their archives a plan of the chapel, and the place where Masse was buried, extracted from the reports which the Mission had sent home; they indicated the spot where beneath the piles of timber would be found the foundations of the chapel, and where the body of Masse was buried, with his feet to the east. The timbers were removed, and the two Jesuits entering into the labour with vigour, removing soil and rubbish, laid bare the footings of the walls of the little chapel, enclosing a space some 30 feet by 12, and digging down for a few feet came upon the uncoffined bones of a man of about 6 feet 3 inches in height, exactly on the spot where their plan showed that the body of the missionary had been laid. They claimed the ground and wanted to remove the bones to the neighbouring chapel. Mr. Dobell insisted, however, on the propriety of the body remaining where it had been originally placed. The village backed him up in his views, and so they referred the matter to the Archbishop, who decided that the body should remain in its first grave, Mr. Dobell offering to give up the site of the little chapel. They put up a fence round the spot, cleared away the remainder of the soil, so as to leave the foundation of the chapel visible, and erected a plain obelisk—a monument—to the earnest missionary, the accuracy of whose reports of his labours had been so authenticated in these particulars, at least, of the reports sent home by those who followed him. Much, undoubtedly, may with truth be urged against the Jesuits and their Indian proselytes in comparing their colonial progress with that of the Protestants in New England. These last have indeed shown more energy and vigour; but the French *habitans* and the Catholic half-breeds of the Canada of the present day illustrate the power of their religion to produce a moral, happy, loyal, and law-abiding people.

Notwithstanding, however, the energy of Champlain and those who followed him, either from the cause I have mentioned, or from a national inaptitude for colonization, no progress attended the French colony; and at the close of half a century from the date of the foundation of Quebec, the sparse population along the river extending to Montreal only amounted to 2,000, and of those the city of Quebec contained nearly the half.

An attempt was made under Louis XIV, by the nomination of a special sovereign council of the city of Quebec, to give further vitality to the colony, and an amount of immigration was carried on for some time, and success might even then have attended the efforts, had it not been for the fatal error in the determination to rule Canada according to the principles of the old French Monarchy. This form of government culminated under Governor Bigot; and to him it has been truly said that, more than to any other man, France owes the loss of her share of the New World. While he himself lived in luxury, the *habitans* were plundered, and reduced to the condition of impoverished serfdom; and while they, under their religious guides, lived lives of abstemious morality, the French seigneurs revelled in dissipation.

It was during this time that Laval, as Bishop of Quebec, carried to its highest point the glory of the Church in this country, establishing seminaries and improving and beautifying the ecclesiastical edifices, and his name still lives in the Universities whose buildings attract the eye on the first approach to Quebec. But the end of the French Government approached. In 1759 Montcalm was Governor of Canada. In England it had been practically resolved that "our northern colonies justly looked upon the expulsion of the French out of the northern continent of America as their only security." And in February, 1758, Montcalm, in appealing to the Minister of France, said: "New France needs peace, or sooner or later it must fall, such are the numbers of the English, such the difficulty of our receiving supplies,"—provisions were very scarce. "The famine," he said, "is very great." On our side Pitt, the earnest lover of liberty, the great supporter of free but attached colonies, determined on the expulsion of France from the Western continent. Lord Howe and James Wolfe were chosen for the command of this great enterprise. It is with the latter of these two that we are now concerned.

General James Wolfe had served at Dettingen, Fontenoy and Laffeldt. He was 31 years of age, and the youngest General in the British Army, and had returned to England in 1758 after the capture of Louisburg and the consequent acquisition by the English of Cape Breton and Prince Edward Island. He was of delicate constitution, but of so enthusiastic a temperament that he had, it is said, on the eve of his departure almost alarmed the Minister by an exhibition of his zeal. James Wolfe on the 26th of June, 1759, arrived with 8,000 men and the fleet of 22 ships of the line and as many frigates and armed vessels off the Isle of Orleans, and next day they disembarked. Amongst those on board the ships were Jervis, afterwards Earl St. Vincent, Cook, the circumnavigator, and "the brave, open hearted and liberal Robert Monckton," George Townshend and Robert Barre, the Adjutant General, with the Grenadiers, under the command of Colonel Guy Carleton. Long and anxious days intervened between that day and the early days of September, and during

9

that time every possible point of attack on the citadel was planned, but each plan was thwarted by the able and watchful eye of Montcalm and of his faithful Indian allies. Wolfe's Brigadiers had advised to convey 4,000 or 5,000 men above the town and thus draw Montcalm from his impregnable position to an open action, and acting under this opinion Wolfe applied himself intently to reconnoitring the north shore above Quebec. With a quick eye and ready of resource he discovered the narrow sentier that rises from the cove which bears his name, formed by the watercourse from the two slopes which bend together toward it, a path so narrow that two men could scarce walk up it abreast. Here then he resolved to land his army, and drawing off the attention of the French General by operations with the feigned object of an attack on St. Charles, he prepared, September 12th, for the attack on the day following. It is related that he had learned by heart Gray's Elegy, which had appeared just before he left home, and that as he visited his ships on the night before the attack, anxiously examining into and ordering each detail, he said to those in his boat, as he repeated stanza after stanza, "I would prefer being the author of that poem to beating the French to-morrow." Who can ever hear the beat of oars on the broad stream of the St. Lawrence, or watch the flash of its waters in the brilliant moonlight, without the picture rising to his mind of the enthusiastic young soldier, with every mark of a vigorous soul in strange contrast to his enfeebled frame, lighted by the brilliance of the great dawn of eternity that was so soon to break upon him as he drew the contrast of his possible future in the verse he was heard to repeat—

"The boast of heraldry, the pomp of power,
    And all that beauty, all that wealth e'er gave,
Await alike the inevitable hour.
    The paths of glory lead but to the grave."

The description of the locality and the account of the fight has been given so well in the pages of Bancroft's 'History of the American Revolution,' and will be read with so much interest by anyone visiting Quebec who may have this book with him, that I venture to extract it.

"Every officer knew his appointed duty, when, at one o'clock in the morning of the 13th September, Wolfe, with Monckton and Murray, and about half the forces, set off in boats, and, without sails or oars, glided down with the tide. In three-quarters of an hour the ships followed, and, though the night had become dark, aided by the rapid current, they reached the cove just in time to cover the landing. Wolfe and the troops with him leaped on shore; the light infantry, who found themselves borne by the current a little below the entrenched path, clambered up the steep hill, staying themselves by the roots and boughs of the maple and spruce and ash trees that covered the precipitous declivity, and, after a little firing, dispersed the picket which guarded the height. The rest ascended safely by the pathway. A battery of four guns on the left was abandoned to Colonel Howe. When Townshend's division disembarked, the English had already gained one of the roads to Quebec, and, advancing in front of the forest, Wolfe stood at daybreak with his invincible battalions on the Plains of Abraham, the battlefield of Empire.

"'It can be but a small party, come to burn a few hovels and retire,' said Montcalm, in amazement, as the news reached him in his entrenchments on the other side of the St. Charles; but obtaining better information— 'Then,' he cried, 'they have at last got to the weak side of this miserable garrison; we must give battle and crush them before midday.' And before 10:00, the two armies, equal in numbers, each being composed of less than 5,000 men, were ranged in presence of one another for battle. The English, not easily accessible from intervening shallow ravines and rail fences, were all regulars, perfect in discipline, terrible in their fearless enthusiasm, thrilling with pride at their morning's success, commanded by a man whom they obeyed with confidence and love. The doomed and devoted Montcalm had what Wolfe had called but 'five weak French battalions,' of less than 2,000 men, 'mingled with disorderly peasantry,' formed on ground which commanded the position of the English. The French had three little pieces of artillery; the English one or two. The two armies cannonaded each other for nearly an hour; when Montcalm, having summoned Bougainville to his aid, and despatched messenger after messenger for De Vandreuil, who had 1,500 men at the camp, to come up before he should be driven from the ground, endeavoured to flank the

British and crowd them down the high bank of the river. Wolfe counter-acted the movement by detaching Townshend with Amherst's regiment, and afterwards a part of the Royal Americans who formed on the left with a double front.

"Waiting no longer for more troops, Montcalm led the French army impetuously to the attack. The ill-disciplined companies broke by sheer precipitation and the unevenness of the ground; and fired by platoons, without unity. The English, especially the 43rd and 47th, where Monck-ton stood, received the shock with calmness, and after having, at Wolfe's command, reserved their fire till their enemy was within 40 yards, their line began a regular, rapid, and exact discharge of musketry. Montcalm was present everywhere, braving danger, wounded, but cheering by his example. The second in command, De Sennezergues, an associate in glo-ry at Ticonderoga, was killed. The brave but untried Canadians, flinching from a hot fire in the open field, began to waver, and, so soon as Wolfe, placing himself at the head of the 28th and the Louisburg grenadiers, charged with bayonets, they everywhere gave way. Of the English officers, Carleton was wounded; Barre, who fought near Wolfe, received in the head a ball which destroyed the power of vision of one eye, and ultimately made him blind. Wolfe, also, as he led the charge, was wounded in the wrist, but still pressing forward, he received a second ball; and, having decided the day, was struck a third time, and mortally, in the breast. 'Sup-port me,' he cried to an officer near him: 'let not my brave fellows see me drop.' He was carried to the rear, and they brought him water to quench his thirst. 'They run, they run' spoke the officer on whom he leaned. 'Who run?' asked Wolfe, as life was ebbing. 'The French,' replied the officer, 'give way everywhere.' 'What,' cried the expiring hero, 'do they run already? Go, one of you to Colonel Burton; bid him march Webb's regiment with all speed to Charles River to cut off the fugitives.' Four days before, he had looked forward to early death with dismay. 'Now, God be praised, I die happy.' These were his words as his spirit escaped in the blaze of his glory. Night, silence, the rushing tide, veteran discipline, the sure inspiration of genius, had been his allies; his battlefield high over the ocean-river, was the grandest theatre on earth for illustrious deeds; his victory, one of the most momentous in the annals of mankind, gave to the English tongue and the institutions of the Germanic race the unexplored and seemingly infinite West and North. He crowded into a few hours actions that would have given lustre to length of life; and filling his day with greatness, completed it before its noon.

"Monckton, the first brigadier, after greatly distinguishing himself, was shot through the lungs. The next in command, Townshend, brave, but deficient in sagacity and attractive power and the delicate perception of right, recalled the troops from the pursuit, and when De Bougainville appeared in view, declined a contest with a fresh enemy. But already the hope of New France was gone. Born and educated in camps, Montcalm had been carefully instructed and was skilled in the language of Homer as well as in the art of war. Greatly laborious, just, disinterested, hopeful even to rashness, sagacious in council, swift in action, his mind was a wellspring of bold designs; his career in Canada a wonderful struggle against inexorable destiny. Sustaining hunger and cold, vigils and incessant toil, anxious for his soldiers, unmindful of himself, he set even to the forest-trained red men an example of self-denial and endurance; and in the midst of corruption made the public good his aim. Struck by a musket ball, as he fought opposite Monckton, he continued in the engagement, till in attempting to rally a body of fugitive Canadians in a copse near St. John's Gate, he was mortally wounded.

"On hearing from the surgeon that death was certain—'I am glad of it,' he cried; 'how long shall I survive?' 'Ten or twelve hours, perhaps less.' 'So much the better; I shall not live to see the surrender of Quebec.' To the Council of War he showed that in twelve hours all the troops near at hand might be concentrated and renew the attack before the English were entrenched. When De Ramsay, who commanded the garrison, asked his advice about defending the city—'To your keeping,' he replied, 'I commend the honour of France. For myself, I shall pass the night with God, and prepare myself for death.' Having written a letter recommending the French prisoners to the generosity of the English, his last hours were given to the hope of endless life, and at five the next morning he expired.

"The day of the battle had not passed when De Vandreuil, who had no capacity for war, wrote to De Ramsay at Quebec not to wait for an assault, but, as soon as his provisions were exhausted, to raise the white flag of surrender. 'We have cheerfully sacrificed our fortunes and our houses' said the citizens; 'but we cannot expose our wives and children to a massacre.' At a Council of War, Fiedmont, a captain of artillery, was the only one who wished to hold out to the last extremity; and, on the 17th of September, before the English had constructed batteries, De Ramsay capitulated."

In the King's speech on the meeting of Parliament, November 13th of that year, his Majesty acquainted Parliament with "the happy progress of our successes, from the taking of Goree, on the coast of Africa, to the conquest of so many important places in America, with the defeat of the French arms in Canada, and the reduction of their capital city of Quebec, effected with so much honour to the courage and conduct of His Majesty's officers both at sea and land, and with so great lustre to his intrepid forces."

The definitive Peace of Paris between France, Spain, England and Portugal was signed February 10th, 1763, under which France ceded to England Nova Scotia, Canada, and the country east of the Mississippi as far as Iberville. A line drawn down the Mississippi from its source to its mouth was thenceforth to form the boundary between the possessions of the two nations, except that New Orleans was not to be included in this cession. France also ceded Cape Breton, with the coasts of the St. Lawrence and its islands, retaining, under certain restrictions which have lately led to so much controversy, rights with regard to the fishing off Newfoundland and in the Gulf of St. Lawrence, at a distance of three leagues from the shore, and the islands of St. Pierre and Miquelon as a shelter for their fishermen. Spain ceded to Great Britain Florida and all districts east of the Mississippi, but she was partly indemnified by receiving from France New Orleans and all Louisiana west of the Mississippi, renouncing all rights to participate in the Newfoundland fisheries. Article 4 of this Treaty is of great interest, and is in the following terms:

"La France renonce en faveur du Roi de la Grande-Bretagne, à toutes les prétentions qu'elle a pu former a l'Acadie ou à la Nouvelle-Ecosse en toutes ses parties, et la garantit toute entière et avec toutes ses dépendances, au Roi de la Grande-Bretagne; elle lui cède et garantit de plus le

Canada avec toutes ses dépendances, ainsi que L'île du Cap-Breton et toutes les autres îles et côtes dans le Golfe et fleuve de Saint-Laurent. Le Roi de la Grande-Bretagne accorde aux habitans du Canada le libre exercice de la religion catholique, en tant que le permettent les lois de l'Angleterre. Les habitans francais du Canada pourront vendre leurs biens; pourvu que ce soit à des sujets britanniques, et sortir librement du pays avec leurs effets, pendant L'espace de dix-huit mois a compter du jour de l'échange des ratifications."

In accordance with these engagements England set to work at once to establish a government in Canada, and a Governor General being appointed, in the month of December, 1763, there were "constituted and appointed Vice Admirals and Judges of the Court of Admiralty, and proper officers to each of the provinces of Quebec, East and West Florida, and also in Granada, St. Vincent and Tobago, in like manner as Vice Admiral, Judges, and other officers of such courts had been constituted by our High Admiral of Great Britain and Ireland for the time being in places in which they had been usually heretofore appointed"; and in pursuance of that authority, so far as regarded the province of Quebec, appointments were issued under the seal of the High Court of Admiralty from 1764 down to 1786.

In 1791 the country was divided into the provinces of Upper and Lower Canada; Upper Canada being the present province of Ontario, and Lower Canada being conterminous with the province of Quebec, and they so remained until 1841.

Then came the Act of 1867, under which—after reciting the desire of the provinces of Canada to be federally united under the Crown, with a constitution similar in principle to that of the United Kingdom, and that such a union would conduce to the welfare of the provinces, and promote the interests of the British Empire—Canada was divided into four provinces with power given to other provinces to join the Union, and to be one Dominion under the name of Canada; and the present government of the Senate and the Legislative Assembly was established under a representative of the Queen, while separate Legislatures were continued to the provinces, the powers of the Dominion Legislature and the provincial Legislatures being clearly defined.

Under this Act, the four provinces, Ontario, Quebec, Nova Scotia and New Brunswick were united, and under it provision was made for the admission at any subsequent period of the other provinces and territories of British North America. In 1870 the province of Manitoba was formed, and, with that portion of the Hudson Bay Territories which lies between Manitoba and the Rocky Mountains, was admitted into the Dominion; British Columbia and Vancouver Island were joined as an additional province in 1871, and Prince Edward Island in 1873, Newfoundland alone holding itself at present aloof and continuing to be administered by a responsible Executive Council and by a Legislative Council of 15 members.

During the year 1881, this great North-West territory was again subdivided into the four provinces of Assiniboia, Alberta, Saskatchewan and Athabasca, and the unification of the whole of the northern part of the American continent, including some three and a half million square miles, with a population at the present time of nearly five million, may thus be considered to be complete.

I do not presume to suggest, however, that there is not still a grave question of the relations of the mother country and the colonies which advances toward solution; there can be little doubt but that Lord Carnarvon spoke the feelings of both in 1870 when he expressed a wish for a state of things under which "the Englishman should feel himself a citizen in Canada and the Canadian should feel himself no stranger in England. It is impossible not sometimes to indulge in the belief—though circumstances sometimes are adverse—that such a great confederation might even yet be achieved—a confederation of which England might be the centre, and of which all the members might be bound to her by a tie which might go on for uncounted generations. Canada, it is true, entails on us political responsibilities, but I believe that the great Dominion which Parliament three years ago built up was erected in the interest of Canada, in the interest of England, and also in the interest of that great continent of which she forms a part." Upon the question of the advantages resulting from the maintenance of British troops in Canada, Lord Carnarvon possibly hung on rather too closely to the antecedent policy, and Lord Granville (the then Colonial Minister) probably took the truer position when he expressed the opinion that "the ties which bound us together are loyalty to the Crown, good will between the colonies and the mother country, and a reciprocity of mutual advantages." It is certainly not least upon the last of these that the other two depend.

In 1870 there occurred the two troubles the settlement of which led to no small extent to the consolidation of the Dominion.

The first of them was from the outside, and was the attempt of the Fenian filibusters to induce and organize a desire for annexation to the United States. Many a tale still is told of the incidents of this campaign.

The other trouble was internal, and will be known in Canadian history as the Red River Rebellion. The following is taken from the "Annual Register," corrected as to some of the details.

The excuse for this uprising was that the Canadian authorities, in purchasing the territorial rights of the Hudson Bay Company, had not provided for representative institutions in the proposed new form of government; the real intention was to erect themselves into an independent republic.

The inhabitants were themselves divided into two fiercely antagonistic parties: the Canadians, almost all half-breeds, speaking French, and professing the Catholic religion, and a minority of English and Scotch. The former rose in insurrection against the proposed transfer. They refused to admit into the district Mr. Macdougal, who was sent by Canada as Governor, so the discontented alleged, merely to get rid of a politician who had been an unsuccessful Minister of Public Works. The leader of the revolutionary party was Louis Riel. He was proclaimed in February, "President of the Republic of the North-West," and he was for a time pretty much of a dictator. A provisional government was formed, the Hudson Bay Company were sent to the rightabout, and certain laws were framed; but as a large portion of the English settlers did not agree with Riel and his ways, and so endeavoured to oppose him, continual hubbub reigned in the country for more than a year. He was a young man of pure French Canadian descent who, "although he had not a drop of Indian blood in his veins, had a large number of half-breed relations and connections, and, in order to identify himself as much as possible with the people, he invariably spoke of himself as a half-breed. He was a man of considerable moral determination, although all who knew him say he was wanting in physical courage. His command of language was great and his power over his audience immense." He and his followers opposed and ill treated the remaining servants of the Company, seized its property, and completed their career of violence by the deliberate murder of a loyal Canadian, "Orangeman and volunteer," of the name of Hugh Scott. This atrocity roused popular feeling in Canada far more strongly than the political acts of Riel and his followers. These had despatched two delegates, Father Richot and Alfred Scott, to Ottawa, in order to negotiate with the delegates there. These gentlemen were apprehended there (in April) as accessories to the murder of Hugh Scott, the Canadian Government having at the time of the murder acquired jurisdiction over the Red River by the Company's cession. They were however discharged, no evidence being preferred. But their mission, the murder of Scott being as yet unavenged, came to nothing.

The Canadian Government came to the conclusion that force must be employed, and the British troops in Canada had to furnish a contingent. One battalion of infantry, two of Canadian militia, and a small party of artillery and engineers, were selected for the purpose, under command of Colonel Wolseley. Between the head of Lake Superior and the Red River about 500 miles were to be passed of country without a road (one had been projected by Canada, but a small portion of it only was even marked out), of a region composed of thick forest, swamp, bush-covered rocks, and small lakes of intricate navigation. The route is described by a member of the expedition as "48 miles by road through the forest to Shenandowan Lake, and from thence about 310 miles by rivers and lakes, with about 17 portages to the Lake of the Woods. Some of these portages were more than a mile in length; and when it is remembered that all the boats, stores, &c., required for the expedition had to be carried by the soldiers over these breaks in the navigation, an idea can be formed of the physical labour which such an operation would entail. From the Lake of the Woods to Fort Garry was about 100 miles in a direct line by land, but there was only a road made for about 60 miles of that distance, the unmade portion being laid out over most difficult swamps"; and ultimately it was necessary to avoid the difficulties of this last portion by a circuitous movement down the Winnipeg River.

The expedition reached Fort Garry, the headquarters of the Hudson Bay Company, and now of Riel and his rebel followers, on the 23rd of August. They were welcomed enthusiastically by the loyal party, and met with no opposition from the disaffected.

Riel abdicated on the near approach of Colonel (now General, Lord) Wolseley and his troops, and from that day to this law and order have existed throughout the Canadian North-West.

About this time the Honourable Donald A. Smith arrived in the country, in the capacity of Commissioner on behalf of the Dominion Government. To Mr. Smith's cool-headed judgement and undaunted firmness, combined with a fine sense of fair play, is due the absence of any very serious scenes of bloodshed; and an Act was passed, giving to the people of Manitoba the same representative institutions as those of the other provinces of Canada, and the British Government did not experience the loss of a single man.

It remains for me to give some account of the origin and proceedings of the great Company which administered with so much success the affairs of the whole of this part of Canada and even a considerable territory to the south of the present boundary line of the two countries, and which existed as the sole governing power until the events of the last few years brought the North-West within the Dominion.

The department of the north consisted of three distinct portions, under the names of the North-West, Rupert's Land, and the Red River Colony. The trade of the North-West was first opened up to our knowledge by the exploring party under Samuel Hearne, who in 1769 set off from Churchill on the Hudson Bay and explored the interior as far as the Copper River. After him the land to the south and west was discovered, if indeed one may apply the term discovered to their visits, by the servants of the North-West Company at certain intervals. That Company was formed in Canada in 1783, with the intention of consolidating the interests of those who since the conquest of New France by England continued the fur trade in this country, taking their name from the fact that, setting out from Canada, they directed themselves toward the northwest of the continent.

After carrying on a ruinous rivalry with the Hudson Bay Company, they became amalgamated in 1821; and obtained together the exclusive privilege of trading in furs with the Indians to the west of Rupert's Land. This privilege was granted in that year for 21 years, but before the expiration of the term, namely, in 1838, it was renewed for another 21 years, expiring in 1859. At that last date the monopoly ceased.

The territory of Rupert's Land embraces all the countries watered by the streams falling into the Hudson Bay, including James Bay, and was under the complete control of the Hudson Bay Company. As the title to their lands has been on many occasions the subject of a very close inquiry, it may be interesting here briefly to state how the matter stood.

In 1626 a charter was granted by Louis XIII to the company of New France granting to them the whole of the territory of the Bay of the Hudson. In 1670 a similar charter was granted by our Charles II to Prince Rupert and his companion adventurers, and it is said that by the treaty of Riswick, in 1696, the whole of this territory was acknowledged belonging to France. But whether this was so or not, the treaty of Utrecht in 1713 ceded to England the coast of the Bay of Hudson, and clearly from that time this country belonged to England. The limits of the French and English possessions were not, however, well defined, and it was not till the treaty of Paris in 1763, under which, as I have shown, the whole of the French possessions were ceded to England, that it can be said that there was a complete and satisfactory title of the Hudson Bay Company to the whole of these possessions.

The third division of this northern land was the Red River Colony. It was in 1812 that an enterprising Scotchman, holding a high position in the Hudson Bay Company, Lord Selkirk, conceived the project of founding a small colony in the middle of Rupert's Land, and for this purpose obtained the cession of a certain extent of land on the borders of the Red River and the Assiniboine, and commenced there an establishment which until recently bore the name of the Selkirk Settlement, the Red River Settlement, or the Assiniboine Settlement. The limits of the land purchased was a radius of 60 miles in all directions from the confluence of the Assiniboine with the Red River; and embraced, therefore, the land northward as far as Lake Winnipeg, and about 30 miles up that lake, and southward to the boundary line.

For very many years the colony was in considerable difficulties, nor can it be said ever to have thoroughly flourished, until at last it amounted to little more than the trading body at Fort Garry, the present city of Winnipeg, where the Governor and the Recorder and his Council formed the principal inhabitants, and administered justice among some few thousand people, consisting principally of the half-breeds and retired Hudson Bay traders who had established themselves there. It was remarked at the time of the foundation of the Selkirk colony that the distance from market would be fatal to them, and it must be observed that though the Hudson Bay Company are charged with having so long kept this great land in its unrecognized and unknown state for the purpose of carrying on their trade without interference, it has been the development of railways that has alone made the North-West a possible country. The company have indeed, whatever may have been their faults, left behind them a character which will ever remain, of having administered their affairs in a spirit of absolute justice to the aboriginal inhabitants.

It may be said that they only acted in their own interest in so doing, as unless the Indians had been kept alive in their rigorous winters and had been paid for their work with fairness and justice, the Hudson Bay Company could not have carried on their very lucrative fur trade; but whatever may have been the motive cause, the result, at any rate, has been that in the long annals of their trade with the Indians not a single charge of injustice has ever been made against the company or of wrong done to the red man; and even now, nothing has more conduced to a complete exploration and to an undisturbed opening up of this country than the absolute security from attack that has been the result of these long years of justice and fair dealing.

CHAPTER II

∿

IN MAKING THAT EXAMINATION of the physical character of the country, without which, as Dr. Arnold well observes, no real knowledge of a country can be acquired, the first thing which strikes one in British North America is its huge area, with the clearly defined limits of drainage of its watersheds. Leaving out of consideration the Labrador or eastern shores, there are four main courses along which this great continent is drained. The first is that of the St. Lawrence, draining an area which Sir William Logan in his Geological Reports estimates at 530,000 square miles, of which about 70,000 are in the United States, and which stretches westward as far as the 94th meridian. The great lakes that feed the St. Lawrence are situated on four plateaux, the highest, Lake Superior, being 600 feet above the sea level, and the lowest, Lake Ontario, 230 feet. Lakes Superior and Michigan, being from 800 to 1000 feet deep, have a depression of their beds of from 300 to 400 feet below the sea level, while Lake Ontario, with an average depth of 600 feet, has a basin 370 feet below that level, and in its greatest depths its depression attains a depth below the surface of the ocean of 1,500 feet. Lake Ontario is about 180 miles long, with a maximum width of 60 to 70 miles. Lakes Erie and Huron are each 240 miles long, and Michigan 320, each of these two last having an area of about 22,500 square miles, while Lake Superior is 400 miles long, with a width in many parts of 200 miles, and a total superficial area of 32,000 square miles. The St. Lawrence and its lakes are estimated to contain 12,000 cubic miles of water, or more than half the fresh water on the globe; the water passing over Niagara is estimated at 20 million cubic feet per minute, and the St. Lawrence receiving all this water, with the addition of the large rivers which run into it from the north to the west of Lake Ontario, the Ottawa, the St. Maurice, and the Saguenai, and from the south the smaller streams of the St. John, the St. Francis, and the Chaudiere, forms below Quebec a broad estuary, and enters the Gulf at Gaspé with a width of more than 100 miles. The second great drainage area in the country is to the western, southern, and eastern shores of Hudson Bay, and is probably double the area of that of the St. Lawrence; it is but little elevated above the sea level, with an alluvial soil, well wooded, and watered by numerous rivers, the Albany, Moose, Abbitibee, Harricanaw, and Notaway on the south, Rupert, East Main, Great and Little Whale on the east, and the Severn, Nelson, and Churchill on the west. The Churchill, 700 miles long, runs through 17 degrees of longitude, and is the outlet of numerous lakes and tributaries, and the Albany is of nearly the same length, and drains the country which lies southwest of James Bay through 10 degrees of longitude.

The third great drainage area is that from which the waters are poured into Lake Winnipeg. The Saskatchewan, "the water that runs rapidly," rises in the Rocky Mountains in two great branches; the streams of its southern branch begin with the Belly River, which has its origin in the Chief Mountain below the boundary line, and gets its name from its passing through the country of the Gros Ventres; it is joined at Stand Off by the Kootenai, which has its rise in the lakes of that name, and further east by the Old Man coming down from the Crowsnest Pass, and bringing with its waters from Fort McLeod those of the Willow Creek, which has its rise a little further to the north. Some 30 miles lower down the Belly River is joined by the Little Bow River, and about 40 miles further to the west by the Bow River, bringing in the streams from the neighbourhood of Calgary. From this last point it becomes the South Saskatchewan, and after receiving a considerable volume of water from the Red Deer or Elk River, which is in fact the bigger of the two streams, it runs in a northeasterly direction to Fort à la Corne, where it is united with the north branch, that has had its origin alike in the eastern slopes of the Rockies, and has run past Battleford and Prince Albert. From this junction their waters run over 6 degrees of longitude through the Cedar Lake into the northwestern end of Lake Winnipeg.

Into the same lake runs from the east the Winnipeg River, the outlet of the numerous lakes and rivers which lie to the northwest of Lake Superior—the Lake of the Woods, Rainy Lake and River, English River, Lonely Lake, and many others. From the Lake of the Woods the Winnipeg River is said to fall 500 feet in 125 miles, and thus is of course not navigable for steamers, though it was, even with its dangerous rapids and frequent portages, the route by which their trade was conducted by the fur companies. Into the southern end of Lake Winnipeg runs from the south the Red River, having its rise in the States from the height of land where its head streams interlace with those which form the first waters of the Mississippi. The Red River takes a direct northerly course through the province of Manitoba, receiving at Fort Garry or Winnipeg the Assiniboine, bringing the joint waters of the Qu'Appelle and Souris from the west, and after a course of about 350 miles falls into the Lake Winnipeg. The outlet of this lake is through the Nelson River and the Hayes River. From the point where the Nelson leaves the lake to York Factory on Hudson Bay, is 300 miles in an air line, or 400 following the course of the river, and for the last 100 miles it is navigable for steamers. At its mouth at high tide it has a breadth of six or seven miles, but narrows rapidly to the head of the tide water, 24 miles up, to a width of 14 miles. Above this it varies from one-half to one mile, with 20 or 40 feet depth, and a velocity of two and a half to three miles per hour. At the mouth of the river the spring tides rise about 12 feet and neaps about 6. It is scarcely likely that this river could ever be used as a waterway between Lake Winnipeg and Hudson Bay, though Mr. Bell (Geological Report 1877–1878) estimates that it has four times the quantity of water of the Ottawa at the Chaudière Falls, or about the same amount as that of the St. Lawrence at Niagara. At 120 miles from Lake Winnipeg all the waters of the Nelson unite for the first time after leaving Play Green Lake, and the channel is there about a quarter of a mile wide, with a depth of from 40 to 50 feet and a current of three miles per hour. I have visited the height of land of all these three watersheds; of the St. Lawrence by following up the chain of lakes to Duluth at the head of Lake Superior, and thence up the beautiful St. Louis, as it falls in a series of lovely cascades, along the line of the railway which connects Duluth with Brainerd, from a small chain of pretty lakes only a few miles distant from those in which, above Brainerd, the Mississippi has its rise; of the Red River in the courses of the high prairies above Braikenridge and Glyndon, and of its affluent Assiniboine in the treeless prairies of the Souris and the alkaline lakes to the east of the Cypress Hills, where it is sometimes not easy to say in which direction the streams run; and lastly of the Saskatchewan, of its head waters on the glorious slopes of the Chief Mountain and the Kootenai Lakes, and of its affluent, the Bow River; but of the fourth great drainage area of the Mackenzie I can speak only by report, and I must hope that life may yet be long enough for me to visit this mighty stream, which takes its rise as the Frazer River in the Cascade range of the Northern Rockies, conveying the waters of the northern part of British Columbia, and cutting its way through the mountains at the Peace River Pass, runs under that name into Lake Athabasca. Here it is joined by the Athabasca River, which has run in a northwesterly direction from the Yellowhead Pass, the pass through which it was originally planned to carry the Canadian Pacific Railway; their joint waters run as the Slave River into the Great Slave Lake, and then flow as the Mackenzie River, receiving in its passage the waters of the Great Bear Lake, into the Arctic Ocean in latitude 70. This stream has a course of probably nearly 3,000 miles, and it is said that 2,000 of this is adapted to steam navigation, and its drainage area is certainly not less than half a million square miles.

Further still to the west comes the Yukon River, which, after a comparatively short course through Canadian land, turns away into the United States territory of Alaska, and flows also into the Arctic Sea.

On going west from Winnipeg we rise by two distinct steps to the plateau of the Rocky Mountains. At Winnipeg the land is at an elevation of 700 or 800 feet above the sea, and so continues from the 97th meridian, on which Winnipeg stands, up to the 101st, with a prairie area of this elevation of about 7,000 square miles. At the 101st there is an elevation of 1,300, and from this meridian, for a distance westward of about 250 miles, decreasing to 200 miles on the 54th parallel, there is an average altitude of 1,600 feet; and thence, for a distance of about 450 miles, the prairie plateau, extending over an area of 130,000 square miles, is 2,000 feet above the sea, attaining at the 113th meridian, at the base of the foothills of the Rocky Mountains, an altitude of over 4,000 feet.

A fuller description of this country will of course appear in my personal narrative.

It remains to say a few words on the system of survey which has been adopted through the whole of the North-West region, and which makes it easy to describe the country with accuracy, and to define any particular locality. A first principal meridian was taken a little to the west of the 97th meridian, at about 12 miles to the west of the city of Winnipeg, the southern foundation of the survey being of course the 49th parallel, the boundary line between Canada and the United States. The whole of this district is surveyed out into blocks six miles square. On going westward these blocks are spoken of as "ranges," and on going north, as "townships," and in their enumeration on the maps, the latitude of the townships is marked by Arabic numerals, the longitude of the ranges being in Roman numerals. From the one principal meridian to the next principal meridian is 33 ranges. The only difficulty arises from the narrowing of the degrees of longitude as you progress northward, necessitating a correction in the western ranges of each principal meridian. Each of these ranges or townships is six miles square, consisting therefore of 36 square miles. Beginning from the southeastern corner of this block, each square mile is numbered; sections 11 and 29 in each township being set apart for the endowment and the maintenance of the schools of the township; sections 8 and 26 being allotted to the Hudson Bay Company in respect of their charter rights; within the range of 24 miles on each side of the main line of any branch of the Canadian Pacific Railway the odd-numbered sections have been granted to the railway, the even-numbered sections being reserved for free-grant homesteads and their attached pre-emptions. Each of these sections of one mile square, or 640 acres, is again subdivided into its four quarter sections of 160 acres each, and every settler has a right to take up as a homestead any block of 160 acres that he may find unoccupied, for which he will have to pay only a small registration fee, and he may occupy for pre-emption the adjoining or any other section of 160 acres, for which he will have to pay at the rate of two and a half dollars per acre at the end of three years from the date of his entry. It will be seen, therefore, that it is within the power of a settler to obtain a farm of 320 acres upon payment of somewhere about £80, the payment of almost the whole of this sum being, as I said, postponed for three years.

It is not my purpose here (for it would take up far too great a space) to enumerate the parts of the country to which I would specially direct the attention of settlers. I think it right, however, to warn such persons that while there is an enormous amount of good and most valuable land in the North-West, there is also plenty of it which is comparatively useless. My best advice to every settler is not to buy a yard of land, or expend any money on any settlement, till he shall have thoroughly discovered its merits or demerits, either by personal examination, or by a report by some person on whose powers of observation he can rely equally with his own, and even in this latter case I should almost as soon think of trusting anybody else to make a selection for me of a wife or a horse, as I should of the land that is to be my home and to furnish the means of maintaining it. The great grain growing country of the North-West is said to be practically illimitable; but as far as I have been able to ascertain, its best land is to be found at the junction of the two Saskatchewans, in the neighbourhood of Prince Albert and Battleford.

There is undoubtedly some fine farming land in the neighbourhood of Qu'Appelle; but in my judgement, from Qu'Appelle westward—the land that is traversed by the Canadian Pacific Railway—to the crossing of the Saskatchewan, is land which requires careful consideration before the settler makes his purchase.

Experimental farms have most properly been laid out along the line by the Railway Company during the last year, and we shall wait with very great interest the report of the produce of those farms.

There has indeed been brought into cultivation in this very country the whole area of land called the Bell Farm, and the reports that are given from this farm seem to be exceedingly satisfactory, and if it should turn out that the land around Broadview, Regina, and Moosejaw, and other sections of this portion of the prairie, is capable of producing high class grain, and that in the majority of years the frosts do not reach too late into the summer, or fall on the crops too early in the autumn, this land will be undoubtedly one of the great granaries of the world.

These remarks will not, I am sure, be understood as in any way pre-judging the question, my only desire being to prevent any damage to the future of the country which may arise from an injudicious and too pro-fuse recommendation of its qualities; for nothing would more surely in-terfere with immigration than a bad report from a disappointed settler, and after all there is no such great hurry in the matter. The experience of a year or two will tell us the capabilities of this district, and meanwhile there is plenty of land of undoubtedly good quality that has yet to be filled up and farmed.

CHAPTER III

∼

HAVING THUS DESCRIBED THE physical character of the land we are about to visit, and having summarized its history, let us take our passage on board one of the boats of the Messrs. Allan, and "ingens iterabimus æquor."

I will not select for my readers any one particular boat of the fleet. I have had the pleasure of crossing the Atlantic in every one of them, and although the first and last, the *Polynesian* and the *Sardinian* are naturally my first and last loves, I do not wish to extol them or their genial captains at the expense of any of the four others. I venture, however, to make this recommendation with reference to all ocean steamers, that it would be a great improvement if instead of the cumbrous marble washing stands in the cabins they could fix some light apparatus, so that it might be possible after every arrival in port to remove it from its place to clean the cabin, and take everything on deck for a perfect ventilation, while all the interior is well scoured out. A very little trouble and a very slight expense in such matters would prevent a good deal of the nasty cabin smell which so dreadfully interferes with the comfort of the intending traveller.

Well, then, it is Thursday morning, and we are on board one of these good ships, and as soon after the hour of noon as the tide may permit, we are steaming away down the Mersey and across the bar. As night comes on we are lighted up by the gorgeous glare of the Hen and Chickens light of the Isle of Man, and then passing along the Irish coast we enter next morning into Lough Foyle, and await our extra passengers and mails off

Moville, with a pretty view of the interesting ruins of Green Castle and the hills that rise behind it. All being ready, the passengers who have had to scurry across Ireland being received somewhat as repentant sinners, away we steam again; and turning round to the west we bear away, leaving Tory Island, the last visible spot of Europe, behind us, and find ourselves in the Atlantic.

There are few more pleasant hours to the busy man than the entire rest and enjoyment of life on the ocean steamer. He to whom, for example, novels are at other times sealed books, finds himself stretched at length on a sofa, and indulging in the full excitement of those wondrous tales. After a while he finds himself promenading and preparing for his next meal, and for excitement there is the sweep on the day's run, with the auction and its attendant fun, in the hands of some good auctioneer; and then the excellent meals provided by the Company, as to which the only criticism is that they would be better if the worthy chef would be content not to attempt too much; but above all there is the pleasant genial companionship of many and many an interesting friend whose acquaintance you there make; and last, not least, there is the concert or mock trial, which brings into play much dormant talent, and in its preparation and discussion ensures many a pleasant hour.

I don't know how it is, but on board an ocean steamer you meet comparatively few disagreeable people. Everybody seems to think that they must try and put on at any rate their best company manners, and to be pleasant and gracious for the short time they are likely to be thrown together; and so the days slip away, varied perhaps by a heavy sea and the glories of the Atlantic rollers, until having passed through "The Devil's Punchbowl" and "The Bearing Forties," we come about the fifth or sixth day into the Arctic current, and the lowering temperature of the water shows that we have passed through the Gulf Stream; a cry is raised of "an iceberg in sight," and we approach one of those most magnificent and interesting of all natural phenomena. If the sun is shining upon it the glorious colours of this wondrous edifice become more and more marvellous, rising as it does occasionally to some 150 or 200 feet above the surface of the water, with the sea dashing at its base and occasionally breaking over it. This gigantic mass, which it has taken, in all probability, centuries to form on an Arctic coast, and which has floated downwards with its glacier stream and then been broken away, is now hurrying; down the ocean current and gradually hastening to its destruction. As to the depth to which the ice may extend below the surface of the water, and as to the consequent bulk of any particular iceberg, it is almost impossible to form any judgement. The height to which it reaches above the water can lead to no conclusion as to its depth below, depending, as it must, on the extent of the submerged plateau from which the peak that we see arises; and as we gaze at this, the first that is called to our attention, probably many others come in sight, and if we are in luck we shall find ourselves coming quite near enough to several of them to look into their crannies and crevices, and to observe the varying strata of their formation. Of course there is the old observation of the various objects to which it may be likened—a huge catafalque with its attendant monks, a giant cathedral, or an enormous beast of prey. These and many more are the images to which resemblance is drawn.

So far as my observation has gone, the three most glorious sights in nature are the iceberg, Niagara, and the prairie and forest fires, each of the three being wholly dissimilar from the others, but each invested with a mysterious, supreme, and majestic power.

After a run of some 1,700 miles we find ourselves, if we are having a good passage, about Wednesday evening approaching the Straits of Belle Isle, and no little credit is due to the Allan Line for having so persistently opened up this route. In 1861 Captain Ballantyne put forward the eligibility of this passage, as being far safer than that to the south of Newfoundland. Admiral Dayfield, however, about the same time entered his protest against it. The experience, nevertheless, of the last 10 years has shown with how great safety the passage may be made, and that between the months of May and November it is safer than the old route, while it has the advantage of saving 120 miles between Liverpool and Quebec. Passing, then, through the straits and leaving Belle Isle on our left hand, we steer into the Gulf of St. Lawrence, and, if we have the advantage of clear weather, we find ourselves passing Heath Point, the easternmost point of Ariticosti, distant from Belle Isle 100 miles; we leave the island on our right, and bear away in a westerly course for the promontory of

Gaspé, a further run of 100 miles. You will be told that Anticosti is a large island, and that it is in the market for any purchaser who may feel inclined to make an investment. I think I may safely warn any such person to inquire more fully into the capabilities of the island for any other purpose than the breeding of a few bears and multitudes of mosquitoes before he is tempted to take any share in such an undertaking.

At a distance of 200 miles from Gaspé we reach Father Point, and close to this at Rimouski we land mails and passengers for Nova Scotia, porpoises and white whales affording us a little amusement as we pass across the gulf, with an occasional visit from a few hawks chasing the small birds, and, if it is clear, a distant glimpse of the wooded hills.

We find ourselves now within the mouth of the St. Lawrence, which is here 24 miles wide, and dotted along the shore are small fishing villages, and little Catholic churches, and patches of cultivated land, backed by hills clothed with woods, the home of the elk and caribou, the former better known to the Englishman as the wapiti, the latter as the reindeer.

Then comes the Isle of Orleans; and as we pass along its western end, upon casting back the eye we catch a glimpse of the magnificent Montmorency Falls, and a few minutes afterwards find ourselves under the citadel of Quebec, and come to our moorings at Point Levis.

It was on the last day of August, in the year 1881, that I landed from the *Polynesian* with my wife at Point Levis; and we were introduced, as a fitting commencement to our Canadian experiences, to a comfortable breakfast provided for immigrants by the Dominion Government. Having filled our eyes with the fine prospect of Quebec on the opposite shores, with its citadel and the towers of the Laval University, we proceeded in the train along the south bank to Montreal. The great quantity of wild autumn flowers, principally the goldenrod and a bright single sunflower, made the banks of the railway gay in the autumn sun. The great booms in the river containing the large rafts of timber that are brought down to Quebec, consisting of many blocks, and with the huts upon them in which the raft men live, present the first spectacle of interest to the stranger. The railway crosses several fine streams falling from left to right into the St. Lawrence, and strikes far into the country, up the Richelieu River, which receives its name from the cardinal under whose auspices Champlain had sailed for Canada. Thence, a somewhat tedious piece of poor land (so far as it is cleared), improving however as we again approach the river, brings us to the site of the great Victoria bridge, which bears us across the St. Lawrence to the city of Montreal.

This very thriving city, the true capital of lower Canada, occupies a position such as few cities can compare with, resting, as it does, on the left bank of the river, and occupying an island formed by the St. Lawrence and the two forks of the Ottawa, of about the length of 10 miles, and a width of 6 or 7, and backed by the wooded hill which gives it its name.

Passing up toward the mountain we are put down at the Windsor Hotel, which may I think fairly claim to be the finest hotel in Her Majesty's dominions. Opposite to the hotel is the Roman Catholic cathedral, begun long ago in rival imitation of St. Peter's; the completion of it would seem, however, to be very remote. I should think that there are few towns containing so many places of worship of various denominations as Montreal; the principal one is the cathedral of Notre Dame, which stands with its two towers as the most prominent object in the city. The Windsor Hotel is the right place for a rest after a sea voyage; its splendid hall, magnificent passages, which, as in other hotels in Canada, are used as sitting rooms, and its *salle à manger*, make a truly comfortable home either for traveller or resident; and if it only had a chef equal in culinary talent and delicacy-producing power to the corresponding genius of its homonym at New York, it would be a perfect hotel. The most interesting object to the visitor to Montreal is the drive up the mountain, laid out in many parts as a cemetery, with the trees cleared and the flowers planted so as to give the prettiest effect in landscape gardening; a more beautiful home for the last sleep could scarcely be imagined.

At the turns of the zigzag road which mounts the hill, views are obtained of the city and the river, with its enormous bridge; and of no little interest to the visitor driving down into the town are the excellent shops, where can be obtained everything that he or she is likely to want during the stay in Canada. Not last among these is the excellent bookshop of Mr. Dawson, and to travellers returning in the latter part of the fall, more interesting, perhaps, are the splendid furs to be found at Messrs. Hendersons'.

Two or three days quickly slip away among our hospitable friends in the city. But it is time that we started for the further West, and after a comfortable dinner at the "Windsor," the eight o'clock train bears us away to Toronto.

The weather at this season in 1881 was terribly hot, and the great drought of the summer being followed by an outbreak of forest fires, we found as we went along at night the fences and the forest adjoining the line blazing all around, and even lighting up the ties or sleepers on which the rails rest. The heat was intense, the thermometer during the night rising to 100°, and we were very glad indeed when our journey came to an end and we found ourselves in the Queen's Hotel at Toronto. For about the first time in my life I was rather knocked up by the heat, but a little interview with the doctor and a quiet day in the hotel soon put me to rights, and we much enjoyed the Agricultural Show and the Exhibition, which were then open. A reception at the Town Hall of the visitors took place, as well as a very interesting distribution of prizes which I was asked to undertake at the school in which my friend Mr. French was a master, and where a number of bright pupils seemed to appreciate the few words which were spoken to them by a university man from the old country.

In taking our journey to Winnipeg the question to be considered was whether we should go by the long land journey through Chicago and St. Paul, or by striking the Lake Superior at Collingwood, sail thence through the lakes to Duluth, and by rail through Glyndon to Winnipeg. We decided on this latter course, and having duly taken our tickets, proceeded on the morning of September 12th by the railway to Collingwood. Here we found the steamboat *Frances S. Smith*, a boat of the half-hotel, half-steamboat class, which no one but an American would ever have devised, and having deposited our luggage in a very comfortable chamber, we remained on deck till dark, as the boat was not to sail until after ten o'clock. As darkness came on we made our way into our cabin. I was not a little surprised, on asking for a light, to be somewhat bluntly informed that no such thing was allowed in the cabin, and that if we had wanted to inspect any of our goods or to do anything else than forthwith tumble into our berths, we should have done it while it was daylight, and that no light was ever allowed in any cabin on any ship. In vain we remonstrated, alleging that we had no knowledge of such a rule, and, as an instance that it could scarcely be universal, we put forward, amongst others, the case of the ocean steamer we had but lately left. After a long parley, however, with the captain a compromise was arrived at, and a boy was told off to stand by with a lantern at the cabin door so long as it might be required. About ten o'clock we got under sail; it began to blow very hard, and we soon found that the *Frances S. Smith* was anything but a good sea boat in bad weather, even in the hands of a skilful captain, and what it might prove in the hands of an uncertificated mariner, such as is allowed by the Canadian Government to take command of a ship in these waters, it was not difficult to imagine. I had an anxious time of it, and thought it the best plan, in order to be ready for any emergency, to sit at the window under the pretext of watching the forest fires which circled the end of the lake. A very rough time of it we had on that dark stormy night, but at last, about three in the morning, all seemed to be quiet, and I tumbled into bed till breakfast time at six next morning. After breakfast we went on the little deck in front of the cabin, and finding ourselves moored, my wife on looking up observed that we were lying under the same elevator under which we had lain the night before; and it turned out upon inquiry that we had been some 30 miles out into the lake, but that the captain, very properly judging the weather somewhat too boisterous for the sea-going capabilities of *Miss Smith*, had turned back again to Collingwood. On putting the question to him as to when we might hope to get under way again, I received a somewhat discourteous reply that it might be a week. Not feeling inclined to spend so much time at Collingwood, we hurried off our baggage into the train, and took our places again in the train, and returned in a somewhat crestfallen frame of mind to Toronto. In the evening we again started off for Chicago. It is a long but not uninteresting railway journey, and at the end of some 24 hours we reached the sandhills which mark the approach to the city.

I need not dilate on the progress of this mushroom city. It is indeed a wonderful energy which has raised in some 15 years since the date of the great fire the vast town, with its magnificent buildings and population of 550,000, and has developed the increasing collection of industry which has grown on and round this great centre. Of its principal building,

35

containing the municipal offices and courts of law, I may speak at a subsequent visit. A first object for the traveller is of course the stockyards, the slaughterhouses, and the meat preserving factories. The sad fate of poor piggie as he passes with countless numbers of his tribe from the stockyard to the bacon warehouse has been often described. The mode in which every part of him is utilized, except, as the saying goes, his last squeak, is indeed a great example of economy, and I think we may fairly hope that he passes to his end with as little pain as possible. I do not think that quite the same thing can be said with reference to the cattle under either of the two processes adopted; the cutting of the spinal column by a stab, or a bullet into the brain, not being so practised as to produce, so far as I could see, as quick and painless a death as could be wished. The manufacture of pepsine from a certain part of the pig's stomach is one of the more delicately conducted operations, and as one of the gentlemen connected with that part of the business said to me, "He guessed that so long as his countrymen ate their meals in the manner usually adopted by them, there would always be plenty of demand for that article." Of course this industry is a thing which every visitor ought to see, but I cannot promise him an unmitigated pleasure from the visit and he will find it many hours before he succeeds in removing from his nostrils the smell of pig which will accompany him from the factory.

Leaving Chicago on the evening of the 14th we found ourselves at noon next day at St. Paul, and after a good wash and pleasant *déjeûner* at the Metropolitan Hotel we took a stroll on the bank at the end of the street where the hotel stands, and obtained our first view of the great Mississippi rolling away down below, and spanned by a long sloping bridge which crosses it at a width of some 1,500 yards to the suburb which connects St. Paul with Minneapolis. The view is truly American. The vast volume of water, the extent of the view, the clearness of the atmosphere, and the already commenced autumnal colouring of the trees, more especially as we found them on our return, made a picture on which we gazed for some time. We then took a carriage and proceeded across the bridge to visit one of the largest flour mills of Minneapolis. The enormous amount of water power obtained from the falls of the St. Anthony, better known to most of our English readers of Longfellow as the Minne-haha, "or laughing water," have made these towns the great flour providers of the States. Here we find, as in most of the other towns of the West, that the last thing that is considered are the roads; and the mud of Minneapolis was something truly dreadful. Into this the wheels of our carriage sank till it reached the floor; and the English traveller wonders how people can be found capable of enduring the discomfort of so much dirt. The interior of the mill presents everything that is attractive in the shape of cleanliness and good machinery. Having completed our inspection we returned to the Minneapolis station, in the waiting room of which I was a little amused with the *affiche* placed conspicuously along the wall, "Gentlemen will not, and other persons are requested not to spit on the floor"; not, however, that this little notice seems to have been productive of much better results than I noticed years ago had followed an *affiche* on the Cathedral at Antwerp, "On est prié de ne pas cracher ni sur le pavé ni sur les murailles. L'église est la maison de Dieu."

Talking of notices, I saw a very quaint one the next day in a small and very unclean hotel in which it was our fate to pass the following night. Over the jack-towel which hung for the convenience of persons who wished to prepare themselves for dinner was the notice, "You are requested to wash before you wipe." A somewhat similar one was an indignant notice by a postmaster in Canada, who had no doubt become weary of acceding to the requests to put stamps on the letters, in which he rather pompously announced that "for the future Her Majesty's postmaster refuses to put stamps on the letters; all persons are therefore requested to lick and stick themselves."

Leaving St. Paul we took our places for Winnipeg, and as we wished to make the whole journey by daylight, we stopped for the night at the halfway place of Feargus Falls. The said falls are of no considerable importance, and certainly do not repay a visit. The place is, however, at the one end of the lake district, the country between it and St. Paul consisting of innumerable lakes, surrounded by woods, and an exceedingly interesting country. The view from the station platform is very characteristic of this exceedingly pretty lake country. From Feargus Falls we enter on the great prairie land of Minnesota, and the line passes over the next hundred miles on the prairie level.

Since I first visited this, at the time I am now mentioning, many farms have sprung up on each side of the line, the small stations have developed into villages and towns, and a great part of the land has been settled up.

Toward the evening we arrived at the boundary between the United States and Canada, with St. Vincent as the last town of the States, and Emerson the first town of Manitoba;[1] keeping close to the Red River, through a similar country to that we had lately passed, after a distance of 60 miles we reached the city of Winnipeg. It was a dark wet evening, and very glad we were to be met by a kind and enterprising young friend who had taken up his home there, and who had secured for us a room in a very makeshift hotel, but the only one to be got. Our earliest experience of the worst feature of Winnipeg, viz., its mud, began on that evening. It is a mud which no person who has not seen it can appreciate. A mixture of putty and birdlime would perhaps most nearly describe it. The wide streets of Winnipeg are, under a baking sun, a solid mass, and as hard as marble. There comes a dripping day or a thunderstorm, and the whole thing is changed into a sea of mud of the character I have given. To walk through it is almost impossible. To keep on your feet on the wooden side paths is not a little difficult, and when you try to remove the mud from your clothes you find it almost equally impossible. It must be remarked, however, that though I am now writing of a state of things which existed three years ago, there has been very little attempt at improvement. I am now speaking indeed of Winnipeg's early days, and the Winnipegians, though with not any great success at present, have begun to mend their ways. At the time of our first visit the old Fort Garry was still standing, and contained the Hudson Bay store, and Indian tents still thronged around it.

Most interesting was it to watch the Indians as they came in, before starting West, to make their annual purchases with the money they had obtained for their skins. An Indian walks into the stores, carefully examines, without touching, however, each of the articles for which he has a requirement, and having at last made up his mind as to his selection, takes the article and deposits it in one corner of the shop. He then wanders noiselessly about in the selection of the next thing, and having satisfied himself as to that takes it and adds it to his cache, till at last, the whole of his purchases being complete, the shopman dots up the amount and the goods are duly paid for. The utmost honesty characterizes the Indian. He would, indeed, very much resent any suspicious watch kept over him, and I believe any attempt during his long wanderings up and down the shop to purloin anything is almost unheard of.

The purchases all being accomplished, and other traders having prepared their goods required for distant settlements, a long train of groaning Red River carts, each drawn by a single bullock, starts off on the westward trail. I believe we saw, in 1881, about the last of these outfits as we counted a train of some 50 or 60 passing Silver Heights, for the railway in that year was completed from Winnipeg to Brandon, and with the completion of the railway the Red River cart became, of course, a thing of the past. The old Red River cart had not a bit of iron about it, and the groaning of the wheels, ignorant of a lubricator, was most melancholy; of late years the cart has been improved upon, and as it carries about seven or eight hundredweight, and a whole train only require some five or six drivers, it was a very cheap mode of freighting.

A few days in Winnipeg were devoted to getting together our outfit for camping on the prairie, and having had selected for me by a kind friend of the Hudson Bay Company one of their most experienced guides, Guillaume Correa, I got together a wagon and a carriage, an additional driver, two pairs of horses, two tents, cooking utensils and stores, and provisions for three weeks, a faithful retriever lent me by my kind friend, cartridges, buffalo robes, blankets, etc., and putting them all into a freight cart, we started for Brandon in the first train that would carry passengers to that new city, which in the September of 1881 was what is colonially known as "the jump-down," that is, the last place that is in course of erection on the outskirts of what is called civilized life, and upon leaving which you at once jump down into the open gulf of unsettledom. The railway from Winnipeg runs in a northwesterly direction along the left bank of the Assiniboine River. The first few miles of the road carry you through a level prairie, which also, since the time that I am speaking of, has become entirely settled; the only place of interest that we passed being a hilly ridge on the right, consisting of stone and gravel, called Stony Heights, from which it is to be hoped that the streets of Winnipeg will eventually derive advantage. On the hill stands a reformatory prison, and in the neighbourhood are to be seen a small band of buffaloes, the property of the doctor who superintends the reformatory; they are said to be tame, but are not very approachable. Upon this subject it is worthy of remark that an animal not apparently of a disposition at all more vicious than our domestic cattle should never have been tamed or in any way utilized by the Indian, who can now fully recognize the value of the ox. This little band of buffaloes remains almost the last survivors of the great family that but a few years ago roamed in such countless millions over this part of the continent, and whose destruction one cannot but think of with regret.

With reference to Stony Heights we indulged in the speculation as to when Winnipeg would find out its value for the construction of a solid foundation on which to found some decent roadway across its sea of mud. To make a decent street is the last thing about which any municipality either in Canada or the States troubles itself, in illustration of which I may give the following little tale of an occurrence while I was out West in 1881.

A most worthy M.P., who had represented a Scottish borough, visited New York. It was a muddy time, and shortly after his landing he was interviewed by the correspondent of a New York paper.

Interviewer—"Well, sir, and what do you think of this city?"

M.P.—"Think of it, mun? It's jest domnable. Yer streets wad disgrace our manest Scottish villages. Ye want a gude Provost, mun. A' weer Provost of _____ for twa years, and ye should jest see the streets in that toon. I tell ye it's simply domnable."

And so the newspaper man went his way, and duly announced in his journal the Scottish M.P.'s views as to the city.

The country is for some distance varied by those occasional scrubby woods of aspen and poplar which, growing generally by the side of the marshes, is all which the prairie fires leave of wood to this part of Manitoba. In some of these thickets the silver-barked poplar, looking more like beech, had grown to a good size, and in some places there were seen stunted oak, all looking, however, as if some giant force of wind or frost, or of both combined, put its veto upon any height being attained of what we should consider to be forest-tree dimensions. We noticed here a fine stubble where wheat had been grown. About Elk River we saw a few pigeons, and everywhere there seemed to be abundance of duck. Elk River is one of the largest tributaries of the Red River, and with the woods at its junction forms one of the prettiest spots on this line, and has some eligible and well cultivated farms in its neighbourhood. Without specifying particularly the names of the stations, which will convey but little information, I may say generally that along the line for the next 50 miles some good land is gone through, with some dark soil, some fairly good cattle, both cows and beasts, the straw of the thrashed-out grain lying in heaps of many hundreds of tons to be burned, and the homesteads about as poorly constructed as it is possible to imagine. After this, at a distance of 60 miles from Winnipeg, we reached Portage la Prairie, where the excellent character of the farms, the far more substantial character of the homesteads, and the ambitious style of stores, municipal buildings and other urban establishments, announce to you an embryo city. Portage is certainly a place of which much will be heard in the future—I believe on its own merits, but even if, without the development of them, history should be silent about it, it will not be from any reticence on the part of the Portagers.

After duly swallowing our noontide meal, and having paid proper homage by an enforced delay of some two hours to the city of a summer's growth, we tracked on over prairie land broken by a few creeks or tributary branches of the Red River, till night fell and hunger came on with considerable violence, and about ten in the evening, after many a stoppage, we found ourselves halted at the temporary bridge over the Assiniboine. We were a long train, and it was not a very grand bridge, and so one part of our train went over first, and then our carriage went over; and beyond the bridge the track, and the passage over it, partook more and more of the character of the pitching of a boat in a rough sea, until at last we stopped, and were told that we were at Brandon and that we might get out.

We got out—into the mud and into the dark, and the colonial "jump down" was never more fully realized. There was no rain, but that was about the only source of discomfort, atmospheric or elementary, that was not present; black darkness and blacker mud saluted some 50 or 60 of us as we struggled on in the direction of where we were led to believe that the hotel lay. Most seriously did I begin to think of the responsibilities of any man who brought a lady to the North-West shod in those unscientific foot protectors which women will profess to believe are "strong boots." At last a kindly spirit passed us with a lantern, and held it low, and I entreated that we might be allowed to follow him. The light proved to be no "will o' the wisp," and led us to a hotel. Ascending the four muddy steps, we found ourselves with many others in a temporary bar, where some had been refreshing themselves, clearly, long before the train had arrived, or perhaps even before it had started from Winnipeg.

"Have you any room here."

"No."

"Can we have any tea or anything to eat?"

"No, there is nothing."

Hunger, a tramp back to the train through the mud, and a long night on those crampy little seats, seemed our only lot, when a door opened, my wife was passed into an inner room, I followed after a little time, and found that tea and bread and butter were to be had, and not a few kind apologies for the slight refreshment that could alone be offered to us. But even better things were in store for us. Our kind friend of the lamp, Mr. Daly, had pushed on to another hotel, and representing to two gentlemen already in bed that an English lady was very tired and had no place to lie down, had elicited from Mr. Roche and Mr. Pearce the expression that if the lady and gentleman really came from the old country, and if the gentleman was an English Member of Parliament, and not "one of our own darned land-jobbing lot," they would give up their bed at once, and we found ourselves by this real kindness with a place to lie down, while our two benefactors took a lie down in an adjoining store, the one on the counter and the other under it.

I need not say how profuse were our thanks to these kind friends in need. A tolerably comfortable night was the consequence, which rested us after a day of considerable fatigue and an evening of no little anxiety.

The next morning we were up early, and after a rough breakfast set to work to get together the stores and outfit, and to look after my men and the dog "Parigi," who was to be the companion of my sport. For some reason or other, best known to the railway managers, the freight car containing our worldly goods had been taken back across the Assiniboine, and there was no little difficulty in getting them back over the skeleton bridge, consisting of lateral beams and iron ties. However, I came across a man who was at work on the telegraph, and who turned out to have been a labourer on a neighbouring farm in Worcestershire, and he kindly volunteered his assistance, and so having brought my goods and dog to the end of the bridge, I proceeded to endeavour to take them across, bit by bit, starting first with my gun case in one hand, and Parigi in the other. Scarcely, however, had we advanced some 15 or 20 yards when Parigi became nervous, and we had to retire again to our starting point. A second journey brought us a few yards further, and Doggy's doubts necessitated a similar return. Starting a third time, I took Parigi with a loose cord, making up my mind that at any rate I would get across myself, and that the dog must look out for himself in the waters of the Assiniboine. The clever dog, however, accepting the position, walked quietly by my side and we got safely across. A return on the second journey brought some more packages, and my friend helped me over with the rest, and then having got them on the wagon we drove back into Brandon, and prepared for our journey into the prairie. Some friends accompanied us as far as the first farm of a Mr. Doran, close up to the Blue Mountains, and having left them there we drove on till after some 12 or 15 miles, which we deemed sufficient for our first afternoon, we pitched our camp by the side of an exceedingly pretty little lake which I christened Lake Mashinka, the Russian diminutive for Mary.

A little bit of clumsiness of one of our men led to two of the horses galloping off over the prairie, and we began to wonder whether we should ever see the animals again, and it was late in the evening when we were saluted by the cheering sounds of our men, whom we found returning with the horses into camp. I need hardly say that precautions were taken to prevent us again being set afoot by a similar accident.

An excellent supper and a comfortable disposal of buffalo robes and blankets introduced us to the first night of camp life on the prairie. Early next morning I took my gun, and, with the assistance of Parigi, brought in three or four ducks from the lake, and on my way home I bagged a couple of prairie chickens. Birds of these two classes form, indeed, in the absence of the bigger game, our principal food on the prairie, supplemented by that necessity of existence, fat bacon, with biscuit and tinned fruit.

After a good breakfast we hitched up, and struck off on our western course. I had intended to have made for the country to the southeast over the Pembina Mountains, and then to take a northeast direction for Winnipeg, but Guillaume had a great desire to take me in the direction of the Moose Mountains, and the Montagne de Bois, as he said that on that line we should stand a better chance of coming across some big game, and that he himself knew that country better. It was a nice bright morning when we left our pretty camp, and struck off in the westerly direction now proposed to me, but in the course of the morning it darkened over, and by dinnertime at noon the rain came down very heavily. Notwithstanding rain, snow, or wind, however, as I found on many occasions afterwards, Guillaume always lighted his fire with his first match, and we cooked our ducks and chicken, and, packing up again, proceeded onwards along the western trail. The rain beat with tremendous force, coming with a very cold wind from the south; and as it was getting dark the driver of our second team became discontented, and almost mutinous, and wanted to know when we were going to stop, and where we were going to camp. As we were in the open prairie, with no wood and no water, except that which was coming on us from the sky, it was of course impossible to make a camp there, but after a few miles' further drive, we saw a shanty that had been erected by some enterprising settler, and magnificently labelled "City of Rosser."

We made up our minds that, though the place did not look very inviting, it was better than stopping out on the prairie or risking a longer drive. We turned in, and having made up for our horses something of a shelter under a haystack, we gladly availed ourselves of a refuge which we found was being shared by some 14 or 15 others. There was shelter from the rain, the settler's wife played us some tunes on the harmonium, and we managed to make ourselves up for the night. Next morning we were up at daylight, and as I was washing, a man shouted out there was a deer close up to the door. Unfortunately he had made so much noise in communicating this piece of intelligence that the animal was well away before I could get hold of my rifle. The rain still came down in torrents, and as my wife was not strong enough for such weather on the prairie, it was clear that there were only two courses, either to give up Moose Mountain altogether, or that she should return to Brandon with Lament and the carriage; and that I, leaving all the things that were superfluous, including our big bell tent, at Mr. Parks', should take Guillaume with the wagon for a fortnight's camping. To this we made up our minds, and at 2:00 p.m., having dined, we parted; my wife to the eastward, and I taking the trail for the west.

The weather cleared up, and we came to an encampment of graders constructing part of the Canada Pacific under contract. This was the place for which Guillaume had been striking the night before, and here we found a store, a large dining tent, and newly baked bread; if we could have pitched our tent here we should certainly have been more comfortable than at the "City of Rosser." I purchased some oats for my horses, and the proprietor of the store might well apologize for the price which he asked for them. It was, however, as he said, very little more than the cost at which they had stood him in. At the same time, 25 shillings for two bushels was indeed a very large price.

I saw here the mode in which a railway was being constructed. The line has to be raised about four feet above the level of the prairie, so as to keep it out of the snow in the winter. In constructing this bank the first thing done is for a width on each side the line of about 20 yards to cut the turf, and to lay it as the foundation of the "dump" which is to carry the line. This having been done, ploughs set to work, and the earth beneath the turf is ploughed up to the depth of 10 or 12 inches. There is then brought to bear upon this what is called a scraper—a big shovel drawn by a pair of horses. The driver puts his horses at right angles to the dump, and digging the nose of the scraper into the soft ploughed-up soil, fills it, and, as his horses cross the dump, he turns it over. Crossing to the other side, and turning his horses, he repeats the same proceeding, and it is wonderful how quickly, with the two span of horses and two scrapers crossing one another, the dump rises to the required height.

When this is done there is of course a considerable amount of levelling to be gone through; but the quantity of spade labour is, by this mode of making a railway, reduced to a minimum. It was a curious thing to see the various men employed in this work. I noticed one man ploughing most energetically, and throwing almost as much strength from himself into his work as he was getting out of his horses. In conversation with Mr. McDonald, the contractor, I was told that this was a medical gentleman, who, not having found any great success in his business, had taken to this new and more active line of life. Another attracted my attention by the curious way in which he was holding his plough, and upon my remarking it I was told that I had no business to criticise his mode of ploughing, for he came from the old country, and I subsequently found that he was a shepherd from one of our western counties. When I add to this that a young man who assisted me in cooking my dinner informed me that he knew me well; that he had been a solicitor's clerk in London, and had been to my chambers with briefs, it will be seen of what a motley assemblage of the "something to do"-seeking waifs from all countries the railway gang consisted. They were, however, happy, active fellows, and were working no doubt all the better from the fact that no such thing as drink finds its way into the Canadian Western railway camp. The weather had quite cleared as we drove on from our railway camp, and the setting sun on the poplars, which were now getting their yellow autumn tint, made a very pretty fringe to the edge of the prairie. We drove into a most snug shelter in the sandhills which we had reached. A little lake and a wood gave us all we wanted for our camp, and we soon had our fire lighted and made ourselves most comfortable. A yell as I put my naked foot on a cactus, and thus made my first acquaintance with a noteworthy member of the flora of the sandy prairies, is a reminiscence of that night, and I realized in a substantial form the nickname that is given to the newcomer out West of "tenderfoot" or "pilgrim." While we were lighting our fire a man came up—he was hunting for some cattle, and told us he was with a settler who had taken up a homestead at no great distance in the woods. I sent him a message, and after our tea he came up and sat by the fire with a pipe, and we discussed the probabilities and chances of success of farming there till the rain began to come down again, and we adjourned into the tent; and about eight o'clock, when our friend had bid us good night, we turned in. The rain came down very heavily, and the wind blew hard, but we were quite comfortable inside our tent. My friend had told me that the cattle do very well here. The land is sandy, but they feed in the woods; and there is a grass which the French call "l'aprelle," which keeps green during the whole of the winter, of a very feeding character. It is an equisetum, and grows to a height of two or three feet. We heard that there were deer in the woods, and that they had been browsing with the cows; and so next morning I was up at sunrise, and had a walk before breakfast through the wood, to see if I could catch sight of any game. I went round the lake and returned my neighbour's visit at his log hut, and had a talk with his cheery little wife. They seemed happy; and he told me that his house had taken him eight days to build, and that the only thing he had had to pay in respect of it was six dollars for the windows. All the rest was made with logs laid on each other, and the spaces between them well filled with mud and clay. His man had an adjoining log hut, and they were then at work on their cow house. I regretted much that I had brought no newspaper, as he had had no news for many weeks, and was curious to hear of the fate of the Irish Land Bill, and had not even heard of the sad murder of the President.

On my way back to my tent, I shot a couple of teal; after breakfast it came on to rain very heavily, and we delayed starting off; but at half-past nine as we had 30 miles to do, we struck camp and hitched up. After leaving the wood we drove about two miles, and stopped to water our horses and to take in wood, as we should find nothing with which to make a fire for the next 30 or 35 miles. We drove along over some sandy and some fairly good land, leaving Oak Lake to our left. On one side of the lake there is an Indian reserve for the Sioux, and a good belt of wood about three miles to our left for the first 10 miles. It seemed to me that a good cattle farm might be placed here, and that cattle would feed well on the prairie through which our trail passed, and where there is an abundance of grass, but it was too wet for wheat, even now, after a dry season.

At the end of about 10 or 12 miles we ascended to a sandy plateau, through which the trail passed for 15 or 20 miles—a thin soil, with occasionally little pools and scattered with granite boulders; hawks, small birds, a few ducks, skunks and gophers being the only inhabitants of this part. Guillaume told me that it had been a great place for buffalo, who were very fond of the grass I have spoken of, and even now their trails may be seen, and many bones, skulls, and horns lying about.

Sunday, October 1st—Up at six o'clock and found it raining steadily, with occasional snow. Having breakfasted and put on our wet clothes we hitched up, and at the end of about two hours we came down a sharp descent into a very wild gully, forming a hollow of about a mile wide before again ascending to the level of the prairie, with a depression of from 80 to 100 feet. This is Stone Pipe Creek, the waters from which run into Oak Lake, to the east of which it is joined by the Souris or Mouse River, and runs into the Assiniboine about 100 miles to the west of Winnipeg. The creek is fairly timbered on the western side, where other cross gullies bring down the water from the higher level. As we approached a large number of Canadian geese rose into the air almost within shot. I was new to prairie life, or I should of course have taken care to approach so good a cover more carefully, and I should certainly have been rewarded with one or two of these most excellent birds. In crossing, the water came up to our axles, but there was a good solid bottom under the wheels. After crossing I got down from the wagon and waded through the long grass up the stream, and was rewarded by getting a couple of ducks. It seemed very strange that in this thoroughly desolate prairie the ducks were more shy, or, as Guillaume called it, more "farouches," than they would have been even in our own country, and I could only approach them by stalking, as if they sighted or winded me they rose from the water before I could get within 150 yards of them. My good dog Parigi having retrieved the birds, we got on the wagon again and proceeded up the slope till we regained the former level of the prairie, and as it began to rain again most heavily we tucked ourselves up as well as we could, though I had got regularly soaked in going through the long grass after the ducks, and so we proceeded on our rather melancholy journey. A little after noon, when the rain was at its worst, as we were near water for the horses, Guillaume intimated that we should halt and dine, and that we should pitch our tent for that purpose. This seemed to me, I must say, a terrible undertaking in a heavy rain, and I suggested that if the horses rested and had their oats we should do better to wait till we stopped for the night. The more practical knowledge of my good friend, however, prevailed, as he argued that it would be better to have our dinner comfortably, and that we must have some shelter; and so the tent was pitched, though my fingers were so cold that I was not of much service; but Guillaume quickly lighted the fire as readily as if it had been a beautiful sunshiny day. We sat in the shelter of the tent and within reach of the warmth of the fire and the incensy smell of its logs. I skinned the two ducks and prepared them for the pot. Stewed with bacon and potatoes, they made an excellent dish, and with some boiling hot tea we had a comfortable meal. The rain abated a little, and we got up at 2:30 and had a tolerably pleasant drive. We saw several skunks on the trail, and one of them trotted along in front of us. One was burrowing away after something at a gopher's burrow. Another seemed to be taking in a leisurely way an afternoon stroll. Poor Parigi, in spite of a warning on the day before, insisted on rushing after this animal. In vain I called to him by every name that rose to my lips, but he still kept on. The skunk then quietly stopped, and as Parigi ran barking up to him, turned round and emptied his skunk bag full over his face and eyes. The poor beast was in a dreadful state, the acrid juice, which must have struck his eyes, being, in addition to the filthy smell, doubtless the cause of considerable pain. I paid the brute off with a charge of shot as I passed him. As to the dog, any further intercourse for a time with him was hopeless, and he had to be exiled from tent and board for two days. The smell of this secretion is truly dreadful—assafœtida, sulphuretted hydrogen, rotten garlic with a strong dash of phosphorus, might perhaps give some little idea of the intolerable stink. It is so bad that I knew of a case where a friend having only come too closely within the atmosphere of the skunk as he followed him up pelting him with stones, smelt so abominably when he came into the hut that everyone insisted on his going out and changing his clothes before he sat down. It would be an interesting thing to ascertain by analysis the exact nature of this liquid, which is the extraordinary mode of defence that has been given to the animal; but I can't help thinking that he would be a bold man of science who could take a skunk's stink-bag and analyze the contents. Some very pretty birds, rather larger than larks, but with somewhat similar habits, rose from the prairie as we

49

passed along, the back of their heads marked like a jack snipe, with some white feathers in the tail and wings. Guillaume called them "goggleux," or goggle eyes, a name taken probably from the ring round the eye that looks like spectacles. I have since found from Professor Macoun's description of the bird that it is the chestnut-collared bunting.

As it grew dusk I shot a pretty brown owl, "sparovigier," and at dark we came on the remains of a camp where some wood had been left. Guillaume suggested our stopping there, but it was a bleak open place, and there was no shelter for the horses, and he had promised that we should reach a wood, for which I pressed on, as he thought it was "pas loin"; to this wood we looked forward on that cold wet night as though it had been the best of hostelries. It grew very dark, and we had some bad places to pass through, narrowly escaping a capsize in one, and at half-past eight we reached some brush and thick grass, and here, as the rain had begun again with snow and hail, we fixed our tent, lighted our fire, and made ourselves as comfortable as we could with biscuits and a box of sardines, and that greatest friend of man, hot tea, and we turned in about 9:30.

There was a downpour of rain during the night. I did not sleep well, and lay wondering much what had become of my wife, and how she would be getting on, and consequently reconsidering my plans as to whether it would not be better to give up my excursion if this bad weather was likely to continue. At last I dozed off, but not into a very good sleep, till six in the morning, when we turned out, put on our wet stockings and boots, and prepared for breakfast. I wrote up my log while Guillaume was packing the things together, harnessing the horses, and hitching up.

Monday, October 2nd—I had already lost count in some way of the days of the week, and under the impression that it was Sunday, made up my mind to make a short Sabbath-day journey. We started, and after a very few miles found ourselves on a beautiful knoll by the side of the trail, with some small lakes in front of us, and two pointed hills with wood creeping up on one side about two miles distant, which Guillaume called "Les Buttes de Coeur." It turned out a beautiful evening, and making a good fire we set to work to dry our clothes, and while this operation was going on I lighted my candle, it being a very still night, for the purpose of writing up my notes.

I had observed during the last three days that though we were going due west my compass seemed to indicate an almost northerly direction, and I wondered very much where the fault lay. Many a time it has fallen to my lot to have to cross-examine the captains of ships as to their not taking note of the variation, and little did I think how easily one who was not a navigator might be found in a similar error.

It was, as I said, a bright starlight night, and guided by "the Dipper," as Charles' Wain is called in Canada, from its resemblance to that most useful article—a tin cup with a long handle, which in every shop and hut in the North-West hangs by the water bucket, so that every visitor may take a drink, I took an observation, from the polar star, of the true north. I was anxious to get the exact bearing of our camp with the top of the hill, to which I proposed making an excursion on the following day. I found on looking at my compass that the magnetic north, instead of being some 20 points to the westward of the true north as it is with us, was 22 points to the eastward of it, and it was this difference of 42 points which had so puzzled me as to our course.

The effect of finding oneself for the first time in the presence and recognition of one of the greatest phenomena of nature is most interesting. A long and thoughtful sit by the fire after Guillaume had turned in, brought the day to its close, and I must have slept pretty heavily, for it was getting toward six o'clock when I awoke, and finding my watch had run down, and knowing that on this day of the year the sun rises at six o'clock, I set my watch by the great luminary as his first edge showed above the prairie; and having breakfasted and taken a full observation of the bearings of the hill and the camp, I set off with my gun and Parigi to the buttes. It was a lovely bit of country, with numerous little meres of from one to 20 or 30 acres, with belts of poplar and cottonwood round them, the brush so thick that it was difficult to work one's way through, and it required all I knew to make sure that I could find my way back. I came to one lovely little lake, and noticed that there was the trail of some big game or of an Indian having passed shortly before in the same direction. I sat down on a fallen tree, as the day was blazing hot; and I must say that of all the exercise in the world commend me to an endeavour to get through the Canadian bush—creeping under one fallen tree, scrambling

51

over another, and squeezing between two leaning close against each other is hard work, and makes progress very slow.

As I sat on the tree I caught sight for the first time of a beaver coming across the pool, and as Parigi and I kept quite still, the little animal came on straight forward, flapping its flat tail in the air. I could not find it in my heart to shoot the interesting little beast, and I left him to follow his own pursuits; not that, however, my tenderness in this respect would be likely to ensure him a long career, now that both Indians and white men are so closely clearing off all the old inhabitants of the lake and the forest.

I had a curious instance of a habit common to wounded animals and birds in the prairie land, of counterfeiting death; I had shot a big mallard, and he dropped as if dead. Not wishing to be encumbered by his weight during my walk, I laid him out with all the gorgeousness of his feathers and wings spread for full display across the trail along which I intended to return. Having thus beautifully arranged the corpse I turned to go on my journey, when hearing a bit of a flap, I looked round, and saw the duck slide away down the bank into the water. From many things I have heard and seen since, I believe that this is a wonderfully developed instinct among these wild animals; who thus make use of their knowledge of the habits of their ordinary pursuers to afford them a last chance against animals which will not touch carrion.

I soon found that the three or four miles to the top of the hill was far more than I could hope to accomplish at the rate at which I could alone proceed; and having got as far as I could up the slope of the hill I turned my way homewards. As this was my first day out in the bush I was not a little anxious as to my finding my way back, and was very pleased to catch sight of my little white tent on the knoll. I found that Guillaume had got everything in good order, and we sat down to our tea and discussed our future plans in a curious language, half French, half English, with a curious admixture of Cree. We had planned to go round the buttes, or get as near them as we could, so that I might perhaps from an easier or less wooded ascent get up and see what view there might be; but on reconsidering our plan after breakfast the next morning, we came to the conclusion that to get through the wood would probably make necessary a circuit of very many miles, and as Guillaume was averse to returning by the same route, which I had rather wished for, as I wanted to see the nice little peninsula in Oak Lake, I gave way to his arguments, and we concluded to go back along our trail for two or three miles, and then to take the northwestern trail for Port Ellice; and so we started at ten o'clock and drove till noon. While we were at breakfast I heard Guillaume cry "Ishqwahanga," and looking up I saw a big fishing-eagle hovering over our fire. I took my chance with my gun, but the shot only rattled against his strong wing feathers, and he sailed away. One of our horses had a sore shoulder, but by packing the collar with my worsted comforter he went tolerably well, and at noon we stopped by the side of a little pool and some brushwood, near the termination of the belt of trees, and took two hours for rest and dinner for our horses and ourselves.

During the previous night I had been interested in watching a big prairie fire in the northwest, the line we had determined to take, and Guillaume had recounted to me his losses in former expeditions and the dangers of being caught. As I walked on I met a man journeying with a cart and a pony and his dog and gun, carrying provisions from Port Ellice to his comrades, who were surveying close down to the boundary line. I had some talk with him, but when Guillaume came up afterwards, he said, "That's the man who lighted the fire last night," and sure enough when we had gone about four miles further we came to the place where he had camped, and from the little circle of his tent lying to the windward of the brule it was clear that he had carelessly allowed his campfire to catch and spread, and it had burned up many a square mile of good prairie grass and useful wood. I had succeeded in getting a considerable number of duck at our camp near the buttes, so that with some bacon we had an excellent dinner.

At two o'clock we started again, and in about two hours recrossed Stone Pipe Creek about 18 miles above the point at which we had crossed it before. We passed through some very good prairie land till six, and I picked up two prairie chickens in my walk after dinner, which gave us a very fair meal at tea time, and with a bright rising moon and amidst the light of a most gorgeous sunset of *couleur de rose* in the north and orange and purple in the west, we pitched our camp, and made a very pleasant evening of it. It soon however came on cold, as, the air being so clear, no sooner does the sun go down than all heat seems to leave.

We tumbled into our blankets with a little concert of a few barks from foxes and prairie dogs and the whizzing of the ducks overhead, and composed ourselves to rest, but it was so cold that I could not keep my feet warm, and did not sleep well in consequence.

We woke about 5:30, and got up a little before sunrise, to find everything frozen very hard, and the rime thick on our blankets. I judged how cold it had been when I found that my knickerbockers, which I flattered myself I had dried yesterday, stood up by themselves, and my sponge in the middle of my travelling bag was frozen stiff and hard. The sun, however, soon began to thaw everything, and we were at eight o'clock ready to start.

Tuesday, October 4—We went on till dinner under a blazing sun, which dried everything, and which gave us a good sample of the wonderful change of temperature in this country.

We drove on till we came to a cross trail, which Guillaume said led back to Brandon. We were then about 12 miles to the south of Port Ellice, and it was about 4:30, so that we could scarcely reach Port Ellice that night. Our horses were getting tired, especially the poor beast with the sore shoulder, so I made up my mind to turn eastward; we drove along over a bad bit of prairie, till we began to be anxious about water, having now got into a very dry piece of country.

The most striking peculiarity of journeying in the prairie is the very short distance that you can see. A mile and a half or two miles at the outside is the limit of your vision in this absolutely flat land. When sitting in your wagon at the height of about six feet from the ground, the prairie gives you the idea that you are constantly rising a gradual hill, and that as soon as you get to the horizon you will get a good view, and for miles and miles this deceptive appearance is continued. A curious little group we must have presented on this present occasion as I drove along with Guillaume standing up on the seat by my side, gazing anxiously to see if he could catch any sight suggestive of water. Presently with great glee he jumped down and pronounced the words "rat house," as he caught sight of one of these curious little conical structures, which told him of a pool.

Having come to it we unhitched on the knoll, which from its complete perforation by badgers, I christened "Badger Hill Camp," and made our camp there and had supper. The water was very thick and dirty, and the only way in which we could make it at all decent for tea was by filtering it through a cloth. It was, however, quite sweet, with no touch of alkali.

Next morning up at six, and a very bad trail for several miles, and after that some 15 miles of the most desolate land conceivable—alkali and clay, with poor, thin herbage, frequent boulders, and occasionally patches of a white clayey mud. No birds or any other living thing, and during the whole of that 20 miles one prairie fox was the only object that we saw. From the tableland we descended to a creek for which Guillaume had no name, and where there was plenty of wood, but no game.

After dinner, I strolled on by myself for three or four miles, and catching sight of an outfit, found, on going up, that it was a friend whom I left at Brandon, with a party just finishing their camp dinner, and bound westward prospecting; but with no very definite prospects before them. Guillaume came up with the wagon, and we went on to the creek, which Guillaume christened "Gophers' Creek," from the number of these little animals that are found there. This seemed an excellent site for a town, and as we lighted our fire, and stuck up a buffalo's head close to our tent, we discussed the future of Gopher Town and the success of the enterprise in the hotel which we determined to establish under the sign of the "Buffalo Head."

A railway camp was at work here, making a crossing for the creek, which was of an unusually heavy character.

In the big tent which was used for dining, around the stove, standing and looking on in their vague listless style, were four or five Sioux Indians. They were of a much larger stamp than the Crees or the other tribes that I have seen. One of them, a fine-looking old hunter, "Chaske," took hold of my gun and examined the central fire breechloader. "I say, boss," said one of the railway men, "who made that gun?" "Boss," replied I. My friend seemed puzzled at the answer, but on looking at the name of the maker laughed heartily at the appropriateness of the answer.

I made out from Guillaume, whose mother was a half-bred Sioux, a few of the Sioux words. I could not however ascertain whether our friends round the fire belonged in any way to the band of "Tanti u tanki," or Sitting Bull, who was at that time a little further to the southwest in the Montagne de Bois. This chief had with his band fled across the boundary line after what has been called the massacre of General Ouster and his regiment.

The story of that encounter as given by Sitting Bull to a friend of mine, Major Crozier, to whom he surrendered, showed the Indian Chief to have had higher military qualities than the dashing but unfortunate officer who fell into the ambuscade.

After dinner and the purchase of some oats we hitched up and went on our journey to our friends at the "City of Rosser." We had a pleasant drive over a good prairie trail, which brought us to the northern side of the sandhills, which we had passed on our journey west. The timber on these hills is principally of a small stumpy oak, with very little grass, the principal vegetation being the *aprelle* of which I have spoken. Crossing once or twice the line of railway which runs here parallel to the trail, we had a drive of about 12 miles, till we reached our destination at Parks', and, camping there, had supper, preferring our tent to the interior of the house.

Sitting up smoking, before retiring, the conversation turned on some poor fellow in the neighbourhood who had been found frozen to death a few days before, and on my asking how it had come about I was told that he had been frozen while out haymaking. This may give a strange idea of the climate. The fact, however, was that the man had gone to sleep in a small bell tent, without taking any care to protect himself against the cold, and had certainly been found dead the following morning. It must not be supposed, however, that haymakers in the North-West are usually liable to such an end in pursuing an occupation which is not generally associated with extreme cold.

Next day I sold my extra stores (which from the shortness of my journey were very considerable) to my host, and started off for Brandon. After a 12-mile drive we come to a good lake and prepared to dine. The grass was very high, and had become thoroughly dry with the frost and the sun, and it was somewhat difficult to prevent it catching fire. We had had several instances of this terrible scourge during our journey, and Guillaume had told me how, in the previous year, the fire had caught the neighbourhood of the camp, and they had lost everything, even including their wagons, except their horses; and I had myself, as I have said, on the day before, seen how quickly an enormous loss in that part of the prairie may be effected in a very few hours at this time of the year. I think I may say for myself and my companions, both in this and subsequent journeys, that no such accident has ever happened to us. The best plan is as soon as the fire is lighted to let it burn till you get a pretty good circle clear, of a few yards wide, burnt round the fire, and by keeping watch with a sack with some grass in it, you can easily prevent the fire from spreading, and after you have got that clear space, of course there is no further danger. Let it, however, once get ahead, and there is no stopping it. Above all it is most necessary that after every camp, before leaving, you should take care that the logs are so far extinguished that there is no chance of sparks flying from them in case of a sudden gust or squall.

After dinner we drove on to Brandon, and arrived there about half-past three, and I walked about till I met my wife coming in from sketching. She had indeed had a dull week of it, and was still suffering a great deal from her cough, but had amused herself with helping a lady, whose acquaintance she had made, to look after a shop and sell goods to the Indians and other customers, of whose honesty indeed, as the customers seemed to have priced and weighed the goods for themselves, they had every reason to speak highly.

Some of our friends had come into our tent, and Guillaume and I got them an excellent tea, and as I must say I still preferred our canvas house to the unfinished and not over-clean hotel, we made up our buffaloes for the evening. It was a lovely moonlight night; but it rained hard, with a good deal of wind, in the morning, and Guillaume and I were up early, before daylight, to get our things together, so as to put them in the train for Winnipeg. Having packed everything, I went into the hotel to see if all my wife's things were ready for a start, and as soon as it was daylight I brought her boxes downstairs and sat down to breakfast.

There was a curious muster of all sorts of people round the table getting their morning meal previous to starting. One worthy man who had seen me hauling the boxes downstairs and putting them ready to go off, remarked—

"I don't know who you are, but you are the sort of chap for this country."

"Why?" said I.

"Because," he said, "you do everything for yourself, and don't call out for help. And I'll tell you what it is, I'll lend you my wagon, and give your things a lift to the station."

This is, indeed, an illustration of what is expected from everybody out in the North-West. Help yourself and everybody is quite willing to help you. Sit down and pray to the gods, and help will not be got either for love or money.

In due course we were under way, and our train having set off eastward, we stopped for dinner again at the thriving town of Portage, and arrived at Winnipeg late in the evening. Here we were met by our good friend Mr. Boyle, who kindly afforded us the hospitality of his pretty little house, with respect to which we only lamented that the dreadful mud convinced us that we must necessarily be giving an enormous amount of trouble; no scrapers, no brushes, no care, can keep you in a condition fit to enter a respectable establishment after a walk through the streets of Winnipeg in wet weather. On one occasion I had gone out to make a call, but on arriving at the door I was so ashamed of the condition of my lower limbs that I beat a retreat without paying my respects.

The second or third day that we were in Winnipeg, about the 15th of October, it turned very cold, and the shops hanging out all their furs as I was proposing to go for a drive to pay some calls, I provided myself with a large racoon coat. Mr. Boyle had a pretty light buggy which he drove, with a good trotter, "Robin"—a steady-looking horse—and he had it prepared for us to go for our drive. On coming to take the reins the horse caught sight of my racoon coat, and was dreadfully alarmed. Thinking that he would soon get over that, I got my friend to hold his head whilst I and my wife got into the carriage, and in that way we drove down to the river, and crossing in a ferry boat we arrived in St. Boniface, and drove up to the house of the Archbishop, Monsieur Taché. Most fortunately I asked my wife to get out of the carriage first, for no sooner had I stepped up to the horse's head and he had caught sight of my fur cloak than he looked almost dazed with fear, and started off along the bank of the Red River as fast as he could go. I kept hold of the reins until catching my foot in something I came a regular sprawler, while the horse went along with the carriage after him till he was out of sight. Hoping that someone would stop him I threw my coat off and followed after him. I found a man driving him hack, but as soon as I got up, either from the smell of my coat or the recognition of my voice as the wearer of the detested garment, he turned sharply round again, and jumped some rails, dragging the light buggy after him. I found he was so thoroughly alarmed that it was utterly impossible for me to get near him, and I was obliged to ask the man who had brought him back, and another friend, to take him out of the trap and put him in the stable. As for us, we found our way back to Winnipeg on foot, and sent the servant for him in the evening, and even when the servant got there he found him still trembling and in a condition of great alarm. I presume my coat had either a wild beast smell about it or it must have given me a somewhat wolfish appearance, for I found that the horse had no such fear of a beaver coat, but that he could not be persuaded to allow any light-coloured fur to come near him. We had indeed a fortunate escape, and I tremble to think what might have happened had I not most fortunately told my wife to get out of the carriage before I myself alighted. These hickory-made little light buggies are wonderful institutions— very light and very strong; the only difficulty about them being that, the fore wheels being the same diameter as the hind ones, they will not turn under the body. The consequence is it takes a larger space than our streets would allow to turn them round.

The evening of this our last day in Winnipeg, October 10th, had been fixed upon for the opening of the club, and an address by the Governor General, who arrived that day. It was an excellent banquet in a most commodious clubhouse, and the Marquis of Lorne was received with much enthusiasm on his return from his Western trip, of which he gave an excellent *résumé*, full of good suggestions and pleasant interchange of good feeling.

The next day we started off on our journey home, and, making another short stay at St. Paul, we ran through Chicago, and found ourselves again in our comfortable rooms in the Queen's Hotel at Toronto. Time, however, was getting short, and we made our way to Montreal, and from thence to Ottawa.

We had hoped to see the Thousand Islands, and to have gone down by Kingston. It was however too late in the season, the last boat having gone; so we contented ourselves with doing the Lachine Rapids, a very pleasant little excursion, which only necessitated being up rather early in the morning; all that is required is to take the train for about six miles to Lachine, put yourself on board the *Corsican*, and, under the careful guidance of the Indian pilot Joseph, you are twisted through the rapids, and, sailing under the big bridge, get back to Windsor Hotel with a good appetite for your breakfast.

From Montreal we ran up to Ottawa, as I wished to make the acquaintance of the Prime Minister—the most eminent citizen of Canada. The Parliament building and the view from the terrace amply repaid a visit to the capital, and it was a pretty drive to Rideau Hall to pay our respects to the Governor General. The glorious red on the oaks and yellow on the maples and poplars in the bright sun of an Indian summer gave a splendid colouring to the woods. We found that the Governor was suffering from that which is the inevitable consequence of camping out, and was confined to his bed with a heavy cold. A pleasant evening at the Prime Minister's brought our visit to a close, and we started off next day for Quebec.

At Quebec we devoted the day following to the Montmorency Falls, and I really think of all the sights in Canada it is one of the most beautiful. The enormous mass of water tumbles over the ledge straight into the St. Lawrence from a height of nearly 200 feet, constituting a fall, though doubtless not so grand, scarcely less beautiful than Niagara, and well does it repay you to wander up the stream above the fall and see the natural staircase formed by the detrition of the rocks, and the pretty path that wanders through the pine wood and gives an air of almost cultivated landscape to the wild woodland.

There was a good deal of snow on the ground in places, and as I passed through one deepish snowdrift my eye fell on a gold bracelet which had fallen from the arm of some recent visitor. Reading its inscription I connected it with a lady whom I had seen in the hotel at Quebec,

60

and who was, I knew, visiting Montmorency that same day. Going up to her on our return to the hotel I asked if she had lost anything, but, being answered in the negative, I produced the bracelet, and found it was indeed hers. She had not missed it, and welcomed its return with very considerable joy.

Next day found us on board the *Circassian*, and a cold day's steam down the St. Lawrence with clear weather through the straits brought us into the Atlantic, where, with a good westerly wind but rather heavy seas, we had a pleasant week, and arrived in the Mersey on the 2nd of November, very well satisfied indeed with our first trip to Canada; pretty confident as to its being a good place for emigrants, and certainly determined to take the earliest opportunity of another visit.

CHAPTER IV

~

AND NOW THAT WE have made acquaintance with the country, and have met a few of the representatives of its earliest races, it may be well to give briefly some details of the divisions into which we find their tribes separated.

The most descriptive generic name that has been given to these races has undoubtedly been that by which they are spoken of by the French as "les sauvages," meaning thereby not what we call "savages," but rather, as the word more correctly implies, the wild men of the country. The word may, perhaps, have too much of the sense in which the Greeks used the word βάρβαος as signifying all who had not attained to their own civilization; but it is at any rate far better than that earliest English name which in all false geography we gave them of American Indian. The name of Redman or Redskin, by which an Indian will in all pride describe himself, in contradistinction to our pale skin "sicklied o'er" he may fancy "with a pale cast of thought," is a far better name.

Whence they came or at what date they had their origin in this land, are questions far beyond the limits of this narrative. Their tribes differ, indeed, between themselves so much in appearance, and so entirely in language, that it is apparent at the first blush, that if there ever were any such common origin, they must have passed through many different stages and undergone the changes of many varying climates before they could have arrived at the completeness of distinction in features, manners, and language which now mark their separation.

Of those with whom my narrative deals, the three principal families are the Algonquin, the Sioux and the Blackfoot.

The Algonquins occupied to the exclusion of all others the district of the North-West between the Red River and Cumberland House, and included the majority of the tribes wandering about the district of the Saskatchewan River and the Swan River, and it is said that some isolated bands have found their way as far north as the Athabaska; if we add to this immense extent of territory the land which the different branches of the Algonquin family occupied in the eastern part of Canada, it is clear that this group of Indians is the most extensive of the whole of the Northern American tribes.

It is said by M. Taché, the very learned and energetic Archbishop of St. Boniface, and one of the truest friends of the red man, that in the Department of the North this tribe in 1869 reckoned not more than 30,000, though tradition tells us that at one time it was far more numerous, but that wars and famine, and above all that terrible scourge smallpox, have reduced it to its present figure.

The Algonquin family consists of three nations: the Saulteux, the Muskegons and the Crees.

The Saulteux occupied in the Department of the North, a belt extending over three or four degrees of latitude to the north of the 49th parallel, from the western limits of Ontario to the eastern part of the district of the river Saskatchewan. The Muskegons occupied the country to the north of this up to the shores of the Hudson Bay, while the Crees occupied a kind of central position between these two tribes to the base of the Rocky Mountains. The Saulteux, who have largely intermingled with the French voyageurs, are of good physique, and are men to whom it has been found by the missionaries to be almost impossible to communicate any notion of Christianity or civilization; proud and superstitious to excess, and, in former days, cruel above all on the warpath, with an inordinate love for adorning their persons and heads with all kinds of shells, jewellery, and feathers. Their name is said to have been given to them as having their headquarters in the land adjoining the Sault St. Marie, the rapids by which the water passes from the Lake Superior into the stream which runs into the Lake Huron, and which the voyageurs knew them to regard as the cradle of their race. The Crees call them Nakaiverniwoh, while the Saulteux designate themselves under the title of Anichineve-woh, both of which words signify men with a qualification attached.

The second branch of the Algonquins, the Muskegons, derive their name from the word muskeg, or marsh; their full name among themselves being Omaskakowoh, or men of the marsh. It is a word with which persons travelling in the west become tolerably familiar, and perhaps none more so than the railway contractors, to whom the muskeg, or bottomless swamp, has been the cause of many a difficulty and cause of failure in carrying out their works.

The Muskegons, called by the English traders "the Swampies," are said in character to be the very opposite of the Saulteux, very easy to manage, and less superstitious; a great number of them have been converted to Christianity. This has no doubt been brought about to a considerable extent by the fact that they have been very largely employed on the boats and in the portages along the trading routes. I may here explain the word "portage," as signifying the land between the two waters, across which the boat and its contents has to be carried, and is equivalent to the Scotch "tarbet," or drag-boat.

The Crees, with whom in my two first journeys I was most thrown in contact, are divided into the two tribes of Crees of the prairie, and Crees of the woods. Their call themselves Neyowoh, or Iyinuwoh. Their Blackfoot neighbours call them Kinistenowoh.

The Cree of the prairie has been at constant war with the Blackfoots. So long as the prairie yielded a good supply of buffalo he was tolerably well-to-do. That time has, however, sadly gone by for him. He is a good rider, and mounted on his little cayeuse is as smart a little figure as could well be sketched.

The Crees of the woods are a very quiet race, living in bark huts, and earning their livelihood by trapping and the sale of furs.

The second great family of our Canadian Indians is the Assiniboians. They are a branch of the warlike family of the Sioux of whom I have spoken in my allusion to the episode of the Sitting Bull, but though of the same family they have ever carried on war to the knife with their relatives; a good illustration of their feeling toward one another is to be found in the name given to the Sioux by the Saulteux, who are in alliance with the Assiniboians. They call them "tewannah," pieces of roast meat; a name which undoubtedly had its origin in the horrible custom indulged in up to a very late day by the Saulteux of cooking and eating those of their adversaries whom they killed in fight or tortured to death as prisoners.

The Assiniboians are, in fact, as their name imports, the Sioux of the Stony Mountains—"Assini" signifying Stonies, the name by which they are called by the English settlers. I have been told that their full name has some reference to their mode of cooking with hot stones in water, but I cannot verify this. These Stonies are also divided into the Stonies of the prairie and the Stonies of the woods. These last have ever been on bad terms with their neighbours, the Blackfoots, who form the third family.

The Sioux proper occupy land south of the boundary line, and it was only after the Minnesota massacre of 1862 that they fled across to the north, and occupied the country in the neighbourhood of the Montagne de Bois.

The Blackfoots occupy the land to the west of the Crees of the prairie and to the south of the northern fork of the Saskatchewan up to the base of the Rocky Mountains. They are, so far as I have seen, men of a better physique and greater capability for cultivation, and have a better notion of adornment and ornament, than any other of the northern Indians. In former times they have had plenty of game both for food and fur, and have managed to acquire considerable bands of horses and other articles which form the wealth of savages. Horse stealing has been, no doubt, their favourite pastime, and one of the great causes of war between them and their neighbours. But in this matter we must not be too hard on the Indians; at the worst they do not in this occupy a much lower position than did our English and Scotch border tribes in the old days, when the harrying of cattle and general robbery and pillage were the modes of life which led to wealth, honour and distinction, and which here also carried in their wake the border wars between English and Scotch just as they have done between Cree and Blackfoot.

The family of Blackfoot consists of three principal tribes: the Blackfoot or Sixika, including the Crows; the Piegans, and the Bloods, or Kinas. These three tribes speak different dialects, but of the same language, so far, at least, as to understand one another; they were allied for the purposes of war. They have, however, marked distinctions among themselves. The Blackfoots are always said to have had the best organization for war of any of the tribes of the north, although in this respect they were far inferior to the tribes on the other side of these boundary lines, both Sioux and Nezperces. The Peigans are excellent judges of a horse, and devoted to horse racing; the Crows are both in language and habits the most grossly immoral of all the Indians.

It is not my intention here to touch upon the Indian rites and ceremonies, on which much has been written. Any person, however, who spends the last days of August or the early days of September in the North-West, will do well to be present, if possible, at the sun dance, their great annual festival.

There is another tribe, the Sarcees, with many of whom I came in contact in one of my journeys, and of whom a few are to be seen in the neighbourhood of Calgary. They are in alliance with the Blackfoots; but are said to have no real connection with them. Monsieur Taché tells us that their language connects them with the tribe of the Beavers, who wander over the land in the north near the Peace River, a branch of those Chippeway Indians who occupy the country to the north of the Athabasca and the Mackenzie Rivers almost up to the shores of the Arctic Ocean. These Castors or Beavers and the Esquimaux are entirely to the north of the countries through which I have travelled. I have nothing therefore to say with regard to them.

The mode in which the Dominion Government has dealt with the Indians is similar to that adopted by the States. In compensation for the occupation of their hunting grounds they have reserved to them large blocks of the best of the land, amply sufficient for all purposes for which they can require land; and for the loss of game, every Indian man, woman, and child, while on the Reserve, receives 1 ½ lb. of beef and 2 lbs. of flour every second day, and a considerable money payment in each year for the purchase of blankets, clothes, and other necessaries. The problem as to how to treat the Indian has been a difficult one, for while undoubtedly these rations and payment destroy every incentive to industry, these

terms honestly carried out have entirely prevented wars and other distur-
bances. They have, in fact, put the Indian entirely on a par with the idle
class in Europe—those "gentlemen" who think that they sufficiently fulfil
the object for which they came into the world by sponging upon their
fellow men, getting themselves up as extremely as their tradesmen will
give credit, betting on horse races, drinking and idling away their hours,
pigeon shooting, and indulging in other low forms of gambling.

Chapter V

~

During my first visit in the Dominion, and on considering more fully what I had seen after my return, I became convinced that there was a great deal to be done in the way of breeding cattle, both for sale there and, if there should be a possibility of surplus stock, for the supply of store cattle to England.

We all know at how great a cost we produce our lean cattle, either as steers for feeding, or as heifers for our milk trade, and it occurred to me that it might be possible to bring across from the West well-bred animals of some two years old ready for such purposes, at a very considerably less price than that at which we can raise them here, and that if this could be done, we should overcome one of the greatest difficulties in the way of cattle farming in England; for undoubtedly with our cheap feeding stuffs, with a well-framed, healthy, fairly bred young animal, the least profitable part of the business would be put on one side, and the more profitable occupation retained. I had kept my eyes open while out on the prairie, to see how this could be done, and while I saw that of course it would be impossible on the prairie itself, where cattle could not winter out, and the expense of wintering them under shelter would wipe out all possibility of profit, yet it seemed to me that where there were woods or coulées available, such as those I had seen in the neighbourhood of the Moose Mountain, these difficulties might be possibly overcome, and shortly after my return home, I made an application for a tract of land in that neighbourhood. I found, however, it had been determined to convert this land into an Indian reserve, and my thoughts therefore were turned to what I had heard of the foothills of the Rocky Mountains, and I applied at Ottawa for a lease of some of the land there. I had my choice given to me of 100,000 acres on the Little Bow River or a similar tract in the Porcupine Hills on the eastern slopes of the Rocky Mountains.

I shall describe both these tracts during the narrative which follows, but I may at once discharge myself of part of this question by saying that the enormously increased demand, caused by emigration, the requirements of the Canada Pacific Railway, and the quantity of meat required for the Indian reserve, had to my mind clearly established the fact that it would be many years before there was any probability of lean animals being spared for the European markets.

Having secured the services of a manager, and having arranged with two friends of mine to share with me in the undertaking, I proposed to proceed as early as I could in the month of August to see this Western land.

The breaking out of the Egyptian campaign having deprived me of the companionship of one whose services might be required in the East, I came to the conclusion that in his place my Westminster boy might be spared from school, with pleasure to me and advantage to himself, and on the 10th of August we found ourselves on board the *Parisian*, with everything duly arranged for a long camp journey, although by no means for so long a one as it turned out in fact to be.

A pleasant and rapid passage found us in the Straits of Belle Isle on Wednesday evening; but when in the Gulf of St. Lawrence, we had to lay to for some eight or nine hours, which prevented this passage being what it otherwise would have been, one of the best on record of the Allan Line.

The morning of Saturday, the 19th of August, gave promise of a nice bright day. We landed at Point Levis at nine, but owing to the great quantity of luggage that had to be examined and put into the train, we did not get off till past noon, and a very slow journey we had of it to Montreal, arriving there at seven in the evening. A fellow passenger having kindly offered to put our names down at the St. James' Club, we drove there and had a good wash and a capital dinner, and back to the station in time for the nine o'clock train. We were speedily put away in our "Sleeper" en route for Toronto. Henry was duly initiated into the charms of a skunk, as we ran over one a few miles outside the city, and we carried away with us the "detestable fragrance" for many a mile.

Sunday, 20th—At daylight found ourselves running into the pretty country near Kingston, which we reached at 6:30. We were getting glimpses of Lake Ontario, as the line ran along its waters to Toronto. Arriving there at one o'clock we went at once to the Queen's Hotel, as our kind friends the Lieutenant-Governor and Mrs. Robinson were absent from Toronto, and so were unable to offer to us the hospitality of Government House. After an early dinner and a good clean up, we took a steamer across to Hanlan's Island (as the sandbank opposite the city has been christened, after the celebrated "oar"), an island which has now become quite the summer abode of the citizens of Toronto, who have built their pretty little villas with every contrivance of verandahs, rocking chairs, and hammocks for avoiding or giving relief in the great heat. We had a long walk of about six miles through the sand to call upon some friends, and coming back to Toronto in the evening, went to the Cathedral and heard a very good sermon from a new vicar. It was exactly 10 days since I had left the House of Commons. As we were coming from the Cathedral at dusk we noticed several nightjars high in the air, with their harsh note and quick flight—an unusual sight in the middle of a town. The bird seemed somewhat larger than our English goat-sucker. Returning to the "Queen's" we had supper, and so to bed.

Monday, 21st—After breakfast, got through our business with reference to ranch matters, and after a morning spent in shopping and letter writing, enjoyed a pleasant dinner with some friends; driving back to our hotel in pouring rain, which seemed to refresh us, as it certainly did the streets and town.

Tuesday, 22nd—Fine morning. In spite of the warning of last year we determined again to try the route across the lakes, so, after a hurried breakfast, we took our places in the Toronto, Grey and Bruce Railway for Owen Sound. The line is very interesting, as it rises up to Charleston by a zigzag corkscrew gradient to a height of 900 feet—with a horseshoe curve up the last part—thence along a piece of level to the summit. The land even at this high elevation of 1,100 feet, appears to be good farm land, and we noticed good crops of wheat. There must be beautiful views from different parts of this high line; but the morning was too thick for us to see much. We arrived at Owen Sound and got on board the *City of Oven Sound* about 1:30, and steamed away up the Georgian Bay. This bay is, in fact, the northeastern part of Lake Huron, from which it is separated by a peninsula running off into a chain of islands, of which the greater and lesser Manitoulin are the principal, the last of the chain being St. James'. The United States have, as usual, had the best of us in, running their boundary so as to include within their territory some islands very convenient for them, but which from their situation would seem more properly to belong to Canada; the boundary being what was supposed to be the deep water channel. The weather was fine; and we were fortunate in this respect, as the *City of Owen Sound* did not seem to be much more seaworthy than our old friend *Miss Smith* of the last year. We had one or two pleasant passengers on board, amongst them an old Charterhouse boy, now living near Toronto. We began to fall into our early hours of the North-West, and tumbled into bed at half-past nine.

Wednesday, 23rd—We woke up at Killarney, where our captain left us. About 10:00 we called at a small place where we left the mails. Amongst our passengers on board was an interesting gentleman, the paymaster of the Indian Department of Ontario; he had a most complete and intimate acquaintance with the Indian tribes dwelling in and around the Manitoulin and other islands; these Indians belong to the Tchippeway race, and live almost entirely by fishing. They are a very steady and well-behaved set of men, and Mr. Percival spoke highly of their accuracy as to the numbers of their lodges in respect of which they are entitled to payment under their treaties. In the evening we reached the Bruce copper mines, and landing there saw large quantities of the ore which had been got and which was lying in heaps on the bank. It is a sulphate of copper; and was formerly worked with very considerable profit. The works are now, however, closed, as the process of producing copper from the sulphate is too expensive to allow the mines to hold their own in the market against the purer or more easily smelted copper which is obtained in the States. It is a beautiful ore to look at, and lies strewed in

71

such large quantities that one cannot but think that at no distant day the mines may upon some cheaper process be worked at a considerable profit. We had only a quarter of an hour to look round, and then went on board, and had a pretty sail through many wooded islands, at one or two of which we called. The scenery reminded us of the lakes traversed by the Gotha Canal in Sweden. Arrived at the end of the lakes we passed into the narrows, where the current being rapid and the channel difficult, we moored for the night at a wooding station called "Richard's Dock." It was a lovely moonlight night, and we intended to start at break of day. At daybreak, however, a fog came on, and the purser, who was then in command, deemed it more prudent to remain where we were until about eleven o'clock, when the fog cleared and we passed up into the St. Mary's River. There are many Indian huts and wigwams on either side along the banks up to "Sault St. Marie," pronounced "The Soo," which we reached at two in the afternoon. The locks are on the American side and there is a considerable town springing up there, while, on the Canadian side, where there would seem to be certainly equal opportunities for a town, there are but a few houses, or small village: little more than a Jesuit missionary station. A new lock is here being constructed large enough to carry an ocean steamer with 16 feet of water over the sill. The locks have been constructed alongside of the rapids, the shooting of which in a canoe is one of the not very perilous, but somewhat exciting, amusements of passengers while the vessel is passing through the lock. One of our passengers performed this exploit in a birchbark canoe paddled by an Indian; we, however, had declined the little voyage, being advised that it was by no means certain that our vessel would take long enough in going through the lock, to insure our being carried on with her. The most interesting part of the proceeding was the cleverness with which the Indian got his boat upstream, taking advantage of all the slack and backwater. We were all aboard again in about an hour's time and sailing out into Lake Superior. The lock raises the vessels to an upper level of about 25 feet. Arrived in Lake Superior darkness soon came on. During the night we stopped at Michipicoten Island to put off a large boiler for use at some silver mines. This operation took about three hours, and the noise accompanying it put an end to sleep, after which at daybreak we found ourselves passing through some pretty islands, many of them flat-topped and of the shape of a raised pie, one of which, especially so formed, has been called "Pie Island," all of them well wooded. Near one of these we saw a deer swimming across from the mainland.

August 25th—We spent this day on the lake and passing between the islands, and at night arrived at a curious little rock which has been made into an island by the spoil thrown up from the workings. Silver Island has been worked most profitably by an American company. Here, again, in the adjustment of the boundary, the States managed to lay hold of this profitable little islet, though it lies close in to the Canadian shore. Passing Thunder Bay in the dark we lost the view of this very fine and interesting headland.

August 26th—After leaving Prince Arthur's landing at 5:00 a.m., we steamed along up the lake and arrived at Duluth at 10:30 p.m. Our skipper was most inhospitably anxious to get rid of his passengers, but we did not see the advantage of being put ashore at that time of the evening, with the possibility of not being able to secure beds, and so refused to leave our vessel before the morning. This refusal was the occasion of a somewhat angry discussion, but we gained our point, one of our friends standing by us, and we had another tolerably comfortable night in our cabin.

Sunday—The skipper managed to get rid of us in good time by refusing to give us breakfast, so we landed at an early hour and drove to an hotel.

Duluth, "the zenith city of the unsalted sea," seems a thriving little place. After a good breakfast at the Hotel St. Louis, which had only been opened about a fortnight, we walked up the hill above the town, where we feasted ourselves on wild raspberry, and took observation of the time with our friend's heliometer. While seated at the top of the hill a real good Yankee sat down by us and had a talk. He was a man of considerable information, and seemed to have visited a greater part of the States. As we were looking at the very pretty view from the spot where we had located ourselves, on a big stump, he came up with the remark, "Say! when this becomes a big city I guess this will be the place where the money will live." And it was indeed a beautiful situation for villas, with prettily wooded hollows and charming views of the lake and with peeps of the St. Louis River, as it throws its waters into the head of the lake. The opposite side the water to Duluth is occupied by Superior City, and a good harbour is formed by a natural mole which runs across the entire width of two or three miles; inside this there is another smaller mole, and still other islands within these, until the water narrows away where it receives the St. Louis River. The doubt as to the future of Duluth arises from the late period of the year at which the ice breaks up at this end of the lake. I have heard of its being there in July. After dinner we took a walk along the mole to Rice's Point, along the first mole, and back for tea, after which we got on board the train at 7:00 p.m. for Winnipeg. The run for the first 30 miles is through beautiful scenery, the line rising by a very steep gradient along the side of the river, which roars away beneath, through pine woods, in cascades and rapids, and the view, as seen by us in the light of a full moon—of the water dashing down beneath the trestles upon which the line is carried—was very striking. After a short time we packed ourselves away in a jolting berth in a "Sleeper," being the top berth at the very tail of the train, and so with all the concentrated vibration arising from our progress. We ran all night through a forest, pathless, except by the railway track, till we reached the height of land on the chain of lakes where the forest ends, and some good grazing and farming land is seen. This height of land is the westernmost point from which the drainage of the St. Lawrence district flows away to the east. Running a few miles further, we reached the southwestern slope, from which the flow is to the headstreams of the Mississippi. We breakfasted at Glyndon, where this Duluth branch runs into the main line of the North Pacific Railway, and shortly after 9:00 a.m. we turned north by the St. Paul, Mineapolis and Minnesota Railway to Winnipeg. We dined badly at Euclid—but who would expect anything better at a place with such a name?—and arrived at Winnipeg at seven in the evening. Our friend of last year, Mr. W. Boyle, met us at the station. As usual in my experience of Winnipeg, the streets were heavy with mud; a severe thunderstorm having come down upon the town on the previous night and producing abundance of that extraordinary material, "Winnipeg mud," to which I have already alluded.

August 29th—Up at eight; after breakfast at our restaurant, we went to see several people on business, and proceeded to get together our train for the journey. Guillaume, my friend and guide of last year, accepted my offer for our present journey. I had written out for our outfit to be ready for us; it had scarcely, however, been advanced so far as I had wished, and I saw that it must take two or three days before we could hope to get under way for the prairie.

August 30th—We spent the day in shopping and getting our horses for the start. We were taking two wagons with a pair of horses for each, and two saddle horses. For a second man Guillaume had engaged for us one whom he recommended as a thoroughly competent guide, a half-bred Saulteux, Joseph Jourdain—a fine dark swarthy fellow, with a good laughing face. As Joseph told me that he wished to leave some money behind him with his wife, I was weak enough to give him 15 dollars for this purpose and for his outfit. The consequence of which was that the next morning, when I went down to the office to see how things were going on, I found my poor friend sitting on the doorstep with a half empty bottle of whisky and his laughing face full of smiles, but himself of very little use. I was very angry, and vowed that I would not have anything to do with him. I was told, however, what an excellent fellow I should find him as soon as I got him away from the whisky. I managed to get hold of the whisky bottle, and get him safely to the railway station, where we had our wagons and freight on board in a big freight car, and Guillaume with them ready for a start. The freight car was to start that evening, and having got hold again of Joseph, who had worked his way back into the town, I sent him off with one of the horses to join Guillaume at the loading stage, which was some half a mile down the line. He managed, however, to elude the vigilance of Guillaume and my other assistant, and as the railway company had refused to allow the freight car to start until both the men were there, poor Joseph's love of whisky led us into much trouble, and caused us very much delay before we managed to get together again. All these difficulties dawned upon us when next morning I found Joseph at the office, not much better than on the night before, and with another bottle of whisky. There was nothing for it but to take him down to the railway, and to start off with him by the morning train for Brandon. I could not help being considerably amused with the poor fellow, who was thus indulging a taste which it really seems almost impossible for these men to resist. He was in the best of good humour, and as we laid down on the prairie, while our train was delayed with hot axles, he introduced us to a gentleman who was lying near, by saying with a broad grin, "This my boss and this his son; I teach him run buffalo." Poor Joseph was most hospitably disposed to our friend, the same gentleman who had come from Owen Sound with us in the boat. In our interest he had deprived Joseph of his whisky bottle, and when the poor fellow put his hand to his pocket, with the intention of treating him to a drink, great was his sorrow at finding himself deprived of the opportunity of showing his friendship toward him. We got to Brandon at half-past two, noticing as we went along a good many farms and settlements that had sprung up since the previous summer. Having dined, we walked up the town, and found how much the hotels and other buildings had progressed during the past 12 months. At 4:30 we left for Broadview. We were offered a place in a special carriage at the end of the train taking down some railway officials. The coupling link broke as we were going along, and there being no means of carrying the information to the driver, we found ourselves left behind for some little time, until the driver discovering that he had not got his load with him, stopped his train and came back and picked us up again. In the evening we reached Broadview, a railway camp, where we were informed there is at no distant time to be a big city, and we went into a canvas shanty which arrogated to itself the name of "Hanwell House." The sleeping places consisted of bunks arranged round the room; there were many other living things in our bunk besides our two selves, and we were by no means sorry to turn out in very good time the next morning. We had been in hopes of finding here our freight car with our outfit, and were much disappointed when we could hear nothing of them. As the "construction train" by which we were travelling had gone on to the Pile of Bones Creek, we took our gun—as we felt bound to pay proper respect to the first of September—and went to try what sort of animal the dog was, whom in default of Parigi, who had engagements with his master, I had purchased the night before we left Winnipeg; "Drake" was a good-looking black and tan setter, but young, and I feared much that we should not find him of great service, and, surely enough, on my shooting a bittern, I found that I had to go into the water to retrieve him for my-self, as the dog sat complacently on the bank and wagged his tail, but was quite unwilling to take any share in the proceedings; however, we hoped for better things from him in future.

The soil here is a heavy friable loam, which may perhaps be found to produce good wheat crops, but as to which I shall wait with some interest to see what is the result of the first experiments. The prairie is a dead level, with but few little pools and no great amount of water. We came back and had dinner, finding the tent of Mrs. McManus, the buxom Irish wife of a *ci-devant* guardsman, who had taken much interest last year in my wife at Brandon, and in the afternoon we took our seats on a "construction train" in a caboose for the "Pile of Bones." The heat was intense. We went on as far as Qu'appelle, where we arrived at nine in the evening. I was very sorry that it was dark when we arrived there, as the country about Qu'appelle is exceedingly pretty, and in fact is the last thing that you see of beauty for nearly 400 miles. We arrived at the Pile of Bones Creek—which is now dignified by the name of Regina, and which for some reasons best known to the selectors has been chosen as the capital of Alberta—about eleven o'clock at night; as we heard the caboose was to stay there all night, we made ourselves pretty comfortable on the floor for a sleep. Our two companions were brakemen on the line, with a very considerable flow of Montana language, which certainly imported into every sentence almost every word which polite ears are scarcely used to, with the names of the Three Persons of the Trinity, and the Day of Judgement turning up in every sentence. A small Jew's harp twanged out "Home, Sweet Home," and songs all round whiled away a good deal of the night, but at three o'clock in the morning some railway officials came up and informed our friends that they had to go back to bring up another "construction train." The language that was used when they heard this order was of the most "winged" character, but being told that the orders were from the "boss," and they would have to go, one of our friends exclaimed, "Do you think I am going to work day and night, Sundays and weekdays, like a 'Goddam' telegraph post?" However, in spite of all these remonstrances, the order had to be obeyed, and so we had to turn out and leave our friends to re-turn upon their unwelcome journey. We found at a short distance from the line a store tent kept by an old Frenchman and his wife, and there we two and Joseph and the dog lay down on our robes, and endeavoured to doze away until the morning, and I listened to the two Gauls discussing the proper sale price of their varied commodities.

September 2nd—Up at seven; our host and hostess having been on the move for some considerable time previously. Turned out and got breakfast in a canvas tent near, and finding, after some difficulty, our luggage, which had been left pretty well at large on the prairie, and having secured a bucket, with some not very clean water, we had a bit of a wash up and changed our clothes, and started off with the gun. It was terribly hot; the thermometer standing at over 100 in the dining tent. Whatever may be the future of "Regina," most certainly, so far as we saw of it, at this time in 1882, it was as little fitted for a capital city as any place could well be conceived to be—an absolute flat, with no wood and no water, and not very promising land; and as a friend observed, you would have to take advantage of the convexity of the earth if you wanted to get out of sight. In the evening we made the acquaintance of a Mr. Conkey, the most spirited foreman of the victualling department of the railway contractors, Messrs. Langdon and Shepherd. Our friend was certainly about as active and energetic a man as ever I came across: when he slept or when he rested was a mystery. Of a stature and appearance not altogether unlike the first Napoleon, he seemed to be possessed of an equally uncompromising restlessness. A word or two to the brakeman in his caboose, then a bound along the cars to the end of the train for a few words with the engineman, and then back again to the caboose. He kindly offered to take us on to the end of the track at Moose Jaw Creek, and about five in the afternoon a train arrived, returning from that place with one of our friends who had been on board the *Parisian*. We all went on together, hearing just as we got under way that our outfit had arrived at Broadview, and sending word back to Guillaume by telegraph to come on to join us as quickly as possible. We got on to Moose Jaw, and there found the boarding cars in which the principal part of the business of the "construction" is locally conducted and where the great proportion of the men employed dine and sleep. The process of "ironing" is conducted thus: To the end of the metals, so far as they are laid, three huge boarding cars are pushed, each of these boarding cars consisting of three stories. On the ground floor are the offices, with the dining rooms and kitchens and berths for the contractors and the principal men, and in the two stories above are sleeping places for the men, with sometimes tents on the roof. The "construction train," containing ties, metals and fish-joint plates sufficient for some two or three hundred yards of line, is brought up to the rear of these cars, and immediately the contents are turned off to the right and left of the line. As this is done light wagons, drawn each by a span of horses or mules, pick up as many of these ties and rails as they can carry, and bear them forward and deposit them by the side of the line to the front of the boarding cars, dropping them as nearly as can be calculated at the points at which they will be required for the laying of the line. As the ties are dropped they are picked up and laid in their places, two men standing by with marked rods and putting them on at distances of two feet apart from centre to centre. When a sufficient number of these are laid, five or six other men carry one of the rails and lay it down upon the adjusted ties, and, as this is placed, it is fixed to the ties by large spikes; a striker standing by with a heavy hammer drives the spike down as it is stuck in by a person to whom this work is assigned. The rail is then fixed to the line of which it forms the prolongation by a fish-joint plate, and as each pair is laid the trolly passes on with other rails, spikes and plates; and these again are laid in exact continuity. The load of the "construction train" that has brought up this material being exhausted, the engine pushes on the boarding cars to the end of the rails so laid, and then returns and carries back its "construction train" to the nearest siding, probably some five or six miles in the rear, whence another "construction train" is brought up, and the "ironing" proceeds in the same manner. The celerity and accuracy with which all this is done is truly astonishing, and the day that we were first there between the hours of eleven and two, a wagon which had been standing by our boarding car at eleven o'clock was at two o'clock nearly two miles behind. One day, when they were working to see how much could be done, five miles of rail were laid; and while we were there the line was advancing at the rate of 20 miles in the week. It may be thought that in this way the "graders" would be caught up, and that the "ironing" would thus be stopped. The grading is however let out in subcontracts, the head contractor always keeping one gang of his own men ready to finish any work that seems likely not to be completed in time for the "ironing," and when it is reported that such an event is likely to happen, this head contractor's gang goes to the front and finishes up the unfinished work, and of course charges it against the subcontractor. We were told, however, that only upon two occasions during the year 1882 had the ironers caught up the graders. When the head contractor's gang is not wanted for this purpose, there is plenty of other work for them to do in finishing and ballasting, as the line being thus rapidly laid, the work has of course to be gone over with care in finishing and fixing, and above all they have to make sidings, the existence of which at every half dozen miles or so is necessary to the construction. We had a comfortable night in the boarding car, and were up early in the morning, and after breakfast returned with our friend Mr. Conkey to the Pile of Bones; here we arrived at five in the evening, and heard that our horses had arrived, and that Guillaume and Joseph had driven out to follow us to Moose Jaw. As the trail ran nearly parallel to the line I got a trolly or handcar and engaged three men to work it for me; they ran it along the rails after the teams, and, coming up with them at about a dozen miles, I sent them on toward Moose Jaw to wait for us there, and returned to the Pile of Bones, where we passed a far more comfortable night than usual in our friend Mr. Conkey's tent.

September 4th—Up at half-past six, and after breakfast, left for Moose Jaw, and passing our wagons, signalled to them to follow us up, and going on ourselves to Moose Jaw, had a bathe and a fish in the creek, and supper and a comfortable turn in with our old friends in the boarding car.

September 6th—Up at six, and after breakfast started off with our wagons at eight o'clock, Henry riding a pacer pony, and I a nice bright buckskin mare. The pale yellow horse called by the French "isabelle" is known in the North-West as a "buckskin"; the chestnut is described under its old English name of "sorrel." It was not very pleasant country for riding, as the prairie had been all burned, and was still aglow in places. We came, however, to a little stream where we found some water, and having dined there started off again at 2:30, and then drove on for another 20 miles or so. The only things that I saw to shoot were some hawks. Seeing some blue hills in the distance, which looked tempting, we endeavoured to make for them for the night. We found, however, that they were much further off than we had thought, so we stopped at a slough. My readers will remember that a slough (pronounced slew) is by no means a Slough of Despond, but a good grassy hollow with a swamp or pool in it; here, as there was no wood, we had to break up one of our boxes to make our fire. The water was rather muddy, but not alkaline, and it made us fairly good tea. This was the first night of our camping, when there is always some little excitement, to see how the things work together, and whether all the requisites have been brought, and what has been left behind or forgotten. We found our tent comfortable, and arranged our plan of sleeping, I on the left, Henry next me, then Guillaume, and Joseph on the extreme right. Our tent was an oblong, with two uprights and a cross pole, about 10 feet by 12, and was a good linen tent but badly stitched. I found it a mistake to have the cross pole fitting on two spikes at the end of the uprights. The holes were constantly splitting out; when this had taken place I repaired the damage by lashing two picket pegs at the end of each upright, so that the cross pole might rest in the groove between them, and bevelling off these splints so as to take the slope of the tent cloth there was no chance of injury by the ends of the poles cutting through. We were much distressed at finding a loss we had sustained. I had brought two pairs of the thickest Hudson Bay "four point" blankets for Henry and myself, and it appeared that Guillaume, while delayed at Broadview, had somewhat incautiously admitted to the freight car a man who was working on the line. He had left the car to get some water for the horses, and on returning he missed the blankets, and sighted in the distance the scoundrel who had been in the car sloping away far down the line with the bundle; and as he could not leave his horses, and never saw the man afterwards, we had to get along without our best blankets. I thought what an action anyone in England would have had against the company, and what "nice questions of law" would have been raised.

Bed in camp is made up by laying the buffalo robes on the ground, and if there are any young pine shoots to be got, placing a layer of them underneath, and over the buffalo a blanket, and then another blanket and then a buffalo, the intervening space between the two blankets being of course occupied by the traveller. The pillow is made up of coats and trousers and other clothes, and our bags placed at the head, with guns down by the side. The back of our tent is to the windward, and the fire—which of course is placed to the leeward of the tent—is made at a distance of some two or three yards from the door. This was the first night in camp, to be followed by many and many an eventful evening, and we found ourselves exceedingly comfortable, although this first was certainly not one of the best camps that we had in our journeyings.

Wednesday, 6th—Up at daylight, and after breakfast I shot a large hawk, which I skinned, but unfortunately lost it out of the wagon, to my great regret, as it was a very fine specimen. I had taken with me for the purpose of preserving my skins a quantity of arsenic paste; in the very dry air this is really unnecessary, as by turning the skin inside out, and placing it for a day or two in the sun, if it is tolerably clean it becomes completely dry, and will keep sufficiently well without any further preparation, and at this time of the year any risk from moth or other insect is at an end. We hitched up at 8:30 and started off—Henry and I on horseback, the other two each driving a wagon. Our animals had not been selected for the prairie with sufficient care; two of them were far too old and two of them much too young. It is a safe rule for anybody driving on the prairie not to take anything under six or over sixteen. We passed a considerable number of alkaline lakes, a feature of this part of the prairie, which may fairly claim some few words of description.

Under a glowing sun an alkaline lake or pool has all the appearance of a rather dulled mirror, with a margin round it of a brilliant green, surrounded by another fringe of red—the colour of the plant which grows in the shallower water of these salty pools—and around this again, a margin of the white alkaline deposit from the evaporated water. The whole affair looks very gorgeous and very unwholesome, by no means of the character of

> —the lake in the waste,
> That "allures the sight but mocks the taste,"

82

and when the wind is blowing from the direction of an alkaline lake the putrescent smell is sometimes very bad.

A considerable number of ducks and waterfowl are always to be seen upon these lakes during the day. No horse who is not used to the country can drink of the water without serious danger to his life, as it brings on a rapid disease in the kidneys, terminating very quickly in splenic apoplexy. I have seen horses that have drank of the water die within a very few hours.

The few words I have quoted from "The Epicurean" brings to my mind the constant mirage. Sometimes, even when most accustomed to it, with the sun at its great heat you would feel positive as to its being water before you. The illusion is caused by the gassy steam which the sun draws from the land, and which entirely obliterates the horizon, without any apparent intervening medium.

After a long ride we arrived at a lake where there was a good deal of grass, and where we tried to bathe; it was, however, too shallow, even with a long wade out, for this purpose. There were a great number of ducks, but we could not get within shot. We found here a sweet-scented yellow water plant with a flower like a small snapdragon. I saw this plant once afterwards on the western slope of the Rocky Mountains, but except upon these two occasions I have never come across it. I mention it here, as if any subsequent traveller should be able to get hold of it, it would make, I think, a very acceptable water plant for our gardens. We stopped at noon to dinner, and hitched up again at 2:30, and had a long drive through burnt ground till we came to a slight undulation round a large swamp, and camped just above a slough, where our horses found plenty of grass. The persicaria in these swamps was the largest I have ever seen, enormous leaves, very big flowers, and the stems nearly three feet high. The water was very bad, but we had our tea of bacon and biscuit, and went to bed about half-past eight.

Thursday, 7th—Up at seven, and rode on in an endeavour to find some place where our horses could get water. We came to a large lake, which is, I believe, called Moose Lake; the mud there was so deep and tenacious that we found it impossible to get our horses through it to the water. We had another couple of miles over burnt ground, the bottom of a dried up lake, until we reached at noon the Lac de Jones, which we were in search of. It is a curious horseshoe-shaped lake, with the bend of the horseshoe to the north and the two extremities to the southeast and southwest. At this northern end there is a great quantity of bulrushes, which gives it its name. On the eastern side it has a cutbank of some 20 or 30 feet to the water's edge. Its western side consists of swampy islands of rushes and reeds, and there is scarcely any of the waterfowl of the West, whether swimmer, wader, or diver, that is not to be found there. Our horses were very glad indeed of the drink; passing through the reeds into the lake they disturbed millions of frogs of different colours— I should think so many frogs were never collected together in any other place since the days of Pharaoh. From the north side of the lake a trail passes off at right angles to that which we were taking, in the direction of Prince Albert, at the junction of the two branches of the Saskatchewan. At the lake we found a camp of railway graders, who called the lake by its English name, "Bulrush Lake"; they told us that it was about eight miles long and three wide. We had a good wash rather than a bathe, as the water was too shallow, though apparently deeper on the eastern side. It was not good to drink, and there was no grass, so we had to come upon our railway friends for some hay and some corn. After dinner we started on our journey, when Henry's pony began to go very lame, from the effects of his having come a regular "cropper" onto his nose in the morning, and appeared to have strained his shoulder. We tied him onto the wagon, and Henry drove, I riding along by myself. In the evening we met a small band of about 40 head of cattle, which the cowboy said he was bringing down from Cochrane's ranch; I have never, however, quite made up my mind as to whose they really were and how they came there, and I was not sufficiently well informed upon the subject at that time to elicit the facts of the case from the cowboy.

He was the first of his race whom I had seen. The costume is an imitation of the Mexican, and so has a dash of Spanish about it. A pair of "chaps" or leather overalls, with tags and fringes down the seams, a pair of big cruel-looking but really very harmless Mexican spurs, a soft felt sombrero hat, and a buckskin shirt, worked probably down the front with some Indian squaw bead work, and a gaudy tie, a revolver in his belt or in a hip pocket placed where fashionable ladies now carry their pocket handkerchiefs; and as he sits his cayeuse, with his left arm on the horn of his saddle supporting his right elbow, the hand of which props his chin or holds his pipe, he has altogether a very picturesque and workmanlike appearance. I say that the spurs look cruel; they are not really so, and in fact the boys call our English spurs cruel; a principal use of these long things being to hold on with by passing them under the belly and sticking them into the cinch of a bucking bronco.

It was getting very dark, and I began to be rather anxious as to a place for camp, as we were on high burnt ground, without wood or water. I rode on ahead to explore, and after a few miles further came to a descent, which brought us to a stream which we recognized as the "Swift Current Creek," a creek which has given satisfaction to other explorers before us, bright clear water running very quickly from left to right. It was quite dark when we crossed the stream and encamped in the neighbourhood of some Cree Indians and some railway surveyors. Some of the Crees— a couple of bucks and three squaws—joined us at tea, and the prairie fires—which had broken out with such vigour in the breeze of the last two days which had sprung up after the tremendous heats—began to blaze close to us; in fact the line of fire was only separated from us by the narrow little creek. I made an attempt to photograph the fire, but of course without success. It brought to my mind more clearly than anything I had ever seen the description of the beacon fire by the Queen in the Agamemnon of Æschylus, as the wind bore it along:

ἀΦθόνῳ μίνει
φλογός μέγαν τώγωνα.

It was, indeed, reaching over a breadth of many miles, "a giant beard of flame."

Friday—Up early, and I took my gun and went after some geese down the stream, but could not get a shot; the Indians had been after them, and they were very wild. At 9:15 hitched up and started, I riding the buckskin "Fan," and the pony being tied onto one of the teams; "Drake" was very unwilling to leave the Indian "teepee," so I had to take him with a cord. After some 15 or 20 miles we came upon a lake literally swarming with duck and geese. As there was no cover round the bank it was very difficult to get at them; I succeeded, however, in shooting a duck; and eight different kinds of waders. I was unable, however, to realize my success, as the ducks were well away from the shore, there was no breeze to bring them toward me, and the mud along the bank prevented my going in after them, and in the matter of our dog we began to realize the proverb as to the inconvenience of keeping a dog and having to bark yourself. This was the only day during this journey that we were troubled by mosquitos, but all along this lake we were a good deal bitten; the bite, however, at this time of year is not very severe, as the cold nights take the strength of the venom out of these troublesome little brutes. I did at last succeed in getting a duck on a smaller pool, riding into the water and getting it out. At night we camped on a slough, where, in the early part of the evening, the mosquitos were again a little troublesome, but a sharp frost came on, and we found a good thick coat of ice on the water in our buckets in the morning.

We rode on next day over a nice piece of prairie, Henry riding and I driving, and we came to a pretty little lake, where I managed to get a couple of duck, but had to undress and swim in and do retriever work for myself. We dined on them, and after dinner Henry shot a large raven. Hitching up at 2:00 p.m., after a long drive we reached, in the evening, a level basin surrounded by sandhills and sandstone rocks; we passed through this for about two miles. Many of the shrubs and flowers were entirely different from any we had seen before, and especially we noticed one shrub, with long straight stems of about two feet, with thorns at regular intervals up the stalk. It covered the ground almost like the dwarf juniper; I did not see this shrub again until we came across it afterwards in Montana, on the headstreams of the Missouri. As the sun was setting we got to the western end of the basin, and camped upon a knoll adjoining a slough with good water. The wind began to blow very fresh, and the sandy ground gave but bad hold for our pickets, and shortly after we had gone to bed down came our tent on the top of us. As one pole remained up at the head end, and it was too dark for us to hope to put matters to rights, we allowed ourselves to lie under the ruins until the morning.

Sunday, 10th—A fine morning, and after breakfast I got out my "housewife" and with some good English thread set to work to repair a big rent in the stitches of the tent, an occupation which took me from one to two hours; we discovered that the creek that we were camped at was not Maple Creek, as we had thought, but a coulée running from the south into one of the chain of alkaline lakes that we had passed on our right hand. We washed up about 10:00 and started on our journey, and had a pleasant drive through the prairie, all of which on our left hand was completely charred. About noon we sighted a stream to our right, with some small wood and shrubs, and picking out a nice little sunny bank, unhitched and made our dinner camp. Henry and I took advantage of a pool that was not dried up, and had a good wash, and after dinner proceeded to skin the raven, and having had a nearly three hours' rest, we hitched up and drove along till we began to ascend some steep hills, which we fancied were immediately above Fort Walsh. Here we met a family of Indians taking their journey east. The woman seated on the horse on the off-side, with her feet resting on one of the travois poles. This is an ingenious Indian contrivance for carrying the children and the household goods. Two long poles are fastened one on each side of the horse's neck and drag behind him; to these is attached a crossbar at a distance of some two feet from his heels, and keeps the poles apart. A second crossbar is placed behind this at about two feet from the end of the poles, and at an interval of about a couple of feet from the front crossbar. A skin or other material is placed between these two, and forms the bag in which the papoose or household goods, or in all probability both, find their travelling carriage. It is wonderful with how little jolting this rude conveyance proceeds along the prairie, and is available in winter and in summer, and the children really seem to enjoy their carriage, and looked far happier than many of our gaudily dressed up West-end children in their more luxurious perambulators. The lady whom we now met had a nearly naked papoose about six or seven months old that seemed to be enjoying its jolting over the prairie. We learned from the Indian buck who was bringing up the procession, which was headed by his boy, that Fort Walsh was still some eight miles off; so, as the sun had set, we camped for the night on a sloping bank with some sloughs in front, and where there was tolerable water, but no wood; so we had to break up one of our boxes to boil our kettle and fry our bacon. An Indian came in to supper, and had a long "powwow" in Cree with Guillaume and Joseph.

Monday, 11th—A sharp morning. On the previous evening, as the water was thick, I had put two of our charcoal filters with India rubber tubes into the bucket, so that acting as siphons they might draw out a sufficient amount of bright water for our breakfast, but I found that the bucket was only about half filled, and the filters must have frozen up at about two or three o'clock in the morning. We hitched up about nine, and after about three hours' drive descended a steep hill, over boulders and big gravel, to a very clear stream, on a knoll above which was an encampment of eight Indian lodges. It was a most picturesque little hollow, well wooded all round; and the sight of the green and the water after the large extent of burnt prairie through which we had passed, was most refreshing. We ascended from the stream up a corresponding hill to that which we had come down—very steep and very rough—it tried the wagons and the horses very considerably. When we were half-way up, the bolts of one of the whippletrees broke, and the binding it up with wire caused a long delay. Some Indian children flitted in and out of the wood on each side of the road gathering chokecherries and serviceberries; these seemed to constitute at present their principal food, as we neither saw nor heard of any big game. The poor little creatures looked very thin and very hungry, and only came out to peep at us from under the boughs or behind the stems of the trees. After ascending the hill, which brought us up again some 200 feet to the prairie level, we came upon a large encampment of Indians, and turning round to the right drove down to Fort Walsh, where we pulled up outside the fort. It was a kind of large stockade, enclosing a number of wood houses and stables, substantially built, with wheelwright and blacksmith's shops, and a large drill square. The ground, having been trodden up a good deal under a burning sun by both mounted police and Indians, was one mass of dust, and as heavy squalls of wind came on from the high land around it, the grit floating in the air was most trying to eyes and lungs. I went in to see the officer in command, and found Major Shurtleff and Mr. Norman, second in command. We went into the fort and were very kindly welcomed. Mr. Norman took us to his room and mapped us out full instructions for our next three days' drive. On coming out, with the assistance of Guillaume and Joseph, we made acquaintance with the Indians, and I persuaded them to let me take their photographs. They were very unwilling to subject themselves to this treatment, as they were not, at the time, on the very best terms with the Government; the Government had refused to give them their supplies unless they would go back upon their reserve, and they had an idea that by sticking out they should get better terms, and they were under the belief that another large band of Crees in the neighbourhood of Regina were coming down and would help in a demonstration to put a pressure upon the Government. It appeared, however, that Joseph had had a good deal of talk with these other Crees, and was able to tell them—and Major Shurtleff requested me to get him to do so—that the Qu'appelle Indians had made up their minds to go back upon their reserve. This altered the state of things, and these men, who were there in the number of about 90 lodges with about five to a lodge, agreed that they would also go back to their reserve if the Government would provide them with food on their way back. We fully discussed this matter with Major Shurtleff, and the conclusion at which they arrived was to send back an escort of police with food to accompany them, and only to give them their day's rations as they proceeded along their journey, and so to make sure of good faith being kept in the matter. The chief who was then in command of the band was "Big Bear"; he, how-ever, has never entered into treaty with the English, and, therefore, is not recognized by the Government. He is certainly not a very distinguished-looking man, and about as plain-headed an Indian as it is possible to see amongst this not very handsome race. The officers and those who were about there considered him a very straightforward fellow, and that he had only not entered into the treaty because he thought it beneath the dignity and to the prejudice of his tribe; there was, however, a considerable feel-ing amongst others there that he was a "bad egg," and they even went so far as to suggest that the sooner he had a bullet in him the better. The acknowledged chief of the band, who had entered into the treaty with the Government, was "Lucky Man," whose photograph I took standing between two young ladies, two of his squaws—one of them really a toler-ably good-looking girl of about fourteen. We had discovered these young

89

ladies, with three or four others, got up in their best finery and engaged in a feast in Lucky Man's teepee. It was not without much coaxing from Joseph that they were persuaded to come out and have their photographs taken. The young squaws, in Cree, "skeni," had their faces painted with yellow, and the cheek bones and parting of the hair daubed with vermilion. After I had photographed them they came up and looked through the camera; like every other person whom I have ever found trying to look at a camera for the first time, they endeavoured to look through the glass instead of on it. It was some little time before they could understand what I wished to show them; when, however, they limited their vision to the surface of the glass, and caught sight of the tent and of one of their friends sitting in it, they laughed most heartily. Though not bad looking, they have rather thick lips and flat noses, but good eyes. The oldest women amongst them are indeed ugly, and no wonder, considering that they have to do all the hard work for themselves, their bucks, their families, and for the tribe generally. As an illustration of the light in which the Indian holds the squaw I may give the following tale.

Amongst the early settlers in Montana was one who was known by the name of "Long Hair"; he was looked upon with much fear by the Indians, the origin of which was the following: In 1871 the Blood Indians were camped on the St. Mary's and Belly Rivers and numbered almost 300 lodges. A quarrel had arisen between a Blood Indian, "Strange Dog," and one of the traders, in which the Indian had shot the white man. On the white men moving off a building had been fired. The Blood Indian, for some fancied wrong inflicted on him by his squaw, drew his pistol and shot her in the hip, depriving her of all power of motion. The poor woman fell beside one of the buildings, and supposing that she was either dead or dying, no one paid any attention to her, and it was not until the burning building was about to roast her that she made any outcry. Upon her crying out, the Indian rode up, pistol in hand, ready to shoot again, but "Long Hair" rushed up, and, standing by the wounded squaw with a rifle, called to the Blood Indian to halt, and in the presence of both whites and reds removed the woman to a place of safety, where she recovered and joined her people. The Blood Indians from that hour entertained a wholesome dread of the man who would fight even for a woman, as amongst the Indians she would not have been thought of sufficient value to be worth risking life for, and they reasoned that if "Long Hair" would fight for a squaw, what would he not do for a horse or a man?

After the photographing, the Major invited us to lunch in his house, which we gladly accepted. Some roast beef and serviceberry jam formed an agreeable change from our usual diet of bacon and biscuits. After dinner, our hosts kindly furnished us with a new whippletree for our wagon, and we hitched up and parted again on our journey. I was anxious to have taken the line almost due west along the Belly River, but I was dissuaded from it, being told by Mr. Norman that it would be difficult to find the trail round the heads of the deep coulées which ran from the south into the river. We many a time, indeed, repented upon our subsequent journey, when pressed by want of water, that we had not followed out my original intention; however, as the Mounted Police have been longer in the country than anyone else, one would have been a bold man to have acted contrary to their advice. So starting off on the trail recommended to us, we began to ascend the hill out of the hollow on the opposite side to that which we had come down. This was like going up the side of a house for about a mile, traversing, in a good many places, piles of rough boulders, until after an even steeper bit than any we had passed before, and which tried to the utmost our own muscles in pushing behind and the pluck of our horses in hauling away in front, we got to the top and came out upon the prairie level. The pretty woods, which clothed the sides of the hollow, had been terribly devastated by fire, to no small extent, the result of the young bucks going in little parties to have their smoke in the woods, where everything is so exceedingly dry that the slightest spark ensures conflagration. On coming up to the prairie we found ourselves in the line of fire, and we had to pass through it. The greater part of the timber at the top had been destroyed, and no wonder, as we were told there had not been a drop of rain here since the end of May. The number of Mounted Police in Fort Walsh was 135; they seemed very cheery and very happy, and are certainly most active in looking after the Indians, in recovering stolen horses, and, above all, in preventing any importation from across the boundary of spirits or other intoxicants. I was riding on ahead when I was called back by Henry, who told me that the old mare was giving out, and so "Fan" had to be taken into harness, and we tied the mare onto the cart; we were thus reduced to our one pair in each wagon. For about a mile she went along in a very tottering condition and at last fell down, so that we took off her bridle and left her on the prairie. We had now got onto a level plain with some scrub, beyond which we could see the wood where we proposed to spend the night. It was a long drive toward it, and it seemed to retire as we advanced, and when the sun went down it was still a long way off. We came, however, at last to an opening which presented the appearance of an avenue, some fire or heavy gale having cleared a wide opening, after going through which for about a mile we sighted a tent, and unhitched, after a long 20-mile drive. This other outfit consisted of a wagon party, a freighter with a heavy load of 5,000 pounds of freight, with two passengers; one of the Mounted Police, and a doctor, with a most shocking gunshot wound that had torn away the upper part of his face. The accident had occurred, as he told us, while shooting with a friend in Newfoundland.

Mr. Mickel, the freighter, was on his way to Fort McLeod, and informed us that Colonel McLeod was encamped close by at the spring. We went there, and found the Colonel already in bed. I apologized for disturbing him, and handed him my card, and told him I had a letter of recommendation to him. He asked us to come in and sit down. Another gentleman was with him, and they were travelling with a wagon and five horses. The Colonel, being Chief Magistrate of his district, was on his circuit administering justice, and making his way to Winnipeg to meet his family. After a pleasant little chat, we left them to their slumbers, and returned to our own camp, where we found the fire lighted and supper ready, and a pleasant night we passed, after our long day, under the pine trees in that very pretty wood.

Tuesday, 12th—Fine morning. After an early visit from Colonel McLeod and a few final words about our route and an invitation to bring the ladies out next year, when we might arrange a pleasant party to the Kootenai Lakes—as to the size of the fish in which we heard some wonderful reports—he left us and we struck camp and hitched up. We began by descending a very steep hill, obtaining a view in the distant southwest of three high peaks, which Guillaume called "les buttes de foin scenté" (or, as they are called in English, "sweet-scented grass hills"), so named from a grass which grows there with which the Indians scent all their articles of clothing and above all their medicine bags. It has a scent like dried woodruff. This was the very paradise of game until the last few years, when all that which lent so much charm to this country and was of such absolute necessity to the Indians has been so ruthlessly destroyed and cleared away. While we were going down the hill, Guillaume ran the wheel of his wagon over a root, and spun himself and Henry and guns and seat of wagon into the bushes. They were not hurt, however, and so, having speedily arranged the seat, the journey was continued. I was driving, with Joseph, in the other wagon, the goods of our outfit being of course pretty equally divided between us. Arrived at the bottom, in a rather pretty meadow, with a stream through the middle, we saw some prairie chicken, and I shot one. The greatest luxury that we found was in an abundance of chokecherry, of which we tore off large boughs as we drove by and plucked and ate the fruit. These berries grow in great profusion on a shrub like a hazel bush; we found here, also, some excellent serviceberries and bush cranberries. The serviceberry grows in clusters of eight or twelve; they are about the size of a black currant. The Indians make a preserve of them, the squaws crushing up the fruit and stones, which give a noyeau flavour to the jam, and, drying the whole in cakes, make an excellent sweetmeat. They also use it pounded up in the pemmican, giving a pleasant fruity taste to this otherwise not very delicate food. While crossing the plain the hind spring of the smaller wagon broke in two, and I was for some time much puzzled as to how we were to get on with this breakdown, there being no blacksmith between this and Fort McLeod. "Necessity is the mother of invention," and, after one or two walks round my wagon, my eye dropped upon the iron footrail of the splashboard; I unscrewed it, and laying it parallel with the broken spring, whipped it from end to end first with a piece of wire and then with strong cord; and so firmly was it done and so well did it answer its purpose, that it lasted and held together during the whole of the rest of our travels, and even was considered a sufficiently good substitute for a spring when we came to dispose of our wagon in the United States. At the end of the plain we came up with the freighter's wagon at dinner, and we all ascended the hill together, and went on about eight miles to what we thought—on the sketch supplied to us by Mr. Norman—was Peigan Creek. Here we made a dry camp, as there was no water, and on continuing our journey we found that the real place that we should have stopped at was a mile further on. We continued our drive for about eight miles and then stopped. During the evening an Indian brought in some fresh buffalo meat, part of which was purchased by the wagoner, who gave us a piece in return for a present of biscuits. Two little Indian boys, very bright little fellows, came and sat by us, looking on as we were eating our supper, and of course they came in for a pretty good meal. An Indian will very seldom tell you his name; they are almost always what we should call nicknames and most frequently of a not very decent signification. These two boys, however, had been rather more fortunate in their nomenclature, and the one informed us that his name was "Thunder Boy," and the other "Stoney Boy."

Wednesday, 13th—Fine morning, and up early, and had a wash in the pools in the Peigan Creek. We made a good fire from the driftwood which we had collected the night before amongst the sand from the wide bed of the stream when in flood. Our two Indian boys took good care to be with us at breakfast, and enjoyed their biscuits and marmalade very much. We started along the prairie, and on coming up to a coulée, we caught sight of an antelope, or, as our half-breeds call them more correctly, "capri," coming toward us; it turned down through the coulée, and over the prairie. As there were some hills at no great distance, and the animal seemed to stop as it approached them, I went for a long stalk for about an hour. I did not succeed, however, in getting near it, as it had turned round the hills, and made away again to the left hand over a prairie bounded by the horizon. About noon we reached a large coulée, which was described to us as the "real Sandy Coulée" in distinction from a sandy coulée which forms a lower bend of the same Seven Persons River. It was very hot, and we found a nice spring at the further edge of the coulée, and after dinner filled up our time with some rifle practice, setting up one of the numerous buffalo heads, whose skulls and bones are strewed over the prairie. This coulée is 36 miles from the cypress wood from which we started the day previously, and as we knew that we should not find any wood for

94

many miles, and it was reported that none was to be got before reaching St. Mary's River, a distance of some 70 miles, we went up and down the coulée and collected a good lot of driftwood to form a provision for our journey. As the freighter's party of three with our own of four made up seven persons, we considered the name of the river quite appropriate. The freighter's wagon started before us, but we soon passed it, and in the evening reached the Forty-mile Coulée. As Guillaume and Joseph were driving ahead, they hurriedly signalled that they sighted some buffalo. We were quickly out of our wagon, and ran onto some rocks with our rifles to get a shot. It was quite in the dusk, and under the hill, as we got up, five figures passed away in the gloaming. On this journey across that part of the prairie, where these animals were a few years ago to be found in countless thousands, these were the only buffalo that we saw. They were away before we got near, and it was too dark for us to see which way they took. We returned to camp and had tea and went to bed.

Thursday, 14th—We were up at daylight, Joseph with a shot gun, and Henry and I with rifles. We took our way across the bed of the dried-up river rising from the coulée on the other side, and just as I was starting off I got a shot at a wolf; I missed him. After that Joseph and I caught sight of a deer; we tracked it for some distance, but eventually lost the track, and returned back, making a long bend up the coulée to our camp. Passing under the rocks where the buffalo had been the night before, we saw their track, and made out that they had taken off to their northwest. We had lost sight of Henry, who had a long prowl after a wolf and got a shot at him; but whether he stalked the wolf, or the wolf stalked him, it did not quite sufficiently appear—he professing the one and we professing to believe the other—however, the wolf seems to have got off safely. The deer that I had been following up had passed in sight of him, and had taken a different turn to the direction in which I had gone. There were also seen one or two antelope, but we did not succeed in getting any of the big game. We had a pleasant breakfast, in camp, at eight o'clock, and after breakfast, Henry and I went to try and get a bathe in a very shallow lake; it turned out, however, to be more of a wallow in the mud than a bathe, but induced to a certain extent a sensation of cleanliness. The freighter had advised us in going forward from here to stop for the night at a point about six miles from beyond the half way to the Chin Coulée, this being the longest drive over the least watered part of the prairie, the route being along the high ground that lies above the Chin Coulée, with one large and several smaller alkaline lakes on the right hand and on the left. After these there is no appearance of anything like water for many miles. He told us that we should find a spring at the place that he had indicated, and that on his eastern journey he had found sufficient water there. Our friends at Fort Walsh had however, advised us that, by looking out after we had made some 20 miles, we should find a trail turning of to the left hand, and that by following it we should find a lake which they had discovered that spring. We hitched up, and after we had gone about 12 miles we met the Indian Commissioner with a large party and two or three wagons, and several horses, looking very much baked up under the broiling sun. They told us they had had no water for 40 hours, and that at the place which the wagoner had told us of we should find the spring dried up. We directed them to the spring that we had left 12 miles to the eastward, and they hurried on at the thought of getting some drink for themselves and their animals. Hearing this account we were of course more clearly resolved to follow the advice that we had received from Mr. Norman. Arriving at the spot where he had indicated, we made out some faint marks where wheels had turned off from the trail, although the trail was three months old. It was indeed a blazing heat, the sun fetching the skin off our left ears. It was at the end of 20 miles that we had taken the turn to the left, and after going about a mile and a half we found a tolerably large lake, but it was absolutely dry. Our indefatigable Joseph ran along, and getting up to a bit of a knoll waved his arm to us, signalling that he had found something. We followed him up and discovered that although the lake itself was dry there was a small spring running into it at one end from which good water was still flowing, and from which we saw at some distance many antelope gallop away as they sighted us. We went on pretty quickly to it, and both our horses and ourselves enjoyed the water. We lighted our campfire, and after a good rest, supine in the cool evening, we had our supper; just as we were turning into bed the freighter and the doctor returned with their four horses, having found after their long day's journey that there was no water at the place that they had made for, and he had to bring his horses seven miles back to where we were, leaving his wagon and one of his party behind. We made up our fire again, and gave them supper and a lie-down in our tent, and the next morning they were up and off considerably before daylight at three o'clock. We had made up our minds also, knowing what we had got before us, to make an early start, and were off at five; it was so intensely cold that sitting in our wagons was impossible, and we had to get out and walk for about three or four miles. This last 24 hours was indeed an experience of the variation of temperature in this climate, where the air is so absolutely dry, and there is so complete an absence of cloud or fog, that when the sun is down all the heat seems to pass away with it, and as soon as the sun is up again there is nothing between its rays and the earth, and so the whole heat comes blazing down. Our route lay over a very similar country to that which we had traversed the day before. The curious hill called the "Chin," which gives the name to this coulée, and which has really the appearance of that part of the person from which it is named, rises with its point to the southeast, and forms the great landmark for many miles round; from this a big coulée runs to the east, forming one of the tributaries of the Saskatchewan. At about four miles from Chin Coulée we passed the wagon, and went down a steep hill into the coulée. We found a spring of water, but somewhat alkaline; we break-fasted, boiling the water and skimming it before we made our tea; we took care, however, that our horses should not taste of it. Henry and I walked on until it came on to rain, when we got into the wagon, and ar-rived at a point where the trail came in from Benton. We got down again, and walked for about eight miles, and then got up and drove along to the St. Mary's River. The last piece of the trail down to the St. Mary's River is over ground eminently suited for cultivation; throwing up very good grass and with clearly abundance of water at no great depth. We had rather a bad descent down the coulée into the river, and had to make one or two attempts before we found a line suited to our wagon, even though these most useful carriages will really go through almost anything. We crossed the river, which was running somewhat high and very rapidly, from left to right, and we pitched our tent at 6:45. This was our longest day's drive—between 60 and 70 miles; our horses seemed about "played out," so we made up our minds to remain quiet next day, and after tea we tumbled into bed, our camp being pitched in a nice quiet bit of thicket at no great distance from the river, with the hills seeming to close in like the sides of a basin all round us.

At a cowboy dance in the North-West, as soon as the sets are arranged, the Master of the Ceremonies, after giving directions to the dancers "Honour your partners," which induces a scrape and a shuffle all round, dictates the figures and the steps, and then enquiring, "Are you all set?" and being answered in chorus, "All set," he orders the music to strike up, with the command to the orchestra, "Let her loose." This formula we adopted in our tent. The last man in enquired, "Are you all set?" "All set," replied the other three, and I gave the order "Let her loose," and the candle was blown out, and a chorus of "Good night all" gave the information that any one was at liberty to doze off to sleep as soon as lie could, whilst the others might carry on "chin-music" as long as they pleased.

We had now finished our journey across the prairie, and had reached more hospitable land in the neighbourhood of the Rocky Mountains. We had, however, a good deal before us, as it turned out, before we reached them.

Saturday, 16th—A wet morning, and the effect of our long drive had told upon us, for we found that we had been asleep for eleven hours and a half, and that it was nine o'clock when we woke up. One of the Mounted Police came into camp; they were encamped near, and shortly after a "Blood," or Indian of the Blood tribe, came to breakfast. We had got out of those tribes with whom we could converse, as the Blood language has nothing in common with the Sioux or Cree—the languages spoken by Guillaume and Joseph. The Blood was really a good-looking fellow, with fine black eyes, good limbs, and a bright face. In the morning, Henry and I took our rods, and went to see if we could pull out any fish, but caught nothing, and after dinner we took a rifle and gun and wandered away through the thicket. We came to an old stockade—one of the forts of the whisky traders, of whom I shall speak hereafter—and learned that the place was named Whoop-up. We then went down the river, and to our surprise found it running in an opposite direction to that which I had thought it would be from the line we had followed. Being very much puzzled by this, we turned back and wandered away and fairly lost the direction of our camp, until night came on, and we began to think of lying down in the thicket, wet as it was, to wait for the daylight, when fortunately we came across the potato patch of a settler. I said to Henry, "The gentleman who owns this potato patch will be sure to have a road from it to his house." So we groped our way round it until we came across a bit of a path, along which we went, and at last to the stockade which we had seen in the morning. Here we met our friend of the Mounted Police, and he conducted us to our camp, which we reached about nine o'clock, quite ready for tea and bed. The mistake with regard to the river arose from my not having been aware of the fact that we were at the junction of two rivers, and that the one which we had come to and found running in the unexpected direction was the Belly River, into which the St. Mary's runs at this point.

Sunday, 17th—We started from camp about eleven o'clock, Henry and I walking on to the fort, where we purchased some oats from the gentleman who lived there. We had an interesting conversation with him about his life when he first established himself as a whisky trader in 1871. He gave a circumstantial account of his life since that time. The whisky traders had first come in from Montana in the year 1872, to carry on a competing trade with the Hudson Bay Company, with whose officials they had had some quarrel. The first thing they did in opposition to the old system, was to trade with the Indians by means not only of the customary flour, matches, beads, &c., but also with whisky. They had established several forts in this part of the country, lying to the east of the Rocky Mountains, being log huts strongly built, to protect them against the anger of their drink-maddened customers. For two years their trade was carried on, and without saying much more about it at present, I think it may be pretty well summed up in the remark that was made to me by one of them, "If they had only been allowed to carry on the business in their own way for another two years, there would have been no trouble now as to feeding the Indians, for there would have been none left to feed: whisky, pistol, strychnine, and other like processes would have effectually cleared off these wretched natives." My friend had a young squaw of about thirteen or fourteen sitting sewing in his log hut, and as he sat, with his long legs sprawling out over his stove, he began to talk to me of his life:

"I tell you what it is, sir, it is rather lonely and dull here, and there is not much amusement of any sort to be got—and she is no company to me."

"Well," said I, "but you find her pretty tolerably useful, don't you?"

"Waal, yes; but then she knows nothing but what I have taught her. I just teach 'em to bake and to make themselves useful about the house."

"Why," said I, "you say *them*, but there is only this one here, is there?"

"Waal, no," he said; "but she is the sixth that I have had. I generally take them when they are about this age. I give the old buck some rubbishing old cayeuse that is worth about four or five dollars, though they've got more particular of late years, and I give the old woman a couple of handfuls of tea, and then they come to me; but I don't generally keep them much above six months, for by that time they begin to know where all the things are kept, and they take your grub and give it to their people, and it is against my principle to beat them myself, and so I just send them back to their own people."

"Well, and what do you suppose generally becomes of them?"

"Oh, waal, you know, they are not thought the worse of at all for having been living with me, and some Indian buck'll marry her; and she has to obey him pretty smart, you bet, or she'll get it pretty warm over the head with a tent pole if he finds anything going wrong in his place; but, as I say, it is against my principle to beat them myself."

I give this little history as an illustration of the manners and customs of the North-West, in the days that are now rapidly passing away; for the squaw man of former days is a little looked down upon by the more civilized settler who is taking his place, and bringing with him those companions and those comforts, in the absence of which the poor squaw was looked to as the only substitute that could be found.

I should perhaps explain that this taking of the food by the squaw for her people has not really the larcenous character that at first sight it may seem to have. A man who takes a squaw becomes one of her family, and the family have all an equal right to any food that any one of its members may obtain, and thus my friend's lady was by Indian law perfectly justified in satisfying the hunger of his father-in-law and mother-in-law and uncles and cousins and brothers and sisters at his expense. In using the word squaw I may add that there is no such word in any Indian language with which I am acquainted, but "sequa" or "esqua" is the termination of words implying the female gender, and so has become the customary English word for the Indian woman.

In our wanderings in the evening before, Henry and I had come across two or three trees in which we had seen for the first time dead bodies, this being the most common mode among the Bloods of disposing of their dead; their practice is to select a tree with two or three branches, usually a cottonwood or aspen tree, either one which is dead or one which they by barking it round soon reduce to this condition; in this they erect a small stage across the forks of the boughs, and place the body upon it, covered with bits of cloth and skins, and a handkerchief is bound round the head, placing round the body any of the articles which have been of particular service to the dead person in this world, and which they hope may be of equal use to him in the "Happy Hunting Grounds"; under the body they place a deerskin, out of which he may get his moccasins made when he arrives in the next world. We asked our friend if he could take us down to this tree, and he seemed to know well the one I had particularly noted.

It turned out that this particular body was one of some little local interest as being that of a well-known Blood. The Crees—who, as I have said before in my account of the Indians, are at continual war with the Bloods—had made up their minds that they would, in respect of his body, be avenged, possibly for some Cree horse he had stolen, or for some other wrong that they fancied the Bloods had done to them, and so coming out on the warpath, they made a descent upon this ground, and by way of revenge took the deerskin from under him, so that he should go barefoot on the other side of the deep waters. The Bloods finding this insult to their dead, turned out also upon the warpath, and followed after the Crees; the Crees, as usual, fled before them. The Bloods coming upon their camp, found only one poor old blind Cree left; this was, however, something upon which they might wreak a little satisfactory vengeance, so they killed and scalped the old Cree. I am afraid that their women roasted and ate some little bits of him as an exhibition of hatred and contempt, and satisfied with this result they retired into their own country.

This little hollow where we were is a favourite burial place for the Bloods. Not only are there many bodies in the trees, but there are also a good many of the teepees of those who have died and who in life had been better off. Of these the teepee is fitted up as "a dead lodge," with the articles belonging to the deceased, the body covered over and placed in the middle in a sitting attitude. For some others regular wooden structures are built as the receptacles, upon or within which the body is also placed in a similar position. From its being the burial place of so many of the tribe, it has got its Indian name of A-Kina s-Kiou, or "many Bloods."

Round the forts at Whoop-up were numbers of Indian squaws busy at work making the jam of which I have spoken, and with them were several of the dogs which they use to work their toboggans and dog-travois in winter. This dog is an animal with about as mean a face as it is possible to imagine, large frames, but a poor, wretched, hungry, half-vicious, half-cowed look. On the cutbanks that border these two streams—St. Mary's and Belly rivers—there are indications of measures of coal, and the coal banks which are now being worked by the North-Western Coal and Navigation Company, and which form part of a very large coal field, begin from the junction of the two rivers, and continue for some distance down the Belly River. These mines have been already worked to a small extent, for local purposes, and the coal has been for some six or seven years used in Fort McLeod. A very enterprising man, Mr. Sheron, who had distinguished himself in one of the Arctic expeditions, had the management of them. He lost his life during the preceding Spring in endeavouring to take a friend across the river, where he was caught by the current, and though a strong swimmer, had not been able to withstand the swiftness of the cold water, sank as his buggy turned over, and was never seen again.

There is no doubt that there is plenty of very good coal, not only at the level at which it is being worked, but also, I believe, to a very considerable extent below the level of the river bed. Having completed our purchases at the fort we had a little snack of lunch, in which the many Indian squaws and children who were around us took no little interest, and started on our journey for Fort McLeod. The first ascent was of a very steep bank, to pull the wagon up which required all the energy both of horses and men. From this we passed along a hot dry plain, and after a drive of a few miles came to the junction of several trails. This of course was a great puzzle to us, as there were no landmarks or anything to indicate which was the trail which would lead us to Fort McLeod, and not having been aware that any such difficulty would arise, I had made no inquiry with respect to our route, and our map was far too vague to be of any help.

We took the trail to the right, and, instead of reaching Fort McLeod, which we should have done, in about 25 miles, we found ourselves at dusk after doing about that distance, at the crossing of the Belly River, just above its junction with the Old Man. The water was rather high, but we crossed pretty easily, and pitched our tent in the corner of a small delta formed by the two rivers. We saw a log hut a few yards distant, from which the settler came out to have a talk to us. I found that he had been there for a few weeks, had erected his log hut, and that in the old country he had been managing a farm for a gentleman whom I knew in Norfolk. He told us that his place was an old whisky fort called Kipp's. Being Sunday he was enjoying a little quiet reading instead of farm work. We had a pleasant evening with him in telling him all the latest news from England. He possessed at present only one sheep, and this was corralled in an enclosure seven feet high, to guard it against the wolves and coyotes.

Monday—Up early. Henry and I had a long walk in the brushwood by the side of the river in search of deer, but we were not successful, and after a bathe in the charming fresh stream, I made up my mind that as we were so near to the Little Bow River, on which one of the ranges that I had to look at was located, it would be better for us to strike out at once and see that range, and then make our way across the prairie to the point on the Willow Creek where I had arranged to meet our manager. Leaving Kipp's I noticed our friend Savery at work with his plough and span of horses backsetting. The process in breaking up the prairie is to turn over the turf with a plough which cuts a sod about 10 inches wide and about an inch and a half thick, and to leave the roots exposed to the summer sun; all the vegetation is thus completely killed, as the grass has little if any seed; as August ends or September begins the settler takes his plough and backsets or turns the sod back again. The winter comes on with all its severity, the frost crumbles the sod, and when Spring comes again in the beginning of the following May he has only to harrow and sow his grain. The quick pace of the horses ploughing was new to an on-looker from the old country, as I am quite sure that Savery's horses were walking over three miles an hour. He complained that he should not do much good till he was able to make an irrigating ditch, and that he must wait till he got some neighbours before he could attempt so large a work. Leaving Kipp's and crossing the river, we worked our way over the prairie along a not very distinct trail. Rising up from the Old Man is the slope of a very beautiful land, under the shadow of a higher ground, well watered by the river, and presenting every appearance of what may be hereafter a thriving settlement. Having ascended to the higher ground we had still a not very distinct trail, but kept the heads of the Belly River coulée on our right hand till we reached the Little Bow River. In going down one of the coulée we observed the fresh track of a bear, who had been after the berries. On arriving at the point where the valley of the Little Bow River trends to the north, we had some difficulty in finding a path down which we could take our wagon to the river. As the gloaming came on Henry and I got off and made an exploring detour to the right, and managed to get well away from the wagons, and had an anxious half hour, until Guillaume, hearing our signal shot, came to the top of a knoll, and took us to the place where they had ensconced themselves amongst the bushes. We found the Little Bow River dry with the exception of pools, but at the mouth of the river there is some wood, not to be found at any other part, and we made a good camp.

Tuesday—Henry and I had a good walk down the Belly River in search of game. It is a very lovely spot; a small delta covered with brush, from which rise little wooded bluffs, and a bright tumbling river at their base. We got some shots at chicken, but saw no bigger game. After break-fast, as our old horse Charley was in a bad condition, I decided that it would be better for me to take Guillaume and the light wagon to drive over the range, and I drew out a map marking a course in a northwesterly direction for Henry and Joseph to take the next day, after a rest of 24 hours, so as to meet us at the elbow of the river, about 12 miles up. To carry out this Guillaume made up "a light camp," and soon after breakfast we started on our journey. After we had left, Joseph and Henry went out for a long walk with their guns. Henry shot two ducks and got back at dark and had tea and went to bed, the only noteworthy incident, as they told me, during the night being the childlike cry of a wolverine.

As we have seen a good deal of the lovely furs of this animal, though I only once caught a glimpse of it living, I cannot mention its name without a notice of its peculiarities as they are told by the trapper. This animal has a character for being the most cute of Nature's creations. He can protect his life against the wiles of the trapper, and laugh over the business; he can steal or sham in a way to beat a London pickpocket or discharged ticket-of-leaver by lengths; and if he thought it would avail him, he would, I believe, swagger and pray worthily of Moody and Sankey; but his knavish tricks—you know Brother John in Dr. Arbuthnot's "Law is a Bottomless Pit," he was a wolverine all over; though other things of the time of good Queen Anne are much admired, I dare not allude to the passage; you will find it in what are called Swift's Works—well, our wolverine is a right down crafty fellow.

Guillaume and I took a course due north, working over a very dry piece of prairie, keeping the Little Bow River on our left hand. The herbage at this time seemed to me very poor stuff indeed; I came to the conclusion, however, afterwards with regard to it that I might have been a little premature as to its grazing capabilities, for I did not then know the excellent feeding quality of much of the grass, which I have since learned to appreciate more highly. The great difficulty there, however, is the want of springs, and any attempt to work this as a grazing range would, in a dry summer at any rate, be a most difficult if not impossible operation. We took a course for about 12 miles to the northward, then turned at right angles to the west, so as to strike the elbow of the Bow River. My readers must bear in mind in taking my description of this land, that we were now in an absolutely unexplored country. After driving about nine or ten miles through similar land—of buffalo and bunch grasses, with no sloughs—along this westerly course, we came to a slope which carried us down toward the bed of the stream, and here, there being no wood with which to make a fire, except some little bits of brush and a box in which was our grub, we made a little blaze with some scrub just enough to boil our kettle, and rolling ourselves up in our blankets had an exceedingly good night under the bright stars and setting moon. It was a most quiet spot—not a single sound of any sort, not a cry of a night bird or the ripple of a stream to disturb the absolute stillness of the night. Up at daylight, and having breakfasted, we took our wagon across the dry bed of the stream and ascended to the prairie level on the other side. We drove away to the south, to make for the point at which we had arranged to meet Henry and Joseph, and for this purpose we took a southwesterly course until we found at the end of about a dozen miles that we were within sight of the Belly River bluffs, where we had been the day before. Seeing that we had somehow overshot or missed their trail, we turned again to the northwest to make for the elbow of the stream which we had left. Just as it was getting dark we came upon the track of our companion wagon, and followed it on its way into the coulée that led down to the stream, and there we found them endeavouring to put up their tent within a very few yards of the place where we had slept on the other side of the bed of the river on the night previously. It appeared that they had started at about nine o'clock on that day, and had at last lost the dog, which, though it had been a pleasant companion, had been of so little use to us. The animal had made up its mind that there was something worth living for at the place where the last camp had been situated, and after one or two fruitless endeavours to bring him with them, they had left him searching for some garbage in a bush at the mouth of the stream. What became of poor Drake—whether he was picked up by some following wagon, or whether he became the associate of coyotes, or the happy companion of some familiar wolf, or whether, as is still more likely, he became a delicate and well-fed morsel for one of these animals, will ever remain amongst the mysteries of explorers. However, after losing their dog and having had a shot or two at some antelope, they had pushed on and arrived at the Little Bow at three in the afternoon, and had endeavoured to put up their tent, in which the wind had proved a too powerful antagonist for them, and as I have said, when we came up they were still engaged in the struggle. With our additional assistance the tent was quickly pitched, fire was lighted, and a good supper prepared, over which we lingered long into the dark, narrating our different experiences since we had parted. We made up our minds, however, that this Little Bow range was not one which we could hope to work at a profit, and having come to this conclusion, we became all the more anxious as quickly as possible to turn our steps to the westward, and to see what Willow Creek and the Porcupines and foothills of the Rocky Mountains would offer us. From the point at which we were then to the point at which I had arranged to meet Mr. Craig was a distance of fully 60 miles, and over land which was described upon my map as a dry, rolling plain, with scant herbage and no indication of water, and so, with our poor horses in the condition in which they then were, it was clearly an impossible journey for us to take. The problem, therefore, was in what way to arrive at our western point. The only feasible plan that occurred to me was to take a southwestern course of some 30 miles, and endeavour to strike a northern bend of the Oldman River, and then from there to take again a northwestern course of another 40 miles or so, and thus to divide the journey, with the prospect of a camping place at which we could rest and refresh our horses. As I had not the exact variation of the compass, and as it was upon so long a line a matter of the very first importance that we should go in exactly the right direction, I had during this two nights to make such observations as would enable me to lay down my exact course. For this purpose, I took a long 12-foot tent pole and got exactly my north and south points, and having thus got my bearings, I laid down another tent pole at an angle to it for the course I wished to take for the bend of the river, taking it as it was laid down on the map. Having thus laid the course, I got Joseph and Guillaume to note the bearings of the bluffs very carefully, with the view of working it out when we should get onto the prairie level. I satisfied myself as to my course by my old friend "the Dipper" on the second evening, and was thus able to feel pretty sure that, unless my chart was very wrong as to the position of the river, we should make the desired point. On this second day we gave our horses a thorough rest.

After breakfast Guillaume and Henry went out shooting, but they saw nothing, and returned to camp. About half-past ten Joseph and I went off for a long stretch along the burnt prairie to the west, after antelope, and also to make sure of the bearings for our course of the next day by observation of any landmarks that we might see. We noticed at some distance to the southward a rise of ground, which was marked on our map as "Black Spring Hill," and we trudged many a weary mile over the burnt prairie without seeming to get much nearer to it, and so we turned at last on a southeasterly course to get to the river. We found that this stream must have been laid down on our charts with no very great accuracy, and we missed the elbow, and it was not until after a walk in this direction of some eight or ten miles under a broiling sun, that we found ourselves by the side of the stream, and then crossing and taking a line somewhat in the direction in which Guillaume and I had been two days before, we at last found ourselves at our camp. The ground was all dried up, and the only game I had seen during the day within shot was a "jackass rabbit," a sort of animal more like the mountain hare of Scotland. I managed to bring him down from a considerable distance with my rifle, and with one or two prairie chickens and duck which I had shot with my gun, we had enough for supper when we got back into camp, and much we enjoyed a good rest and a smoke after our trudge of about 24 miles, with nothing to eat since early breakfast.

Friday was a fine morning, and we were up early, and having hitched up, leaving on our left hand the Black Spring Hills, we came to a basin of about a mile in width, enclosed by very low hills. After this we reached what was marked on our maps as a lake; it was not only dried up, but the bottom was an extraordinary mass of granulated clay split into small cubes, into which the wheels of the wagon and the feet of the horses sank to a considerable depth. Here we sighted a band of eight antelope, and Henry and I got off for a stalk. We lay for a long time under a most broiling sun, and at last were able to approach nearer; and there we lay watching, till one, having caught sight of us, with that curiosity which frequently brings them within shot, marched up toward us. We lay perfectly still, in the hopes that he might have been tempted to come well within range, but at a distance of about 350 yards he was satisfied that there was danger—in all probability winded us, although we had done our best to keep to leeward—and he turned back at a trot. I gave him a parting shot, but the hazy gas that was rising from the ground prevented me from taking a satisfactory aim, as he seemed, in that atmosphere, to be almost dancing in the air, and away they galloped, without giving us another chance. After this we toiled away slowly, and Guillaume, having dropped some of our maps, added to the length of our journey by having to go back a mile or two to pick them up. About half-past four I began to get a little bit anxious at our not sighting the elbow of the stream that I was in search of, and it seemed clear, that either we had taken a course a little different from that which I had laid down, or that our map was again in fault. We concluded that our course should have been a little more to the southward, and as we had some high ground in sight in that direction, we changed our course and took one due southward, in the certainty that we must then at some distance or another strike the river. As it turned out afterwards, if we had only had the patience to keep on for another mile and a half we should have struck the point for which I was making, and for which our course had been correctly laid and properly worked out. As it was we went on with no little anxiety, Joseph running on foot some mile or so in advance, Henry and I driving our wagon, and Guillaume following us with his played-out old horse Charley and Fan. We kept on pretty well in advance till it was dark. We crossed three trails, and came in sight of some bluffs. These bluffs were very misleading, as they induced us to believe that we were near the river long before we got there, and it was quite dark before we made our camp. We fired a shot to show Guillaume where we were, and soon after he turned up, unfortunately, however, with only the mare—the old horse had been played out some six or seven miles back, and he had taken him out and left him on the prairie. After supper at eight o'clock there was a bright moon, and as I had told Guillaume that the horse must be brought into camp, I felt that I was not going to ask him to do what I would not do myself, and so I started out with him to see if we could find and bring in the old horse. We trudged over the prairie seven miles, I picking out in the moonlight the trail of Guillaume's wagon with no little difficulty. We came across the place where the horse had been taken out, and we made a circuit of nearly a mile in diameter wandering round to see if we could come across him. He was not to be found, so after a long and fruitless search, as the moon was getting low, we turned back toward camp. I was as usual making my way by the stars, Guillaume in Indian fashion was looking out for trails which he had noticed as we came out, and which therefore we should cross on our way home. The effect of some little mistake of his in this matter was, that we got close up to the river without finding any indication of our camp, and we wandered about backwards and forward, until at last the moon went down and we were very much out of it. It got very dark, and at last, as we again approached the river, Guillaume agreed there was nothing for us but to lie down until daybreak, and so we tried to make ourselves comfortable in some wet sage brush, in a little bit of a hollow leading down to the river. I had not been lying there many minutes before I began to feel that after the hot fast walk in the thin clothes I had on, it would be a case of rheumatics or mountain ague, or some other equally bad complaint, if I lay there, and so I jumped up, telling Guillaume that we must find our way down to the river and get some wood and make a fire; we groped about until at last one of us laid hold of a bush, when Guillaume taking my big knife cut off some branches, and very soon made up a roaring fire, by which we toasted ourselves, kneeling and sitting, and sometimes ineffectually trying to lie down, for the next two or three hours, until the welcome sound of a signal shot indicated to us that our camp was after all at no great distance from us. It was still so dark, however, that we agreed that it would be better to stop where we were until daylight, and although we heard another shot fired we stuck to our resolve. Day breaking we most gladly pulled ourselves together and started off for our camp. We found that we must have been at one time within a very short distance indeed of the tent, but that we had taken a wrong direction afterwards, and had wandered away for nearly a couple of miles. Very glad we were to get into camp to find Joseph with a good hot jorum of tea, after which I laid down to sleep; but Guillaume, being rather put out at the thought that I was annoyed at the horse having been left out on the prairie, started off again, and within a couple of hours came back with old Charley safely into camp. It appeared that Henry had fired several shots during the night, but we had not noticed any until nearly four o'clock, and it was his last shots that we heard. Altogether we must have had a walk during that night of about 20 miles. It is strange how short a distance the sound of a gun extends on the prairie; as soon as you get into the coulées and hills, it is of course different, but when a gun is fired on the prairie, even close to you, the sound is of the most popgun order.

After breakfast Henry and I walked down to the Oldman River, and had a bathe, and then, as clean clothes were beginning to run out, we did a real good morning's work in the washerwoman's business in the clean stream, and, having spread our washed clothes upon the shingle by the side of the river to dry, we walked back into camp and took a photograph of the group at dinner, getting Henry to take the shot, so that "the boss" might be seen in the companionship of his much prized teacup.

After dinner we took a long walk down the Belly River. Between the bluffs and the stream there are on the left side well-wooded patches of dwarf cottonwood trees, and the oleagnus, the bush which bears at this time of the year the grey berries of which the prairie chicken is very fond. On the other side of the river the banks rise pretty gently to the prairie level. The stream itself was here about 50 or 60 yards wide, and tolerably rapid, clear and not very deep; as in this month it is about at its lowest, the streams of this country being only in flood when the melted snows and summer rains swell them into big rivers, and make them then impassable. We lay for some time on a very pretty grassy hill overhanging a bend of the river, and, not having succeeded in getting any game, began to return to camp. On our way back we saw two porcupines walking leisurely along by the side of the bush. We hardly recognized, at first, what they were as they walked with their backs hunched up, making themselves as high as they could, and we at first thought they were small bears. Henry shot one, and we tied his legs together and proceeded to bring him into camp. The other porcupine we chivvied into the bushes—although he did not seem disposed to run away from us. The one which we had killed weighed about 40 pounds, and we slung him on our rifles, but had had quite enough of him before we got into camp. We had a very pleasant tea, and Joseph skinned the porcupine, which looked very good meat and was very fat, and would at any other time, no doubt, have been much relished; but as we, had at that time plenty of meat, we did not regale ourselves upon him, but were satisfied with his skin.

September 24th—Hitched up about eleven in the morning, and Charley, the old horse, being still in a very feeble condition, I arranged that

Guillaume should take him with the old mare and the wagon, as lightly loaded as possible, to Fort McLeod, and that we ourselves should strike off in the course which I had previously indicated. I had intended that Guillaume should have come with us up to the elbow of the river, and then have turned down to the southwest. Shortly after we had got under way we saw him moving off in the opposite direction; and it seemed that he had observed that down below the point to which we had walked on the day previously there was a ford by which the wagons carrying coal from the coal banks into the fort had crossed the stream, and he had made up his mind to try this trail. We drove along for about eight miles, and came to the bend of the river which I had intended to have struck on leaving the Little Bow, and continued our northwest course across the prairie. It came on to rain, and at times with such cold squalls mixed with snow that we had to pull up and turn our backs to the violence of the storm. At the end of another eight or ten miles we came to a place where there had been a recent encampment, and a good deal of hay had been cut; it was so cold that we unhitched and made our camp. We had heard that my manager had been cutting hay near the Willow Creek, and as the place where we had pitched our tent was close by a much used trail, we concluded that it was the Calgary trail to Fort McLeod and that a few miles west would bring us to the creek. Shortly after camping a party of Indians came up, consisting of a brave with four squaws, a younger brother, and three papooses. They had a wretched outfit; the squaws put together their three travois with a small quantity of cloth to windward to protect them from the rain and sleet. The children, in a manner that is not usual amongst Indians, squalled a good deal. It was "a dry camp," and we had only one small stone jug of water; as the Indian begged for a little for the children we gave them all we could spare, and then letting the children and the squaws come into our tent, we made them very happy with some good big handfuls of biscuits and marmalade, which they greedily devoured. Joseph declared they were the only Indians he had ever known to beg. The buck made himself very much at home, and pointing to the apology for a tent in which were his squaws and papooses, signified to us by signs that it was too cold a place and not fit for him to sleep in, and that he would rather come and lie down in our tent. We asked him where he was going—although as a Blood, he spoke no language which our half-breeds could understand, the unmistakeable language of signs takes well the place of spoken words—and he showed us by a slow motion of his hand, that he was going for two days, bending his head down on his hand and closing his eyes to indicate his two camps, and that then he should cross the mountains, and that he hoped to get over in four days, and by slowly circling his hand, pointing out how many times the sun would set before he should arrive at the place to which he was going. I showed him a corner of the tent where he might sleep, and he then begged that his younger brother might be allowed to come in and lie there too. This I was not disposed to allow, and holding up one finger indicated to him that there could be only one to sleep there, and pointed out to him the spot where his "lie-down" should be. This he accepted, and we were all very glad to turn in, for during the day there had been a very considerable amount of walking, both for the purpose of resting our horses and keeping ourselves warm, and at parts where the wagon being ahead had disappeared from sight, Henry and I had had very considerable difficulty in picking up the trail over the dry and not easily marked ground.

Monday—About daylight the Indian roused himself, and signed to me that he wanted to borrow my knife to cut some part of his clothing. Here I had an instance of the utter want of forethought of these people, as having borrowed the knife, he cut off a strip of the blanket, which he could ill spare, to make a piece of a belt to keep his clothes up round his waist. Having gone out of the tent he returned with a big log on his shoulder, and in the most gentlemanlike way, pointed it out to me as being the only recompense that he could offer for our hospitality. He had of course noticed it at some little distance, and had brought it in, knowing well that we should want a bit of wood to make our fire in the morning. We quickly got up and struck camp, hitched up, and went along the trail to the north for about four miles, when, examining a surveyor's post to which we came, I made out that we were on the Blackfoot-crossing trail, and finding pretty clearly from the look of the hills opposite the point which I wished to make, I struck a course west by south, and kept an absolute line by one of the hills in front of us—which formed an excellent landmark. We went on till three o'clock, and our horses had now been for 30 hours without water, and we had had nothing to drink since our very limited tea of the previous evening, and very much delighted we were when we caught sight of a large herd of cattle, and on coming down to meet the wagons that were with them, we heard that we were close to Willow Creek. The herd which we had come across was one of 4,500, in two bands nearly equally divided; they had been bought down in the south for Mr. Senator Cochrane, and were being driven up to his range near Calgary. This was my first view of a large band of cattle, and a very beautiful sight it was; they were being herded pretty close, and looked fairly well, considering their long drive. They were accompanied by many wagons, a large staff of cowboys, and a big band of horses for the purpose of driving. Having had a drink from their tub, we made our way down to the creek and camped, on a lovely afternoon, by the side of the water— the very sight of which was a relief and a great pleasure to our horses, at any rate, after their long fast. After dinner we waded the stream to a small log hut about a mile off, and found there a little half-bred Indian boy, who said his father's name was Bill Wagner; his mother, a Blackfoot squaw with two papooses, could not understand English or Cree. He told us that the place belonged to Captain Winder, and that there was a house about seven miles off, which had been bought from the man who had originally built Wagner's house. We were satisfied that this was the place which we had heard our manager had lately bought for us, and it was most satisfactory to find that I had after all struck the exact point at which I had arranged to meet him. Satisfied as to this, we went back to camp and soon turned in.

Tuesday—Fine morning. As we were bathing after breakfast we saw Guillaume and Mr. Craig coming toward us on horseback, and leading two horses, so we struck camp, hitched up, and Henry and I went off with Craig, leaving Guillaume and Joseph to follow with the wagon. We heard from Craig of the distress that he had been in on our not having turned up or being heard of at Fort McLeod. He had expected to meet us at the point where we were then at nearly a week before, and when I had not arrived, he had gone into Port McLeod to make inquiries with reference to us. Here he came across the freighter who had parted with us at St. Mary's River, and who had quite concluded from our nonarrival that some evil had befallen us, and arrangements had been made by the kind officer in command of the Mounted Police to send out bands of Indians down the river, and several of the Mounted Police across the prairie to endeavour to obtain information with regard to us; as it had never occurred, of course, to our manager that I should have turned off to investigate the Little Bow Range before meeting him. When nothing was heard of us, Craig's anxiety was still further increased by a little conversation which he had with Mickel, the freighter.

"Well," said Craig to Mickel, "what do you think has become of them?"

"Oh, not much doubt as to what's become of them" said the wagoner, with a mysterious look.

"Why—what do you mean," said Craig.

"Well, you should have just seen the two bad-looking half-breed fellows they were in company with—just the chaps, if they got them out on the prairie, to cut their throats and leave them."

This, of course, considerably increased poor Craig's anxiety. When I came to hear of the charge that had thus been made against our dear good friends Guillaume and Joseph, I felt indeed, how easily a bad character may be given without a sufficient foundation. However, just as the Mounted Police were starting out on their exploration, one of Craig's men had met Guillaume, and had seen my name on one of the boxes on the wagon, upon which there was great rejoicing, and Craig at once turned back to see if I had arrived at the point where I had indicated I would meet him. We rode along pleasantly up the Willow Creek, enjoying much the prospect of the hills on our left hand, and hearing the accounts of what had been done with reference to our range, and making our plans for exploring the range and purchasing cattle. Three miles up the stream we came upon the log hut which had been purchased by Craig as our ranch and headquarters, from a settler, Kounts, to whom I was introduced, and who we found discharging the duties of cook. The place had hitherto been called "The Leavings," a name common to many other similar places where the trail leaves the water, as indicating by its name to those travelling along the trail that they must take water and wood from this place, as it might be some time before they came across either of those useful articles again. I christened it there and then New Oxley Ranch, a name by which it will doubtless continue to be known for many and many a long year to come. Amongst those whom we found in the ranch was a rascally looking half-breed Indian boy whom Mr. Craig had taken in hand, and of whom he was going to make a good cowboy; in this, however, as we shall see hereafter, he did not meet with very signal success. During our dinner hour we had a long talk with Mr. Orr, an old Montana rancher, who was driving up the band of cattle we had seen. He gave us his experience as a cattle breeder of some 30 years' standing, and it was pretty clear, from his description, that the overstocking which has been the result of free ranching in Montana had completely destroyed the grass there, and compelled them to sell off. The band that he was driving had been on their journey for some 90 days, with occasional rests, so as to make the whole drive last over three months. They had been doing about 10 miles a day, and had undertaken to deliver on a certain day on the Calgary Range, the price to be paid being so much per head for the cattle delivered, and a certain added sum per head for the drive. After a most excellent dinner, in which hot rolls, fresh butter, and molasses played no inconsiderable part, we started off for a ride round a big canyon about three or four miles distant. We rode as far as the top of some low hills near to a small ranch occupied by a settler named Lindon, and having seen the excellent quality of the grass on top of the Porcupine Hills, where even at their highest points it was up to the horses' knees, we returned home at dusk. After tea and a pleasant evening's talk with some new arrivals who had come with the mail, we retired to our beds in our tent, as the house seemed pretty full. Amongst those who had come in was an old French horse dealer named Beaupré, who became afterwards our companion for many days.

New Oxley lies on the banks of the Willow Creek, in the lower ground which forms the glacier valley, and which is about half a mile in width, from which the bluffs rise to the prairie level, at a height of about 80 feet. On the east side these bluffs slope down somewhat gradually, but rise more precipitously to the west. The stream flows through the middle of the valley, with a good deal of the brush and willows on each side which give the creek its name, the valley narrowing up on the northern end to quite a gorge, and on the southern end spreads out until the river runs between cutbanks, the whole of them on the prairie level. Toward the northern end there is a very curious formation of blocks of sandstone loose in the clay, from which by the frosts and rains they are separated, and fall down in enormous squared blocks of sometimes 12 or 20 feet long, 6 feet wide, and a couple of feet in thickness, ready to be sawn for building purposes and most conveniently adapted for this, when some labour shall have come in in the shape of stonemasons and others who can construct some more solid building than the log huts, which are, however, most valuable to us at present, and than which there can be no better protection against the summer's heat or the winter's cold.

Wednesday, 27th—Up early, and after breakfast walked about the ranch and inspected the ground that had been broken up for potatoes, and made a good examination of the grassy bottom which I have just described; after this I spent the morning in going through my manager's accounts. A little before noon, our four-horse wagon having been provided with the requisites for our journey, with two men upon it and saddle horses for five others of us were to complete the party, we started for our inspection of the Porcupine Hills range. The eastern boundary of our range was reckoned to be about 18 miles from the ranch, and the block of which we had the lease was 9 miles wide by 18 in length, and consisted of land which had never been yet surveyed or inspected, and upon which in all probability no white man had ever yet set foot. We had a pleasant ride over the prairie, as firm as a well-kept lawn, rising gradually from the western bank of the river, until we came into a broad valley, where grass of two or three feet deep promised excellent fields for hay. Riding about through different parts of this valley and inspecting the condition of the land and drawing every bit of bush and covert in the hope of turning out some deer, we arrived in the evening by the side of a branch of the creek, where we camped, and after a good tea went to bed. The place where we had camped was a knoll, rising to some 60 feet above the stream, along which the brush extended for a mile or two, affording capital cover for deer and other game. On waking on Thursday morning, we found that the snow which I had seen on the highest ground in our ride of the day previously had reached us, and there were several inches on the ground, and it was still snowing. I was up very early, and went with my rifle along the edge of the wood, but finding the snow coming down very heavily I thought it prudent to return back into camp. After breakfast Henry and I took our rifles and gun and went to look for deer, but found none, and having waded through the creek at least five or six times in our zigzagging about through the bush, we returned and had dinner, and afterwards left to try to get to the forks of the creek at night. By the forks of the creek—although they were at that time not surveyed and very little was really known about them—we understood a division in the Willow Creek, or rather I should say a union of two branches; one coming from the north and the other from the south. At these forks we arrived about five o'clock; a very pretty little pool near the forks seemed full of trout, and Henry, having put a little bit of bacon on a hook, in about 10 minutes returned with seven trout averaging one pound apiece. These helped to make an additional and excellent dish at our evening meal, the other items on the menu being prairie chicken and bacon. The snow, however, was getting deeper and deeper, and made me rather anxious as to our onward progress.

Friday morning Henry went out to fish, and came back with a very good load of trout. After breakfast he and I and Craig and Kounts went off to look for a surveyor's post, to see if we could make out whether or not we had yet arrived at the eastern boundary of our range; we arranged to join the wagon at night a little further up the creek. Our search after the post was not successful, and at four o'clock we joined the wagon and camped for the night on the south fork of the creek, at no great distance from a lake covered with duck and other water fowl. Kounts and I went off to look after some deer, Craig and Henry went to the lake, where they shot 10 ducks, but not having the dog with them had not been able to get any of them, as they fell in the water, and it was too cold to go in even if they had not been hindered by the deep mud that lined the shore. Kounts and I had had a beautiful ride up into the foothills, but did not come across any big game. There appeared an anxiety in Kounts' mind as to its being necessary to obtain some provision; this being so I went off to see whether I could not be more successful in getting duck off the lake, but not being more successful than the others, we came home and went to bed, arranging to go out very early and see whether we could not do better in the morning.

Saturday—Still snowing hard; we were not, however, to be driven back from our exploring expedition, and arranged that the wagon should go on under Beaupré's guidance to a fixed point, and that Henry and Kounts and Craig and I should go and get some duck. We walked up and down the lake—which is here a long sheet of water lying between two low hills, and forming the headwaters of this portion of the creek. Going further up the lake, we found that there was still another lake lying to the north of it. After passing through some very swampy ground, and still further to the north, we came to the conclusion that this chain of lakes must reach up almost to the neighbourhood of the sources of the High River. We only succeeded in getting a few waders, and then rode on to join the wagon, and picked it up at three in the afternoon. We found them camped in a sheltered place with a high hill behind it, and close to what we considered to be the north fork of the Willow Creek. So beautiful were the festoons of snow that were drooping from a big cotton tree that overhung our tent, that I wished to take a photograph of the scene, and upon enquiring from Kounts as to my plates, I found that they had been left at the ranch. I was very disappointed at this, as one of my great objects was to take some views of our range, and especially of the wilder portions of this part of the Rocky Mountains, as we got further up. So I told Kounts he would have to ride back to the ranch the next day and fetch the glasses, and he could at the same time bring up any further provisions that we might be in want of.

Sunday morning, snowing hard and blowing. Upon enquiry of Kounts as to our provisions, he told me that they would come to an end that night. This was indeed a very serious business, as it was quite clear, that to endeavour with the wagon to retrace our steps in the present condition of the snow was absolutely impossible, and that an advance was equally hopeless. I told Kounts that he must therefore start at once for the ranch, and as he knew the hills better than any man, he must do his best to get down there, and at once come up with two or three pack horses and some grub, and that we would wait for him until Wednesday morning. As he was going away he told us that he saw some deer in the distance, and we went out, but found when we got up that it was only the bushes, which in the driving snow he had mistaken for game. We went up the creek a little way, and endeavoured to find some game, wading through the snow, but we found none. We found that Kounts' account of the provisions was not overstated, for, with the exception of three small tins, which we thought best to put by for a last emergency, and a half bottle of Lea and Perrins, we had come to the end of everything, biscuits and all.

Monday—It was still snowing hard. As it was absolutely necessary some food should be got, it was agreed that we must all go out and look for game. So Henry and Beaupré and I started off on horseback to shoot, and Craig and Cottingham and Joseph went to fish, but took rifles with them. A difficult ride we had for some two or three miles through the snow, which was at least two feet deep, and of course in places had drifted to a very considerable depth. I managed, however, to shoot two prairie chickens and two ducks, and Beaupré shot two chickens; Henry had carried the rifle, so had no chance of getting a shot at the smaller game, and bigger game there was none. We rode sometimes into drifts that took our horses over their backs, and which required much plunging to extricate, and as it kept on snowing all the time, and got very thick, we were glad to get back to camp, where we found that our other friends had returned, but had only got a few trout.

Tuesday—Still snowing. The men had amused themselves during these two days by carrying in huge logs, there being plenty of dead pine in the neighbourhood, and I must say that the loads our little Beaupré—a stiff little Frenchman—and our other men carried in seemed enormous. We tried to make ourselves as happy as we could, and many a French song arose from Beaupré and from ourselves, and many a tale passed round the huge fire which we kept up in the camp, and considerable skill was shown in economizing every single bit of chicken and the ducks, and that half bottle of Worcestershire sauce did more, I believe, to win to our meagre meals an aspect and a flavour of abundance than anything else could have afforded. Amongst other tales that were told round our fire in "Snowy Camp"—this being the name which I preferred to give this place of our imprisonment, rather than "Starvation Camp," by which name some of our party less euphemistically designated it—was a wonderful story which was told by Beaupré of one of the incidents of his earlier life.

He had been for some 30 years travelling in all parts of the northern continent, and it was during the first explorations of Colonel Fremont, when he was surveying for a transcontinental line, that old Beaupré was working his way with a team from San Francisco eastward; his horses had either got played out or were stolen by Indians, and poor Beaupré found himself "set afoot" in the middle of the prairie. An old voyageur is not, however, to be put out by anything so long as he has his axe left him, and using this to some purpose Beaupré broke up a part of his wagon and constructed a wheelbarrow; on this he put a little flour, his frying pan, his kettle, and two or three other things of which he was most absolutely in want, and proceeded to trundle the barrow across the prairie. He had gone many hundred miles when he was met by the Colonel, who offered to give him some opportunity for better locomotion; but Beaupré, having got so far, determined that he would do the rest in the same way, and trundled along his barrow for the remaining three or four hundred miles, until just as his food was played out, he reached the settlements where he could renew his stores.

Many tales were told of the difficulties of travelling in the old days through Montana and the States, and even in this part of the country it was not very safe for many years to travel during the day, when a man might be seen by hostile Indian tribes. The practice always was to work as far as you could during the silence and almost darkness of the night, and then to lie perfectly *caché* during the day, and so to make up the journey from point to point. No more exciting stories were told than those of the Road Agents, the Younger Brothers, and the Brothers James, the highwaymen of Montana, and the Lynch law that was administered at Helena and Virginia City. I shall, however, allude more particularly to these worthy citizens when I come to describe the country where most of their exploits were performed.

The thermometer was not low, in fact, scarcely below freezing point, so that the camp very soon began to be very slushy. I had given to every man some grand title as official of our municipal body, sanitary inspectors, and other officers, to each of whom was allotted some particular duty with regard to the camp. The poor unfortunate horses remained pretty close round us, eating the browse and occasionally digging down to a bit of long grass near to the roots of the bush.

Wednesday—Beaupré and Joseph and I went out to shoot, while Henry and Cottingham fished in turns. We rode out somewhat in the same direction as that which we had followed yesterday, but bending off a little bit more to the eastward, along some brush which lined what seemed to be another branch of the creek, and we came home with exactly the same amount of chicken and duck that we had got the day previously. This, however, only lasted us for tea that night and breakfast the following morning. During the night I began to feel the effect of the storm on my eyes, and waking about two o'clock in the morning found the eyeballs itching at the back to such an extent that I could almost have rubbed them out. Shortly afterwards they began to water very considerably, and at last I dropped off to sleep, to wake in the morning, however, and find that it was almost impossible to open my eyes. Feeling that this snow-blindness was coming on I remained in the tent, and sent out Beaupré and Cottingham and Joseph to shoot; they came back with empty bags, and Henry and the others having got only three trout. We finished them that night, and thinking that we had got to the worst, eked out our meal with a few provisions which we had hoarded for cases of emergency, with a good supply of the Worcester sauce, and now we were with an entirely empty larder.

On waking on Thursday morning, my eyes were worse, and the running during the night had been more extensive; we woke to find that it had been snowing hard during the night and was at it still. Having nothing to eat there was no object in getting up, so we lay in bed until after 10:00, when there being no prospect of Kounts' return, we fully agreed that some steps must be taken to obtain food, so we arranged to shoot one of the horses. In these days of hunger the whole thought and conversation turns on food in all its aspects. We wondered what they were having for dinner at Oxley, whether our friends in England had as good appetites as we had, and whether really beef steaks or mutton chops were the better, and how about a gigot—and long had been our discussions as to what was best on the prairie. Beaupré had eaten everything "good to eat" on the prairie, and I think about this time we had come to the conclusion that he was right, and that everything was good to eat except perhaps crow, which somebody objected to; wolf was pronounced to be "bully meat," and as for dog, if we had had one he would have had very little chance indeed of saving his life; a horse's paunch, however, seemed to be the favourite idea, and as we had now arrived at a position in which it seemed possible that we might be kept here for weeks, I began to feel some little anxiety as to the possibility of a stampede amongst the horses, in which case we should have been left with no possibility of food. So we agreed that we would kill the least useful of the horses, and it was carried that the animal we could best spare was a rather respectable old buckskin horse—that we would cook his paunch that day and would try our best at making some pemmican and suitable joints of the rest of him. Henry had proceeded to get my rifle and one of the men was starting to bring in the poor animal for slaughter, when suddenly a prairie chicken flew over my head into the tree; I seized my gun, which was standing close by, and shot it; three others went into the bushes, and Beaupré diving into the snow after them managed to get the rest. These four chickens served for food for our dinner and tea, and I made up my mind that come what might we must try to get out the next day. This was almost impossible so long as the snow was coming down; however deep it might be we could still try to get through it, but while it continued to fall it was so blinding that it was almost an impossibility to keep the direction in which we might wish to go. That night, I must say, I began to be some-what anxious about the fate of our little band. I cannot say that I ever felt frightened for myself, but it must be remembered that all those who were out there with me were there for the purpose of helping me in my own work, and I felt, therefore, that if any ill fate fell upon them it would be to a certain extent properly laid upon my shoulders—although so far as the want of food went the only blame that could be attached to me was, that I had not taken care to enquire before we started what amount of food we had with us in the wagon. Very careless indeed it was of those to whom I trusted, as having so much more experience in these matters than I had, and to have left behind us some four months' provisions at the ranch, and with a whole wagon at their disposal, not to have provided a greater amount for the possibilities of our journey. There is this to be said, however, in the defence, that Kounts had thought that we should have arrived at an earlier day at some ranch in the mountains, and that at any rate we should have been able to pick up a good amount of game on our journey. It appeared, however, that the Stony Indians had been down in the neighbourhood, and had shot and frightened away the game of which otherwise there would have been an abundance, and the snow had, of course, prevented us making more rapid advance, and the storm was too severe to allow even game to move. However we were getting very anxious about Kounts not having returned, and as I lay awake that night I heard the thuds of snow dropping from the cotton tree onto our tent, and on looking out once or twice saw that it was falling fast. I must say that the probability of our being able to get back to the ranch seemed somewhat remote. My eyes, the next morning, were a little better, and so making a very meagre breakfast on a few trout and the carefully put away remains of the previous meal, we got together the horses and packed the bigger tent on one of them, with our frying pan, kettle and teapot and a few other articles on another, and each of us mounting his horse, we sallied forth in the direction of the ranch. Before leaving I got Craig to cut a good broad blaze on the white wood of the tree; in case anything should happen to us, we left a memento which some future traveller might discover, in the following description:

"No provisions.

Kounts sent Sunday, did not return.

We have killed 25 chickens and four ducks; have come to an end of all.

Saturday, September 29th, arrived Staveley Hill, and party.

Leaving for our last camp this morning, Friday, October 6th.

We shall try to reach the forks tonight."

We were sometimes a little tinged with melancholy, especially as the men began to get weaker and less inclined for the amusement of carrying in big logs and seeing the big blaze. It was the last night of the month, and Beaupré, who had been sitting more pensively than was his wont, looked up from the campfire and said to me, "Demain, Monsieur, c'est le Jour des Morts." "Non," said I, knowing well as a lawyer the *cras animarum*; "demain ce n'est que le premier Octobre." "Ah!" said he joyfully, "alors nous sommes sauvés, s'il avait été le premier Novembre, cette niège ne nous aurait pas laissé échapper. Ah! mois d'Octobre—il va dégeler bientôt."

In order to enforce the very salutary rule which enjoins the never bringing a loaded gun into the tent, I may here narrate a narrow escape from a bad accident. One of our friends, being very anxious to do something toward helping the larder, had strolled off with a gun, but returned into camp with his fingers so cold that he could not take out the cartridges. He laid the gun down, therefore, close by where Henry and I were lying, and having warmed his fingers some little time proceeded to do the extracting—Henry and I got up from the place where we were lying. I suppose that the fingers were still pretty numbed, for in a few seconds we heard the gun go off, and most fortunate it was for us that we had moved, as the whole contents of the barrel went through the top of my photograph case, on which our heads had rested, and had cut half through the tent pole against which it had been propped. It was a merciful escape from what would have been a most tragic end to our journey. One morning we had a real disappointment. Craig had gone out, during one of our worst days, to see if he could pick up some game, and returning loaded into camp, a cheer was raised that he had got a porcupine. I need not say that had this been the fact, the delicacy would not have been left as much neglected as it was on the Oldman River; it turned out, however, that the load he was bringing into camp was a papoose bag made of a buffalo skin stuffed with hay which he had found hanging on a tree, the cradle left behind by some squaw on the break up of an Indian encampment to dry; though it was not good to eat it was good to laugh at, and so, no doubt, was useful in its way. And now for our sortie.

Leaving our wagon and the small tent we started off in Indian file in the following order. First, Beaupré, as the oldest voyageur, led the way, Joseph, Henry, myself, a pack horse, Craig, pack horse, and Cottingham bringing up the rear. In crossing the first plateau as we came up out of the bed of the stream, we found the snow very deep, in some places in drifts into which the horses plunged over their backs, and it took very nearly an hour and a half to get over what was scarcely more than three parts of a mile. Here we got to the base of one of the hills, and upon consultation, we came to the conclusion that we should find the snow less deep on the summit; we began therefore to toil up the hill. Head over heels most of us went many and many a time, but the snow was so soft and so deep that no harm was done. It was very hot work, as the greater part of it had to be done on foot—pulling our horses after us. Zigzagging the slope, we must have made nearly two miles in getting to the top, with the snow very frequently up to our shoulders, and lying down frequently in it to rest and get our wind, until we almost despaired of getting to the top. At last we reached the divide, and to our dismay found the snow deeper than it was in the bottom, and having expended all this labour in getting up the hill, there was nothing for it but to go down again. The hardest work fell to the leading horse, who had to break the trail, and Beaupré's being done, Joseph and his animal had to take up the work. We toiled along, however, and when we had done about seven miles we came again to the north fork of the creek. Beaupré, who was again leading, caught sight of a wolf by the side of the stream, and came running back to tell me to come and have a shot at him. I had unfortunately, in trying to get my horse out of one of the deep snowdrifts, knocked the front sight off my rifle, so was obliged to have recourse to a little Winchester which Henry was carrying, but having had nothing to do with this rifle previously, I put the sight at an elevation of about 700 yards, and stealing through the bush got a capital view of the wolf. He was a big blue-grey wood wolf, and the cunning rascal was fishing, holding his nose close down to the water, and waiting till a big trout came near him, and then digging his nose into the water fetched out the fish. I watched him for a few seconds, and getting a capital broadside view of him, fired at him. Unfortunately, from the sighting of my rifle, I saw that my shot went over his back, and as he bounded off I got another shot at him, but with no more success, and as he dived first to the right, into the bush, and then, catching sight of my companions, struck across the stream, and off to the distant hills, I fired three or four wild shots after him. Great was the regret of the camp at missing what would have made an excellent supper, but we had managed to kill some chickens and a duck during the day, and we knew that where the wolf could get fish the probability was that we could get plenty also. We found a nice flat place upon which to pitch our tent, and rolling away the snow scraped it clean with our frying pan, which we used as a shovel. Our tent being pitched and fire made, Henry and Craig went to fish, and came back in a few minutes with some seven big trout of at least a pound each, and these boiled down with our prairie chicken made us a soup which we pronounced excellent, and which stood in good stead now that we had not got any tea, and so we made a sufficient supper. We arranged two big logs as benches, and had a good dry of our clothes, and so to bed. In giving the account of our food, I have scarcely sufficiently evinced the gratitude which we owed for the bottle of Worcester sauce. When everything else was very scarce it had added a most satisfactory relish to what would have otherwise been very poor and watery diet; this, however, had, amongst our other good things, come to an end.

Next morning, Saturday, Henry and Craig went again to fish, and came back with six trout, and having boiled them, we made our breakfast of fish "straight," a North-West phrase expressing the absence of any farinaceous or other addition.

Saturday—We started soon after daylight, as we hoped to get to the ranch that night. There had been after the thaw in the hot sun a little freezing again of the snow, giving an icy crust which sadly troubled the shins of our poor horses, and along a great part of the journey the snow was so deep that we made but poor progress. We stopped in the middle of the day to rest the horses on a little bit of an islet in the gravel bed of the creek, which we struck again at the forks, and Henry and Craig caught nine trout, which gave us again our dinner and some good fish broth. This was the same place where we had camped on our way out. I had here a curious experience with regard to my snow-blindness; I had been very bad during the morning, but on walking down, while dinner was being got ready, to the stream and looking into the running water as it danced over the pebbles, I found my eyes suddenly completely relieved, and the pain wholly gone. As long as I continued looking at the stream the eyes seemed perfectly well, and I rejoiced in the fact that I was completely right again; the relief was, however, but temporary, for I had scarcely turned away from the stream for more than two or three minutes, when the pain and weakness came back again as bad as ever. Again I turned and for nearly a quarter of an hour I looked at the water with a complete sense of relief, but on turning from it the snow-blindness returned in all its force. I had not heard then of the plans adopted by old voyageurs and trappers to prevent or alleviate this trouble; but these are one or two useful hints. One plan suggested, which it is said gives some relief, and perhaps, if taken at an early stage, would prevent the blindness coming on, is to take the charred end of a stick and to blacken the cheek-bones and upper part of the face round the eyes and close up to the eyes themselves. But the better plan by far is to cut out a thin piece of wood to the shape of a pair of spectacles, and in the round pieces which cover the eyes and take the place of the glasses, to cut a slit for each eye, and with a piece of string fastened to each end of the piece of wood passing round the head to wear it as spectacles: the small amount of light which is thus allowed to come in through the crevices will, it is said, entirely protect the eyes against the glare which produces the snow-blindness. Of course if you have the luck to have some blue or green goggles you are all right. I fancy that the angle at which the sun's rays strike the snow has a good deal to do with it, as we have generally had attacks in the early and late snows, and seldom in mid-winter. At three we started again, and I rode along for some time with my eyes almost closed; toward the evening they began to get better, and I managed later on in the afternoon to shoot three prairie chicken. We worked up to the top of a hill and camped there, some little distance away from the creek; having lighted our fires, we melted snow for water, and boiling our prairie chicken, drank the broth and picked the bones and went to bed.

Sunday, Oct. 8—Up at seven. A fine morning, but very cold in the exposed place on which we had advisedly pitched our tents, as the snow was still deep in the bottom. As our larder was empty and we had nothing to cook, I bade the boys not waste their time in making a fire, and we started off at once, being relieved from any trouble as to preparing breakfast. We rode on till twelve o'clock, when coming to a stream we stopped and made an attempt to get fish. As we had nothing to eat for ourselves, so also we had nothing wherewith to bait for fish, and the two or three trout which we saw in the stream steadily refused to yield to the temptations of an artificial fly, which was all we had to offer them. Having rested for an hour, we resumed our journey, I think a little out of spirits. The horse which we had intended to kill and eat, and which we had chris-tened "Pemmican," from the use which we had intended to put his better parts, began to show signs of being played out. I got on him and tried to make him go, and managed to get another two or three miles out of him, but the poor beasts were necessarily very thin and getting very weak. We came here to some chokecherry bushes, and it was a curious sight to see the whole of the cavalcade jump off their horses as one man, jumping up at the boughs, and ravenously devouring the berries without troubling to spit out the stories. Riding on we came to a camp of Stony Indians, and as we were descending a coulée, "Pemmican" and Craig's horse completely gave out. As for poor "Pemmican," he stood still in a deep snow drift on the edge of a little runner, and I could not push or pull him either forward or backward. No threats, no cajolery or adjurations availed the least. He looked the very ideal of hopeless and helpless obstinacy. I could not leave him where he was, so as he stood on the edge of the bank with his forelegs planted out stiff and pressing his whole weight upon them, I took a good swinging drive at them with my arm behind his knees, and thus with his front legs knocked from under him he was obliged to give a spring forward to save himself, and the exertion took him over the brook and up the bank on the other side; here I took off his saddle and bridle, and Craig's horse being equally played out, we took our tent and other goods off the two pack horses and, as it was now a case of home or nothing, we put our saddles on them, and leaving our goods with the two played-out horses, we continued our ranchward course.

We rode on into the darkness, but we were now in a country that we knew, and home was within reach, and at eleven o'clock we were close down to the Willow Creek, and finding its welcome banks we got the best we could out of our horses in riding up to the ranch, where we were received with considerable delight; we ourselves were most pleased to sit down and get that which is the greatest luxury that anyone can have under these circumstances—a cup of real good tea; hot, strong and sweet, and plenty of it. After this the supper provided us by our excellent cook kept us ringing the changes on the luxuries of hot cakes, bacon, and beef, and we ate away till one in the morning, when we retired to bed. We heard with some little anxiety, that Kounts had arrived at the ranch during the night of the day in which he had left us, and having worked hard at baking and preparing food, had started with it with one pack horse back for "Snowy Camp" on the following afternoon.

Monday—Up at eight, and after a breakfast which even after the supper of last night was no small treat, we walked about the ranch with Craig. It was curious to see to what an extent, we had been reduced in flesh during our six days' abstinence, Henry remarking as we were washing when we were stripped the next morning, that we looked like two starved Indians, the effect upon our other men having been at the end of the third or fourth day a depression of spirits and an unwillingness to do hard work, and it was clear that ducks and chickens straight, although they may be admirable food for invalids, have very little sustaining power for men.

In the afternoon, Craig and I went out to ride over a part of the range, having sent Guillaume and Joseph to bring in the tent and the two horses; Henry walked up the creek with a gun, and succeeded in getting two prairie chicken and one duck. In the evening the stage arrived, and put up at the ranch, and as six people came in the house was pretty full.

Tuesday—Up at seven, and walked about the ranch all day with Craig, and planned a house and a sawmill, and heard that morning that a herd of buffalo had been seen on the trail between Fort Benton and Billings—the road we were intending to take. I was getting now anxious as to the fate of Kounts, and I was determined not to leave the country until I had ascertained his safety; so on Wednesday I sent off Cottingham with a horse and some provisions to search for him, taking the route which he had told our men that he should take, and Joseph started on the line by which we had returned, as I hoped that by these means we should find some sign of him.

Thursday—Henry's eyes became bad with snow-blindness, and he was out of order with the starvation and subsequent filling up, and so leaving him for a day's rest at the ranch, Craig and I started off after dinner on horseback for Fort McLeod, and had a pleasant canter for the first 12 miles, after which we got into the remains of the snow. It was curious to note how on this first piece of the prairie the snow had entirely departed. The Chinook wind which we had felt on our second day after leaving Snowy Camp had melted the snow and so licked it up that it had left the ground dry underneath. We found several indications of the stress to which the people who had been caught by the storm had been reduced; in one place there was still left a pile of snow 10 or 12 feet high, which had been formed to windward of a wagon that had been caught there; and another had had to break up the chest of his wagon for fuel. Many other incidents were told us of the severity of the storm, than which none more severe at this period of the year has ever been recorded in the North-West.

After passing the cutbanks, the place where we again approach the Willow Creek on its passage down to McLeod, we caught sight for the first time of the range of the Rocky Mountains, extending along in a magnificent series of snowy peaks standing out against the pure blue sky, with snow clouds gathered around their summits, and bearing out more fully than I had ever seen before the Homeric phrase of the hill of cloud-collecting Jove. They form at this place as beautiful a panorama as could be found of scenery of this character. Between us and the greater heights there are the low-lying foothills extending away in continuation of the Porcupine range on the right to the northward, but toward Fort McLeod the prairie itself seems to touch the base of the mountains as they extend far to the southward to their terminating peak of the Chief Mountain. After a pleasant ride we reached Fort McLeod, and I made my first acquaintance with that somewhat grandly named town, the big type of whose name on the map had inspired me with a certain respect for its importance, and I was not a little surprised to find the town represented by a wide, muddy lane, with a row of dirty, half-finished wooden shanties flanking each side.

In these wooden shanties, however, an amount of business is done which would, I daresay, gladden the heart of many a decent shopkeeper in a country town in England; aye, if only he could put his net profits at even one-fourteenth of that which rolls into the pockets of the possessors of one of these shanties.

The trade that has been done there during the last few years by one firm that has been energetically "running" the North-West is something enormous. Oh, my Hudson Bay Company, all this might have been yours, if you had not sat by with folded arms and allowed your own legitimate business to have been grabbed by some Montana adventurers! Having made the acquaintance of Major Crozier, then in command of the Mounted Police, and inspected a band of horses which had been brought into McLeod, and as to which I tried to make a deal, but found the owner opening his mouth too wide, we found a comfortable shakedown on the floor of a friend's blanket store, and next day I made a more complete enquiry as to the probability of purchasing cattle and horses. Having finished a good day's work, and picked up a wagon which had been left by Craig in his previous search for us, we hitched our saddle horses to it, and started off after tea back for our ranch.

We had a pleasant but rather cold drive home. As we did not leave until nearly eight o'clock, we barely got across the rivers and through the thicket which lines the banks, before darkness had set in. We had, however, carefully noted the ford, and the water barely came up to the floor of the wagon. When we got out on the prairie it was a lovely starlight night, and we drove away till we reached home about one o'clock. It was very interesting to watch the stars during those long hours rising and getting well up in the sky, and it was with difficulty that we could persuade ourselves that stars which we saw high up in the heavens at the close of our drive were those we had noticed rising one after another above the horizon like lights on the prairie. On we went over the beautiful sward, as level as a billiard table, the snow almost entirely gone, until at last we were both somewhat alarmed as to whether we had not passed the turn down which would take us to the lower level to our ranch. However, after a mile or two further we satisfied ourselves that we were all right, and were very glad to find ourselves at last at the ranch, when I bent my steps gladly toward the tent, and turned in between the buffalo robes. Henry had been bad during the day with a considerable increase of snow-blindness. I found him better, however, for rest and an early bed. We heard from Cottingham, who had returned, that Kounts had left Lindori's ranch on his way for Snowy Camp on the Wednesday in pretty good spirits as to his being able to reach us. I cannot say that I was very much relieved by this information, as it seemed to me that under these circumstances we ought long before this to have heard of him, as it was now nearly 10 days since he had started out from Oxley Ranch.

Saturday—Henry and I said goodbye to the ranch, and with Craig and Cottingham left for Fort McLeod at two in the afternoon. We had a pleasant drive across the prairie, which I began now to be pretty tolerably acquainted with. On arriving at Port McLeod, Henry and I had a pleasant little dinner with Major Crozier, and then went back to the blanket store at our friend Captain Winder's, where we turned in and had a good night.

Sunday—Up early, and went to breakfast at the only hotel that there is in McLeod, if, indeed, one may dignify by the name of a hotel a very common wooden shanty. The gentleman who keeps it goes by the name of Kamoose, and as he himself told me his own story of the origin of this name, I don't know that there is any reason why I should not narrate it to my readers.

Mr. Henry Taylor had originally begun life as a missionary, but, having given up that profession, had come in from Montana with the whisky traders in 1872, and had distinguished himself a good deal in that line in his dealings with the Indians. Upon the Mounted Police coming into the country in 1874, he had given up the whisky trading in common with all the rest of the crew, and had started a small hotel in the fort.

While engaged in business as a whisky trader, he had stolen a squaw from one of the Bloods, though according to his own account he had not stolen her, but had "traded her" for a gallon of whisky; but however that may be, he was not allowed to remain in peaceful possession of the lady, as the Blood from whom he had stolen her was on his trail, intending to kill both him and the squaw; and, as Kamoose prudently observed, that there was no use in having anybody killed about it, and he thought that the best thing he could do was to pass her on, and so he traded her to somebody else—perhaps one of the Bloods—for half a gallon of whisky. The Bloods, however, nicknamed him "Kamoose," signifying in their language "robber," and the name has always remained to him, and by that title he and his hotel are known.

If the outraged Blood husband had caught them he would have been entitled to kill Kamoose, but his punishment of his wife, according to Blood custom, should have been, with either his strong teeth or his knife, to have taken off her nose. This mode of punishment seems to commend itself to the savage, because while the loss of the nose does not at all impair the usefulness of the squaw as a drudge, it puts her out of the pale of those who might be likely to obtain attention, either from a husband or from anyone else. The sentiment of the Indian is, perhaps, a little in contradiction to the habits of some civilized countries, for while infidelity in a wife is by them looked upon as an outrageous offence, the young un-married lady is allowed the most complete freedom in every respect with-out the slightest damage to her reputation or matrimonial prospects.

Kamoose was a kind, genial, square built man, with a considerable attachment to the Indians, and more especially to a lot of little Indian children who seemed to make their home of his house, and I am bound to say this for Kamoose, that I only wish that hotel keepers whose bills I have had the honour of making acquaintance with in European lands deserved the title of "robber" as little as he did in that respect. The house consisted of a kitchen with a very good stove, where the cook produced very good meals, and not least to be remembered is that great luxury of the West, the slap-jacks, the cakes either of flour or buckwheat, which are sent up in little piles of three deep at the end of every meal, and which are eaten with butter and molasses, fresh and hot as they are required; the same that in Russia, our European land of most excellent bread, are called "bleenie." Adjoining the kitchen was the dining room, with three or four tables and benches in rows, and next to that a large low room, which was the sleeping room, accommodating 30 or 40, and where every-body, whites and Indians, slept on the ground, wrapped up in such buf-falo robes or blankets as they possessed. The terrible smell and horrible dirt of this dormitory was such as to frighten any person from sleeping there unless they were to the manner born; it was through this dormitory that we had to pass to go into the dining room. The meals were indeed excellent, and well worth the 50 cents which were paid for them. There was another establishment in McLeod, of a very much higher character, kept by an old woman of colour, known by the familiar title of "Aunty"; we went there to dinner. She had been, I rather fancy, in some good fam-ily in the South before the troubles when so many of the Southern people came up into Montana, and from there migrated into this part of the Dominion. She spoke in the most pleasant voice, and used exceedingly good language, somewhat in the style of a well-educated housekeeper in England. She was very glad to see us, and I think was a little jealous of our ever dining at Kamoose's instead of accepting her hospitality. She told us with much sorrow how she had her house all in order to give breakfast to Lord Lorne when he was making his trip last year as Governor General. She had got up early to prepare the breakfast, but her man made too big a fire in the stove, or in some other way the house got on fire, and she lost all her little property. This loss did not seem so much to have affected her as the consequent inability to provide the breakfast. In the afternoon we started west for the Crowsnest Pass. I had succeeded in purchasing, in addition to the horse that we had brought to McLeod, a pair of very good chestnuts, for which I gave 300 dollars. Henry rode one of these, and Craig rode an old white horse[2] that was considered to be one of the best herding horses that I had got in the Barton band, a band of horses I had bought on the previous morning. I rode the other chestnut, and, as we did not start till about four in the afternoon, we felt that we had not too much time to get before dark to Captain Stewart's ranch at Pincher Creek, for which we were bound, and as none of us had ever been in the country before, it was not unlikely that if we loitered much on our road, we should find ourselves for the night on the prairie. We started along the Oldman River, which we had seen at so many points from its junction with the Belly, and which we were now following toward its source. Leaving the stream we struck across up into some higher ground, passing by an Indian Reserve farm; after this we found ourselves in an exceedingly wild part of the prairie, when darkness came on, and we had done about 20 miles, and we knew that there were about four miles still to do. We should have been thoroughly set afoot, as there was no landmark and very little indication of any trail, but fortunately a settler came by on a buckboard, going in our direction; he gave us our line, and we took off for Captain Stewart's, where we were very glad to arrive about nine in the evening. We found that threshing was going on, and not the least interesting part of the proceedings was to find so many men there, coming in from all the different places round to assist at the threshing—sitting in the barn when their work was done, and having the usual harvest songs, but with nothing except tea to drink, and yet the cheeriness and joviality seemed by no means less than I have seen it at an English harvest supper where there has been far more stimulating drink provided. Captain Stewart's was a comfortable house, with buildings and corrals round it of a very good character; it had been put up for a Police farm, where the horses were to be reared and the corn grown for the provision of the Mounted Police in Fort McLeod; in addition to this Captain Stewart had added to the house, and had had the good fortune to have a most excellent manager, whose wife assisted in looking after the comforts of the establishment. We made ourselves very comfortable on the floor of a large room, rolled up in our blankets and buffaloes.

Monday—Up pretty early, and having looked through the corrals and generally over the farm buildings, we started for the ranch of a friend of ours about 20 miles further up the valley, in the direction of the Crowsnest Pass. We picked up a man who was going into British Columbia to Okanogan, near Kamloops; he was alone, riding a cayeuse and driving before him a pack pony loaded with a little flour, some bacon, and his kettle. He was making his way through the "Rockies" by himself, with a journey of 600 miles before him, which would take him about two months. The only difficulty which presented itself to him was the first few days across the mountains, when it seemed not impossible that another snowstorm might come on, or that he might find a considerable amount of snow still remaining from the previous storm; however, he was very cheery about it, and seemed to be looking forward to his solitary ride with no little pleasure. He had of course a gun with him and looked forward to picking up a good deal of game. We had a long chat, and a very pretty ride it was, under the side of the mountains; after crossing the southern fork of the "Old Man," we ascended a steep bank to the prairie, when we found a plateau with a good deal of scrub upon it and very deep grass, and an enormous quantity of peavine, indicating the excellent feeding quality of the ground, and trotting over this for about a couple of miles further we found ourselves, at the end of a ride of some 20 to 22 miles, at the ranch of our friend Mr. Garnett. A more lovely spot it would be difficult to pick out, as we stood at the door of his ranch; the view of the Rocky Mountains rising from the plateau reminded me very much of the view of the Alps from the terrace at Berne. I think, however, that the comparison is in favour of the view that I am now describing, though the hills are of course not so high. Beginning with the Crow's Nest Hill, which gives its name to the pass, it is a curiously roundheaded hill, and rises above the pass on the right hand; from this point, running the eye from right to left, comes a bold pyramidal peak, after this one or two finely outlined conical heights, and next the Castle Mountain, looking like a rampart, walls with high round towers rising at each angle; next to this, further to the south, is Victoria Peak, also a fine pyramidal hill, until the view ends in the Chief Mountain, with its squareish head, something like that of Ingleborough, in Yorkshire. All these at the time I am describing were covered with snow down to the base, fringed along the bottom with good pine and spruce forests draped with snow, while dotted over the plain were some very fairly large black pine, and along the edge and by the side of the plateau ran one of the branches of the Oldman River; the whole of the plateau itself being apparently about six miles wide. The range of the Messrs. Garnett is very well bounded by the two forks of the Oldman River; on the other side of the fork is the range of Messrs. Jones and Inderwick. Mr. Garnett had two brothers with him at the ranch, and as I had had the pleasure of meeting them in Staffordshire, we had a very pleasant evening after the work was done, sitting by the stove and talking of all our friends at home, and all the gossip of the Old Country. Very charming it was to find young men able to do everything for themselves, for they had built their own log huts, and done the principal part of the building of a very useful and pretty frame house which they had erected to take the place of the original log hut; they had built their stables, cow house and dairy, they made their butter, soap, fishing creels, and last, but not least, were each of them very good cooks. The cooking was taken in turn for a week by each, and of course whoever had the cooking to do was obliged to get his own meals after everybody else had finished, our practice in the North-West being that everybody, small and great, sits down to the table at the same time so long as there is room for him, everybody eating of the same dishes and having exactly the same food. Our hosts told us that the fishing in these streams is most excellent, a very few hours' fly-fishing producing some 60 or 80 pounds weight of trout. On the walls of the log hut there were many trophies of bear, elk, and other game. In the neighbourhood of the ranch a band of Stoneys were hunting under a chief, Jemmy Dickson. These people are certainly a long way ahead of most of the other Indians, and Mr. Garnett told me that he had every reason to believe that they knew something of a written character. They refuse any Government assistance and endeavour to keep themselves, and so long as there is any game in the mountain, they will be able undoubtedly to hold their own. They also, no doubt, are beginning to feel the pinch, now that the buffalo has passed away, and they cannot look forward for any further sustenance from that most useful animal, and are now obliged to follow up the deer and the other mountain game. After dinner at about half-past one, we rode off to try and find the Police camp, which we had heard of as stationed in the Crowsnest Pass, and a gentleman in partnership with Messrs. Garnett kindly rode with us to help us on our road. Henry's sorrel began to show his bronco characteristic, and gave a rattling good buck, and placed him on his back on the prairie. He was soon in the saddle again, and we rode about eight miles up the pass; a very wild ride it was, over a good deal of rocky ground, but exceedingly pretty, with several lakes and streams, and good-sized Scotch fir. One place we came to reminded us of the Roodee racecourse on a most extensive scale, a piece of circular prairie about two miles in diameter, with a mound rising near the edge of it in one place, which would have made a most excellent natural "stand." The settler who had for some time had a ranch further up in the "Crow's Nest" had located himself here, and was breaking up some of the ground. We rode on and on, still hoping to find the Police camp. We heard that it was pitched some little way off the trail in a wood, and we kept up a pretty continual shout to try if we could get any response. As night was coming on, and we found no clue to the camp, we had a long and somewhat anxious consultation as to what was to be done; I myself was in favour of making a night of it where we were, to lie down and make the best of our saddle blankets, and picket our horses, and try on a little further in the morning. I found however that the majority were rather anxious on the subject of possible wet and snow coming on, as we had nothing but our light riding coats with us, and so it was resolved, in obedience to the will of the majority, that we should turn back again to the Garnett's ranch. We learnt afterwards that a couple of miles further would have taken us to the camp, which had been pushed forward. In returning we had to recross a stream which we had noticed to be deep in mud, where the waters had been pounded up by a beaver dam.

Wishing to make the best of our way without going round over the dam, the course we had taken in going up, I sent Henry, as the lightest weight, first into the brook to see if he could get across, but his horse got so deep in—up to the neck—that it was with difficulty that he got him out on the other side, and it was quite clear that all of us, who were heavier, would have had a very poor chance of getting out of it at all, so leaving him there we turned back, and worked our way across the Beaver Dam. Getting to the place on the other side to which he had crossed, I was not a little horrified to see Henry's horse come galloping toward us with his saddle turned under his belly; however, I was rendered more easy by hearing a shout from Henry some distance up the hill that he was all right. It appeared that as the horse was fidgety at finding himself alone, he had tried to take him along the trail, which led up a very steep hill, and getting him a little way up the brute had bucked again, and turning smartly round had slipped at the same time down the hill, when the saddle had turned, and Henry had come off, but had fortunately not been hurt. It was very dark; we managed, however, to catch the horse and to put the saddle on again, and to work our way with him up to the hill, when Henry mounted again, and we proceeded on our journey. Riding along through the dark, we came to the place where we had seen our friend who had ridden with us in the morning camped for the night. He was proceeding in a very ingenious way to keep himself safe against the possibility of an attack from a grizzly, of which there are a good many in this neighbourhood; he had covered himself over with boughs, and had got his gun by his side, and as we passed by and saw the remains of his fire, we called to him to see where he was; we were saluted by a voice coming from under the heap of sticks and pine boughs and brush. Here he would be pretty safe against the chance of a grizzly picking him up while asleep, as the disturbing of the sticks by the enemy would wake him up in time to protect himself. The plan adopted by our friend gave a pretty good insight into the possibilities of many an exciting adventure before he reached his journey's end. Leaving him, we rode on, and found ourselves at Garnett's between eight and nine, when we had a good supper and went to bed.

On the day after our arrival at Oxley, on our return from Snowy Camp, we had, as I have said, passed one of the mornings in looking after a site for a mill, and in our exploring expedition for that purpose, we had crossed a stream of snowy water; taking off our boots and stockings for that purpose, a chill from the very cold water must have caught my feet, tender from their having been constantly wet during oar stay in Snowy Camp, and they began now to be very painful. Whether it was that the feet had been rather frostbitten, or that it was a very bad sort of chilblain that came on, I know not, but I had been suffering from them for the last 48 hours, and now they began to be so bad that it was with difficulty that I could walk. My kind friends, who seemed always to have everything that was necessary, provided me with some opodeldoc, and this gave me a little relief. The next day they were no better, and it was with difficulty that I could move about with sticks; I was, however, able to sit on my horse, and the big wooden stirrups afforded me pretty comfortable places for my feet.

Tuesday—After breakfast I had driven up for me a large band of horses, which had been brought across the mountains a short time previously by a Mr. Rush, and the inspection of which was one of the principal objects of our visit to Mr. Garnett's ranch. A band of unbroken horses, under the charge of the old stud horse, is a very interesting sight; the mares try to break away from the band, picking out some young stud to go with them, and if the old stud catches sight of him a pretty good hammering the young usurper gets, and not less the ladies, a smart bite over whose withers and a good rattle into their ribs from the heels bringing them back again into the band; and the old Sultan wanders round them, keeping his eye on them, and picking an occasional mouthful of grass, taking care to keep them all together. If another band should come near, and he sees a mare that he thinks he would like to have in his own band, it is curious to watch how he will dodge away and steal her. If he can separate her from her band, he will soon have her in amongst his own harem, and will take good care that she shall not stray away from him again. By this means a clever stud horse will quickly increase his own band until he will get sometimes 60 to 80 or even 100 mares in it. They are not very pleasant gentlemen to come across out on the prairie, and I would not advise anyone to go into the neighbourhood of one, such as I am describing, on foot without the opportunity of beating a safe retreat.

We had the whole band driven into the corral. The owner, Mr. Rush, worked the lariat with very great dexterity, the noose flying from his hand and falling with very great quickness and precision round the head of the horse that was wanted, a very skilful part of the operation being the easy way in which he approached the poor frightened beast he had in the noose for examination. We spent a long time without coming to a bargain, and generally in the North-West, the price that is asked is the lowest that will be taken, the probability being that if that is refused, the next price that will be asked will be somewhat higher than the one to which you have previously objected. I spent pretty well the whole of the day pottering about this corral, and examining all the horses, and it was not until tea time, when we had a little more talk, that at last it was arranged that I should have the horses at sixty-nine dollars fifty cents per head, and we made further arrangement as to the band, numbering about 250, being driven over along the hills to our ranch, a shorter way than they could have been taken by going through McLeod. I need not say that in the North-West a pretty considerable additional sum had to be paid to those of our friends who were willing to undertake this job.

Thursday—We started at four in the afternoon back for Captain Stewart's, and had a quick ride, arriving there at six o'clock. In crossing the forks of the Oldman River we saw a beautiful piece of prairie, a sort of delta that had been formed by the two forks of the stream, and a great quantity of duck and grebe and other waterfowl were flying and swimming about the different streams. At the ranch we found a young Englishman who was out prospecting for a cattle range.

On each of these nights on the Old Man we had been much interested in the view of the magnificent comet which was an object of so much attention both in America and England, and which was most beautiful at this time, a little before the break of day.

Friday—My new acquaintance and I went to shoot geese on the Indian farm, Craig and Henry riding on to Fort McLeod. The geese were on the small lakes to which we went, in thousands, a good many of them the Blue Canadian, but more of the White Waver, both of the smaller and larger kind. They were very difficult to approach on the lake, as there is no cover of any sort; they flew from there to the stubbles on the Indian farm, and could easily be got by any person lying cached as they went over early in the morning or late in the evening. We, however, unfortunately were not there at the right time, and we found it impossible to approach them, and as we could not wait till the evening, after an afternoon spent in a somewhat tantalizing attempt, we got on our horses again and started off for Fort McLeod. On arriving at Fort McLeod we were delighted to find Cottingham and Kounts, and to hear from the latter the interesting tale of his journey and of the hardships that he had gone through. The account which he gave me of his expedition was in the following words:

"After I left you on Sunday at Snowy Camp, it was blowing and storming very severely, and I had some considerable difficulty in getting through the drifts. I struck the creek eight miles from Oxley going down, and seeing a band of cattle in the bottom, my horse turned to go down with them. I went off from them, and after travelling three miles my horse turned round to get back to the cattle. I knew I was going wrong, but it was so thick storming and blowing from the N.E., that I let him take his own course, which he did till I had got back the three miles to the band of cattle, and then we turned round and I followed the creek down to the house, eight miles, and I arrived at the house about 1:00 a.m. It stormed all that night and the next day, and I got the things ready and packed for a start. Next day (Tuesday) I started to go a route which would not be quite so lonesome, and I had a very bad route, and I had to break the trail where the snow had drifted down in the canyon with my hands and feet, walking up and down before the horse, and this I had to do for a couple of hundred yards, and after that I kept on the S.E. side of the canyon, which is very steep, to get out of the way of the snow, till I got to the other end of the lake, when I came upon better ground, and I thought I should have no more trouble. Crossing the summits of the Porcupines I came across plenty of snow, which was deep but not hard enough to bear the horses; one of the horses was weakening, and I had to go four miles to reach Linden's ranch. It was dark when I got there, and I had only done 10 miles during the whole day. I stopped there that night. Next morning (Wednesday) I thought of leaving one horse, but I changed my mind, as I thought with one horse to break the trail for the pack horse; it would be only six miles to Quin's ranch, where I could leave him and where there would be hay. Those six miles were the hardest part; the further I went up the creek the deeper the snow, about 3 feet 6 inches, and the drifts some 10 feet deep. Within half a mile of the house, when it was after dark, 'Fan' gave out, and I had to take the saddle off and leave her there; next day I went to look for her, and found her dead, and covered over with fresh snow; with the other horse I got over to Quin's about 8:00 p.m. Next day (Thursday) I was told of an Indian camp about two miles further up. I thought to get there, and to get some Indians to help me to break trail and pack over some grub. I found the snow still deeper, and it was storming, and I could not find the camp, and had to turn back, and when I got back to the house I was told that I ought to have gone further; I had slipped into the creek through the snow, and had got wet through. After dinner, again I started back to try to find the Indian camp, and found it in a clump of pine trees by the edge of the creek, but there was nothing there but a bitch with a litter of puppies, and I could not see the trail which they had taken. I got back to the house it was dark. Next day (Friday) I made up a pack of 25 or 30 lbs., crackers, tobacco and woollen socks, and started off. I took the trail which I had made the day before for the Indian camp. I was going at a good rate, and calculated to reach "Starvation Camp" in a day and a half at most. After getting to the end of my trail of the day before, I found that with the pack on my back I struck through snow to my waist, and sometimes to my armpits. I took the strap from my neck, and raised myself by the pack to the top. I saw that it would not work that way, and as my pack consisted of blanket, pants, socks and other things, I thought I could trail my pack. It did very well for a little while, but I was getting the provisions all wet, so I wrapped the blanket (the only one) round the pack, but I found that this was wearing my blanket out. I was very wet, and as the day looked like bad weather I thought of striking camp for the night. I did this in the snow, and made a fire after treading and scraping through to the bottom for half an hour, and breaking off some dry limbs of trees I kept up a large fire; so by the time I got dry, I had room enough to lie down alongside the fire. That night I had only the snow which I had caught in the rim of my hat from the snow drift hanging over, so I had a comfortable night with a wall of snow all round me, which kept me out of the wind. Next morning (Saturday) I started off again with my pack. I had a very long hill of two miles to climb, and the snow was very deep; the further I got up, the deeper the snow, and before I got up to the top I had to place part of my pack away in a tree to lighten me. I thought I should have enough to help them away from camp. I felt myself beginning to get blind from the reflection of the sun from the snow drifts; feeling the burning sensation, and the eyes blurred, I kept up my hand to my face, as I knew I should get blind. I suffered intensely from thirst, which eating the snow did not quench, and I only got to the top of the hill, and I was still in sight of Quin's house, and I could see away to the camp. I camped again for the night in the same way as the night before. My eyes were very sore. Next morning (Sunday) at daylight I thought I could get over some ground before the sun rose, and the snow would be harder. I got about four miles that day, and I got within two miles of camp. I was very tired and wet. I camped at a little creek that runs into the south fork. Next morning (Monday) I got to "Starvation Camp" at about eight. My eyes were very bad. I read what was written on the tree. I lay in the hut, and remained in camp nearly blind till Wednesday, when Joseph came about 6:00 p.m. Thursday Joseph and I left. He had come in with one horse, the other having given out. We went home, reaching Oxley in three days."

The other account which was given by Joseph of how he found Kounts, and how they came home, he also narrated to me, and I give it in his own words. These little narratives may perhaps remain as an interesting story of the North-West in its earlier days when the country shall have become settled up, and such events as are here narrated may be perhaps scarcely likely to recur:

"After I left Oxley Ranch with 'George' and 'Charley' (the two horses), I went to the forks; there was no snow very much to go to the forks. I camp there and make fire, and was pretty comfortable. Next morning I started, jist about daylight; there was deep snow, and I camp where you had shot at wolf, and I jist take a bit of food, and then I start from there, and I make two miles, and I leave 'George, he was played out; he had been carrying pack, and I jist thought take one horse to go journey camp, and I get there about two in the afternoon, and I jist see a leetel and a leetel camp smoke, but I see nobody, and I jist take the saddle from the horse, and I find Kounts, who was inside the tent; I call out and then I throw saddle down, and he came out, and he was snow-blind; he said, 'I'm glad to see you, Joe, because I can't see anything, because I'm snow-blind.' Kounts was quite blind, and he was crying, and I said, 'Kounts, don't cry, I am here, and we shall be all right now.' I make fire and stop all night. I had left all my blankets and coat with 'George.' We just had only one blanket that night. We had biscuits and bacon. Next morning I pack all, and as I was afraid 'George' would be played out, I carried my pack myself. Next day we start about seven. Kounts could see then pretty well, Kounts led the horse; we make two miles, and leave again the horse, and we carried our packs to the forks, and we packed the things on 'Charley' and we think to come on the second night to our hut to Oxley. We had one chicken for supper. Next morning we had nothing, and so we start with nothing, and about two in the afternoon I shoot one chicken, and Kounts take off saddle to make fire, as he was glad I shoot him, and we had him for dinner, and we start off for ranch, and get there about half-past six, Kounts and I and 'Charley.' Kounts had got on Henry's moccasins, which were burned at the end, and so turned up and carried him like snowshoes, while I sink through much."

Saturday—As I had now recovered my stragglers I made up my mind to strike down into Montana, where I had heard of a band of cattle that I thought would suit me, and to proceed on thence to Fort Benton, and so down to the North Pacific Railway at Coulston or Billings. This was in fact the shortest way home and the nearest railway station. It will, however, a little surprise those who are not acquainted with the enormous distances of the North-West, to hear that for Craig to drive me down from our ranch to the railway station and back again to Oxley, involved a journey of exactly 1,000 miles. We made up our minds, however, to start, and as we had only three horses that were fit to go to Fort Benton, and we wanted three more, Craig and I and Kounts drove down to Kipp's, the place where we had camped before turning off to the Little Bow River range, to have a look at some horses belonging to a Mr. Saul. I went down and found that he had some really good horses; we bought two unbroken chestnuts, and two others. Henry had been meanwhile to look at some other horses on the Old Man, but did not find that they were adapted for our purpose. Poor dear old Saul, he was about as respectable and honest a trafficker in horseflesh as any I ever had dealings with. After a rather disappointing winter he had made up his mind to go home in the spring to see an aged mother in Ontario, when he was drowned crossing the Old Man near to Fort McLeod.

Sunday, 22nd—After breakfast we put the two chestnuts to our wagon, and Joseph and Guillaume drove them about the town, and found that they went pretty well for broncos. At half-past three, after a farewell dinner at Kamoose's, Henry and I rode and Craig followed, driving one wagon with the broncos, and Guillaume and Joseph driving the other wagon. We reached the crossing of the Kootenai River after dark. We were making for a place called "Standoff," between two rivers, the Belly and the Kootenai, belonging to an old settler, Fred Wachter; we crossed the Kootenai, finding it rather heavy water, and made our way to the house, distant about a mile from the bank. About half-past eight we had supper, and as Craig and the other wagon had not come, I went with Henry down to the crossing, and we saw them encamped on the other side. Arriving at the river after dark, they had very prudently thought it better not to cross at night, as they did not know the best ford nor how deep it might be. These streams are a little dangerous at the best of times, although at this period of the year they are about at the lowest. In the months of June and July, when the snows are melting on the hills, they are impassable.[3] Standoff is 22 miles from McLeod, and has its name from the fact that in the earlier days Wachter and two or three of his comrades had "stood off" the United States police, who had come up to serve some process, under the impression that it was south of the boundary line. The word implies the resistance which had been offered.

Monday—Craig and Joseph and Guillaume arrived to breakfast. I endeavoured to enter into some dealings with my friend Wachter in the matter of some Indian curiosities. "Dutch Fred," as he is called by his friends, had refused the night before to sell any of his articles, but the following morning found him more amenable, and I succeeded in obtaining an excellent mountain sheep's head with the skin, and also the skin of a Rocky Mountain lion, as the puma is called. I only persuaded Fred to sell me the skin of the cub; the larger one of the old lioness he refused to part with, as he said he was going to keep it to present it to the Queen. This was our first introduction to a place which we afterwards bought, and which will, I hope, become one of the best breeding farms in the North-West. We started at nine in the morning, mounted as yesterday, hoping to reach the crossing of the St. Mary's River to dinner. After crossing the Belly River, on leaving Standoff, the trail runs through the Blood reserve, and we passed some Peigan Indians, going to the agency for the payment of their allowance. It was a very pretty ride through some good land on the reserve, some of the best land in this part of the country. At about 14 miles we came to a creek, which at first we believed to be the St. Mary's River, but which turned out to be a branch running to the west of the river, and called Lee's Creek, and from there we had a long ride, reaching the St. Mary's River at a distance from Standoff of about 20 miles. We decided to stop there for the night, as the weather began to look a little threatening.

Tuesday, September 29th—It had come onto snow rather heavily, which was all the more awkward as our journey for this day was across the very worst piece of ground in stormy weather that is to be found in this country, the high land called Milk River Ridge, which forms the real dividing line between the Dominion and the States. We decided not to attempt to cross this ridge while it was snowing. About eleven, however, it cleared, and Captain Stewart rode on ahead to find the crossing of the river, Guillaume and Henry following, and Craig and myself driving together, and Joseph alone. I found my feet had got so bad now that it was with difficulty that I could sit with them in the stirrups, and I therefore was obliged to give up my riding and to get my boots off and sit in the wagon with my feet wrapped up in a blanket. As we were rising the Milk River Ridge, and in the middle of a smart snowstorm, we met a little Indian squaw riding a horse and driving a pack horse with a colt before her. Anything more lonely than the poor little thing looked, in the middle of the snow in this rough piece of country, it was difficult to conceive. She seemed, however, perfectly contented, and I have no doubt was as full of self-confidence as if she had had her whole tribe with her. It came on to snow much harder, and just as we were on the worst part of the ridge one of our wagons broke down. We patched it up and got across the highest part of the ridge and down to the north fork of the Milk River to camp, having done about 17 miles from the St. Mary's River.

Wednesday—We had a very steep hill to get over, after which we reached the south fork to dinner; here we were in a warmer and brighter bit of country, and we went on to the Cut Bank, another creek of the same stream, having done this day a distance of 22 miles.

Thursday, October 1st—Up pretty early, and rode and drove to "Two Medicine" River. The origin of this name I don't know; it is connected, however, I suppose, with some great gathering of the Bloods or Peigans. We reached this at dinnertime, and then went on past the old Black-foot agency. We were now in the States, and this is one of the Government Agencies, where they have erected a sawmill and placed a settlement to look after the Indians. From this we went on to another creek, called Birch Creek, where we found a small settlement of half-breeds; we crossed the creek and camped; we found very little grass, but had a pretty comfortable location on a gravel bed surrounded by the stream, and with two or three good cottonwood trees near us; fortunately for us we had this shelter, as it came on to blow tremendously hard, and it tried our tent pegs, which had not got very good holding ground. From Cut Bank to Birch Creek we had done 21 miles.

Friday—We started at noon for McCleane's ranch on Dupuyer Creek, the location of the band of cattle that I was looking after. We had only 12 miles to do, and got there by two in the afternoon, and made our camp in a nice little corner of an enclosure, and not very far from McCleane's log hut. My feet were now so bad that my friends insisted upon my taking up my quarters in the log hut, and as I found an old cowboy, Turner, very hospitably disposed toward me, and quite willing to take an interest in my poor feet, I turned into the bunk there, and lay as still as I could, considering the great pain in which I was. It seemed to me, however, that my rest here would give me a capital opportunity of doing that, which I was not slow to avail myself, to come to terms with my host for his ranch and his cattle. I found that my feet were indeed very bad, and old Turner upon looking at them gave me a melancholy account of a similar condition in which his own had been, and from which they had never recovered, illustrating his lecture by an exhibition, and showing me how "pieces of bone kept continually coming away": he proceeded to give me the same remedies, which I am bound to say, however, did not appear to me to have been altogether successful in his own case, and rubbing the feet first with skunk oil, proceeded afterwards to bathe them with some mixture of his own. This gave me very considerable relief, although Turner's account, especially of the blue colour which had come over parts of them, made me a little anxious is to the result.

Saturday—After breakfast, Henry rode out with Craig to look at some horses and some cattle that were in the neighbourhood, and returned about five, I sticking, of course, to the log hut, from which I was only able, with the assistance of a couple of sticks, to wander out for a few yards. Captain Stewart had left us that morning, having gone on to Port Shaw, where he had some business.

Our breakfast, dinner, and tea consisted of beans, by which I mean what we call in Europe haricot beans, and some very indifferent bacon. As I was a guest I could not complain, but it was not nice, and the coffee was very much ditto. On the second day, I got McCleane to drive some of the cattle into the corral, and he shot me a nice two-year-old steer. For help in skinning and cutting up the animal, the services of a lazy, pockmarked, half-bred Mexican greaser and two squaws were called into requisition. The former was a consummate little vagabond; as old Turner told me, with a good many Montana expletives, he had offered to pay him to make him a lariat, and had cut up a cowhide for it, and had given him the brains and the fat to dress it, "but the doggarned skunk was too darned idle to twist it." The meat of our steer turned out excellent— the brains fried with crumbs make an excellent dish—and the meals improved considerably; we took an ample provision of the best cuts for our journey, and which, as the first fruits of the ranch, was duly appreciated. The Indian squaws and children have a great partiality for the entrails and kidneys, which they prefer to eat raw, a taste as to the latter of which delicacies seems to have some survival among the frequenters of London chophouses. A poor fellow who lived in the adjoining log hut at Dupuyer Creek, Jemmy Grant, and who had an affection for one of these squaws, and with whom my party spent one of their evenings, had a sad ending. Shortly after we left, he had gone off for a few days, and on his return had reason to suspect that his squaw had been too intimate with an Indian buck, and not being so philosophic as my friend at Whoop-up, had drawn his six-shooter and given him a bullet in the arm; the Indian went off, and returning with his rifle shot poor Jimmy through the heart; the white fellows some days afterwards followed up the buck, and disposed of him; and when I last heard of them, the Indians were looking out to carry on the quarrel by a shot at one of the white men.

Sunday. My feet began to get better, and having had many opportunities of talking to my host on the subject of the cattle, and having come very nearly to an agreement as to price, we decided to start next day. And so an agreement was at last drawn out and settled, but the execution was of course postponed to a weekday.

Monday—I found that my host was all the more inclined to deal from having received letters from his wife and daughter and son at Missoula, where he lived, entreating him to come home, and as I had finally arranged with him as to the price which I would give him for ranch, cattle, and all about the place, or, as I said, I would buy him out, "lock, stock, and barrel," the agreement was duly signed, and possession handed over to Turner in my name. We hitched up and started off for one of the frontier settlements in Montana, known as the Old Agency, a distance of 30 miles. Our journey from Dupuyer was first along the side of a hill, round which two or three coyotes were prowling; from this we passed down very steep slopes into the wide prairie, with some stony knolls scattered about at distances of 15 or 20 miles. Here for the first time we saw a flock of sheep, a large number in most excellent pasture; two or three little streams run through this vast prairie, and it was clear that there is more rain here than on any other land further to the south. We arrived at the Old Agency at four in the afternoon, and found a good store, kept by "Alf Hamilton," and we picked out a capital place for camping in among some brushwood, down by the stream. I had the great satisfaction of feeling my feet so much better that I was able to walk about with tolerable comfort.[4]

Next morning, *Tuesday*, we started to see a "roundup" which was going on at about 15 or 20 miles to the southeast, on the Muddy River. "We were told that we should find everybody there, and should be able to get a full account of the herd of cattle that I had bought. Having crossed the stream, we ascended a steep hill and got onto the prairie level; we had very considerable difficulty in making up our minds which of the two trails we were to take. We found ourselves, at last, close to a corral which had been lately used, and Joseph and I with the first wagon arrived at the stream which lay between us and it. It looked quite clear water, with an appearance of white pebbles at the bottom, and Joseph was so taken in by the appearance, that he put our horses straight at the stream; in we went, and down we sank, and found ourselves, at about two yards from the bank, deeply imbedded in the mud, and our horses incapable of dragging us out. This was an unpleasant position, especially for me, who was still very helpless for locomotion. We could scarcely, however, help laughing, as Henry and Guillaume remained with their wagon on the bank behind us. Our horses having at last broken their traces and got out on the other side, we laid our tent poles from the bank onto our wagon, and I slid along them down to the bank; having unloaded the heavy articles from our wagon, we hitched the horses on from behind and dragged it back up the bank. Joseph found a place a little lower down the stream where he could manage to cross, and striking over, brought back our horses, traces were mended up, and we again, after a considerable delay, found ourselves able to proceed on our journey. It was still cold and snowy, and having gone on for about four miles, and finding no trace of the "roundup" party, we camped for the night.

Wednesday—Craig rode off, immediately after an early breakfast, to explore, and found the party at the next corral and had a talk to them; the snow there was so deep that they had come clearly to the conclusion that the storm was too much for them, and they had determined to break up the "roundup" and not proceed further with any herding or branding.

Craig's account of the "roundup" was curious. As work was out of the question the boys were amusing themselves with poker and euchre, and some of them had very quickly indeed got rid of every penny that they had earned during the whole of the "roundup"; in fact, the condition of a cowboy seems either to have his pocket very full of money or else to be in a state of absolute impecuniosity, as the moment he gets his wages, his natural tendency is to gamble them away. Nor is this the case with the cowboys only; the Indians have just the same passion for gambling, and it was upon this ride that we came across a whole party of Peigan Indians, shortly after we had left Standoff, the greater part of whom had been set afoot by losing their horses and every bit of property that they possessed in gambling with some of the Bloods with whom they had come in contact. The Peigans had at this time a very good racehorse, and one of them had made a considerable amount of money upon him; the horse was supposed to be the fastest in that country, and there were almost incredible stories of the large amounts that had been offered to the Peigan who was his possessor, it was said upon one occasion, his teepee being strewed with dollar notes; but the Peigan had, with a considerable amount of common sense, said: "You want Indian's horse to make money; Indian keep horse and make money himself."

I decided to start away down the Muddy for Fort Benton, hoping to reach the Teton River, where the Muddy runs into it, that night. We drove for about 16 miles, when one of our horses giving out, we left him on the prairie, and put the remaining saddle horse into the wagon in his place, We drove on and reached the Teton about six, after a drive during that day of about 33 miles. It came on very cold indeed during the night, and we heard the wild swans going over our heads with their curious weird sound which we interpreted into "G-o-o home, Go-o home." We managed to keep ourselves pretty comfortable, as we had plenty of buffalo robes, but I found the next morning that the thermometer indicated 10° below zero, or 42°F of frost. After breakfast Joseph went to fetch in the played-out horse, and we started off at ten for the crossing of the Teton. A very pretty bit of country along low ground till we had crossed the river, from which we rose again to the prairie level, and found that we were out of the snow; it is a curious thing in this country in what narrow belts the snow lies; frequently for about 10 miles you will have deep snow, and then find yourselves suddenly on land where there has been no fall at all, and then after a few miles you come into it again. We got at dinnertime to a ranch belonging to Messrs. Hunt and Richter, and found Mr. Richter ready to do the hospitable to us, and we had an excellent dinner. I looked over some of his big band of sheep, and discussed with him the merits of his plan of crossing the Angola with the Shropshire Down, and inspected with much interest the arrangements which he had for housing his sheep during the winter. We did not see his partner, Mr. Hunt, as he was out on the prairie. I mention him as it was but a few days after we had left that one of those events happened which illustrate in a very marked way the difference between the condition of things in Canada and the States. Poor Hunt was riding over the prairie and looking after his sheep. A couple of days had passed, and on his not coming back to the ranch, his men went to look for him, and found his body lying where he had been shot, with three bullet holes in him. His horse also was dead, but the saddle had been taken. I don't know that the murderers have ever been discovered. Of course it was put down to the Indians, but I am inclined to think that it was one of that band of scoundrels that was at that time infesting Montana, and had I known to what extent they were carrying on there I should have had very much hesitation in taking with me the great amount of money which I had at that time in my possession, and was carrying for Messrs. Baker down to Fort Benton. After leaving Richters' we came to the crossing of the Teton, and camped about six o'clock. The descent down to the river was very awkward indeed, and our horses being rather tired, we had no little difficulty in keeping them along the ledge of a stony ground along which the trail ran before descending to the level of the stream; we managed, however, by "putting our shoulders to the wheel" in good earnest, to keep our wagons level, and to get them safely over the bad piece, and we camped in a comfortable little corner under an old log hut at a little distance from the stream, after a drive of about 30 miles.

Friday morning we crossed the river and did the remaining 11 miles into Fort Benton. After reaching the high ground we found many acres almost covered with cactus, to the exclusion of every other plant, and thence after a few miles along the lower prairie the trail ran over the high bluffs beneath which the Missouri runs; it was here very soft, sticky soil, and very bad travelling. The descent into Fort Benton is exceedingly wild—down clay bluffs with occasional rocks and boulders—a most awkward descent for the last mile and a half, when a level bit of prairie is reached, upon which the city stands.

I think I may take the opportunity here of describing the great territory of Montana, of which Fort Benton, if not the capital, is at any rate one of the oldest places of interest. The territory is bounded on the north by the boundary line of the 49th parallel and on the south by the 45th, and extends, therefore, over four degrees of latitude. On the east, at its furthest point, is Fort Buford, at the junction of the Yellowstone River and the Missouri on the 104th meridian, and from there it extends west to the Bitter Root Mountains (a branch of the Rockies), running from the 116th meridian in a diagonal line to the 113th, the southern part of the territory being conterminous with Wyoming, in the northeastern corner of which is the famous Yellowstone Park, which here runs up into Montana. A great part, perhaps almost a third, of the territory is at present in the possession of the Indians as reserves under their treaties: very nearly the whole of the north for more than one degree of latitude having been handed over by a treaty of 1874 as a reserve for the Gros Ventres, Peigan, Blood, Blackfoot, and River Crow Indians. A large block on the south, extending down to the edge of the territory, being the reservation for the Crow Indians, and another considerable block in the west, to the south of the Flathead Lake, of which I shall speak in my journey next year, having been reserved by the treaty in 1855 to the Flathead Indians. The rest of the territory—speaking generally, the whole of the western part—is mountainous, and contains great and most valuable deposits of minerals, consisting of Choteau county on the north, Missoula on the west, with others which I need scarcely name here. The whole of the western part of the territory is prairie, with a few buttes, rising into and watered by the great streams that I have mentioned and their tributaries. The whole of this country has a very small rainfall, and but little of it is available for agricultural purposes, except where the streams descending from the mountains may be utilized. This is practicable, however, over a large area of level land on either side of them, and the productive quality of the soil is of an extraordinary character. I have seen nowhere a country of which on the whole I can say that it has more of beauty and more of promise than the territory of Montana, and, glad as I am that it should be in the hands of its present enterprising citizens, I cannot but deeply lament the want of judgement which allowed the boundary line to be placed so far to the north as to have shorn the Dominion of Canada of this beautiful province. It is with Choteau county that I am dealing now, as our route, after crossing the St. Mary's River, lay through that county until we were some 30 miles to the south of Fort Benton. The whole of the territory of Montana is about 600 miles from east to west, by about nearly 300 from north to south. The creeks across which we had passed in travelling from the boundary line down to Fort Benton are all tributaries of the Marias River, a stream which runs into the Missouri at Ophir, some 20 miles below Fort Benton. Choteau county has indeed been truly said to command a generous supply of timber, and to be watered by numerous rivers, creeks, and springs, which present to the emigrant advantages unsurpassed and perhaps unequalled by any other section of this territory of Montana. It must be remembered, however, that although there is an enormous area of grazing land, supplying an abundance of nutritious grass, this grass has in itself in ordinary years very little seed; it spreads principally from its root, and, consequently, it may very easily be overtaken by an excessive amount of stock, and I cannot but think that a good deal of the land through which I passed has sustained serious, if not permanent, injury from the system of free ranging, which has induced the keeping of an excessive amount of stock.

Old Fort Benton was first founded by employees of the American Fur Company, and a very lonely life they must have had there, continually defending themselves against probable attacks from Flatheads and Peigans and the other Indians. At that time "Little Dog," although at peace with the employees of the Company, was accustomed to lead his braves into the country of his enemies, and sometimes against parties of white traders, trappers, or hunters on the Oregon trail, along the waters of the Snake River. The raison d'être of Fort Benton has been its position at the head of the Missouri navigation. Whether it will still maintain its value now that the navigation is superseded by the Northern Pacific, which has left it on one side on its course to the Western Ocean, may be seriously doubted; it must, however, always be a considerable distributing centre for goods for the great cattle and agricultural districts around it. The two capital cities of Montana are Helena, in the western mining country, and Miles City, on the Yellowstone; the territory, however, is so enormous that there is plenty of room for both these and for other cities. The old fort, which still remains at Fort Benton, was built with adobe in the lowest corner of the town, and will, I presume, like Fort Grays at Winnipeg, soon pass away, although it seems a pity that these interesting records of the first beginning of the town should not be kept for future ages, to which they would undoubtedly afford considerable interest. But, to continue my narrative, descending the hill, we reached Fort Benton about three in the afternoon, and put up at a new hotel, the "Grand Union," of which we were the first registered visitors, as it had only been opened the day previously. Very glad we were to get a letter from home at last, but not recent; we had not had any intelligence from Europe of a later date than August 10th, (these indeed only came down to August 15th), and it was now November 10th. We had done here our 290 miles, the longest part of our journey, leaving us 218 miles still to do to Billings, where we expected to strike the North Pacific Railway. I purposed to wait here until I should receive some telegrams in answer to those which I had sent with reference to cattle; the working, however, along these wires seemed to be of a somewhat uncertain character, and I had to wait several days, and at last to leave without my replies.

Saturday, November 11th, we went to the excellent stores of Messrs. Baker, Messrs. Power, and Messrs. Neil & Murphy, not forgetting also the very useful stores of Messrs. Herschberg & Nathan, where Henry procured a magnificent buffalo coat and Mr. Craig followed suit. I was able to buy several good skins, and having laid in a certain amount of beaver at Standoff, I made up my quantity with additional purchases here, as I found that the prices were very considerably lower than those which I should have had to give further east. We spent the rest of the day in purchasing a Schutler wagon for the ranch, and looking at some horses, and buying some stores for the remainder of our journey.

Sunday—We went to church in the morning, a small building, and had a very good service and a capital sermon, although it was somewhat devoted to an elaborate description of the probable future of Montana and Fort Benton. Our preacher drew for us several sketches of cathedrals in the air, of spires pointing heavenward, and peals of bells and beautiful ecclesiastical accompaniments. A great deal of this, I am bound to say upon reflection, seems to be in the very far distant future.

I cannot say that I endorse as amendments the small changes in the language of the service imported into the American Prayer Book. The change of terms in the Te Deum, "Thou did'st not disdain to be born of a virgin," may be a concession required by the finer feelings of American modesty, but it does not entirely represent the sense of the original; and the change of "health and wealth" to "health and prosperity" may perhaps be a fitting concession to the universally recognized maxim of the American code of manners never to allude to a man's pecuniary means or to his dollars under any circumstances; but the use of "those" for "them" is not right, and the change of this word in the Lord's Prayer grates unpleasantly upon the ear, and seems somewhat pharasaically to place in a category as separated from ourselves many whom we may after all find somewhat nearer home.

We had heard of the capture of some Indians who had been brought to Benton the night previously, charged with killing some thoroughbred cattle belonging to Mr. Conrad; so after church Sheriff Healey, the principal officer in Benton, came and asked me whether I would like to go to the prison to see his prisoners; I readily accepted the offer, and started off with Henry and Craig, Guillaume and Joseph, to look at the incarcerated men. We found the jail a new square building, without any great appearance of strength, which I must say in that lawless district, where an attack upon any prison either for rescue or for execution of Lynch law is not uncommon, was somewhat surprising. On going through the door, however, we found where the real strength lay; the whole of the inside of one part of the building is occupied by a huge cage, with strong iron floor, iron roof, and iron bars, standing away from the wall on every side; outside this are posted the warders, inside the prisoners, so that it is utterly impossible for a prisoner to pass out without the complete consent of those who hold the keys of the cage. The cage itself is separated off into four or five compartments, but every part of it is as open to the view of the warders as is the interior of a canary cage to any lady who may have it in her room. The door of the cage being opened, our friend the sheriff walked us into the interior, where everybody seemed to be on the most friendly, not to say familiar, terms with the prisoners. At one end of one of the compartments was a good-looking, well-built young man of about 23; he was a Scotchman, who had only been in the country for about two years, and who, having had a quarrel with his brother and partner in some ranch business, had drawn his pistol and shot him through the head. As it appeared that he himself was the first party to the quarrel, he had a narrow escape of being lynched for this murder. He had, however, been safely deposited in the cage, and upon my asking the sheriff what might be the probable result with regard to him, I was answered, "Well, the judge will come down on his assize soon after next March, and he will just be hanged." I must say one could not but feel, even under these circumstances, a sort of pity for the wretched life that this miserable fellow would have during the following six months, locked up in an iron cage, and which, apart from any moral feeling, would be the more galling, from the utter change from the open prairie life that he had been leading. Another denizen of the cage was a square, rather villainous-looking man, with whom Joseph got into communication, the man telling him that he was there as a warder to look after the other prisoners. The real story of the case pronounced the gentleman to be in custody as one of the most notorious horse thieves that had infested the country for some time. He had stolen from the Mounted Police at Fort McLeod a band of about a hundred horses, and had brought them across the boundary line. Some little international difficulty was raised by Sheriff Healey, upon which I was glad to be able to offer him my opinion as to the handing him back for this offence; however, as they had got charges against him of horse stealing within the territory, the sheriff came to the conclusion to keep him and try him there, and I saw by the paper afterwards that when the judge did come round, this great violator of North-Western law got five years' penal servitude; a sentence which was also accorded to the fratricide, the jury having been able to find that there was a serious quarrel existing between him and the poor fellow who was killed, which led them to think that there were extenuating circumstances for the sudden ebullition of anger. I took more interest in the other prisoners in the cage; they were six Indians, one of them a young fellow of about 17, "Little Yellow Wolf" and another, "Little Weasel," both of them sons of chiefs of the Peigans, and four others. Sheriff Healey, than whom a more cool minister of the law has, I should think, never existed even in the North-West, on hearing of the killing of the cattle, had, with a small company, gone into the Indian camp and had brought out these six men. There had been, at the first sight of him, some intention to resist, but on his producing his pistol and at the sight of a Winchester rifle on his saddle, the Indians, knowing who he was, had thought it better at once to give up their prisoners. The killing of cattle has, down in Montana, become already a serious difficulty with the Indians now that the buffalo and the big game is nearly killed off; the Indian has, indeed, very little food, and one cannot wonder very much that he looks upon the cattle that are feeding on the ground where the buffalo roamed as very little less his own property than the buffalo had been from time immemorial; of course, however, in the interest of the country, it is absolutely necessary that the killing of cattle should be put a stop to. I noticed that these Indians received a punishment of two or three years' imprisonment. In conversing with my friend the sheriff on the subject of one of these young men, I could not but be struck by the great difference that there is in the relations of the whites with the Indians in the States, to that which exists in the Dominion. I asked who Little Weasel was, and was told that he had been doing some work at one time for our friend at the Old Agency, and that his employer, finding that he bore no good will toward him or his cattle, suggested to the sheriff that it might be as well to put a bullet in him. "Oh, no," said the sheriff; "don't do that; he has got no reason to love you, because you got his father hanged; but you just catch him out in some crime of some sort and hand him over to me, and I will, get him a pretty sharp turn of imprisonment." So Little Weasel was handed over to the authorities, and for the moment escaped a bullet, which in all probability, however, will be his fate some day. Sheriff Healey gave me an account of the commencement of whisky trading in our Canadian territory in 1872, which as he allowed me to take it down from his lips, he will not, I think, object to my narrating here.

"In 1863 I fitted out an outfit for prospecting in the Hudson Bay Territory. The Hudson Bay Company found that we should be their competitors, and although they had promised that they would sell us provisions, and I took excellent horses and a $10,000 outfit, when my men got there they refused them food during the winter, giving them 1s. a load for cutting wood, and selling them provisions at 6d. a pound. They were starving, and had to come home. I met them here (Fort Benton), and I sent up word to the Hudson Bay men that I would be even with them, and so in 1869 Alf Hamilton and I got up $25,000 and started at Whoop-up with the Indians. We got all the trade, and as the Hudson Bay men looked to the Bloods to supply them with meat for their northern stations, and we got all they had, we were starving them out. We took up 50 gallons of alcohol, not so much for the value of the goods it would bring in, as thereby to secure the Indian trade; we carried this on till the Hudson Bay Company made a handle of this whisky business and got the Canadian Government to pass the prohibition law and send down the Mounted Police. Wonderful stories were then got up about us in the New York papers; it was said that two notorious and powerful desperadoes of the names of Healey and Hamilton, with known men of a most daring character, had seized artillery belonging to the United States Government, and were prepared to hold the country against the Canadian forces. I was never intending to resist them or the law in any shape, so on the arrival of the police I at once struck out for Colonel McLeod, and went to him. He could not believe that the small man whom he saw before him was the gigantic outlaw of those New York stories, but I soon satisfied him. I gave him up all the whisky there was there, it was all spilled, and the whole thing came to an end. I have never been one to resist the law, and as I told the boys when I was standing for sheriff, 'If any of you is going to steal horses during the next two years, he had better vote against me, for by God! if I catch him, whether he's voted for me or against me, I'll hang him.'" Thus began and ended this worst period of Indian trading.

Monday, November 1st—About Fort Benton all day. We took some interest in the proceedings preparatory to the General Election, which took place the following day. The contest lay, of course, between the Republican and Democratic tickets, each ticket embracing a nomination for all the offices, from the Delegate to Congress down to the constable. The principal office, as to which the contest was likely to prove most severe, was that of Judge of the Probate Court; this judge has not only those duties which are assigned to him here, but is also the principal judicial officer in all other matters. For the office Mr. J.W. Tatten was nominated for the Democrats and Mr. Max Waterman for the Republicans, the former being the existing and outgoing judge. The contest was severe, and the speeches that were made were of a most exciting character. Already the Choteau county had been stumped at three or four of its principal—

not to say most populous—points, but it was at Fort Benton that it was felt that the real struggle would take place. We had not, of course, been able to attend previous meetings, but hearing that Judge Tatten was to make his great speech in the Court House on this evening, we got one of our friends to secure us good places in the room. The judge proceeded to go through not only his own merits, but very strongly to criticize the demerits of his adversary. The whole question seemed to hinge upon personal fitness, and I must say that, in listening to the speeches which we heard, there and on the other side, one would certainly have come to the conclusion that both parties must in their nomination have selected the greatest scoundrels who could be found in America. Judge Tatten proceeded to prove that his antagonist, as a barrister practising in the court, had been guilty of gross perjury, and showed from the documents that he had in his possession, as judge of the court, that Mr. Max Waterman had, on one occasion, when defending a prisoner, received the fee which he was entitled to from the State for that defence on making a declaration that the prisoner was without means, he having at the time received from the prisoner a large fee, to be still further increased in case of his acquittal. I have not the slightest doubt that Mr. Max Waterman had a full and complete answer to the charge. It was a curious illustration, however, of the bitterness with which political contests are carried on in the States, and would have a little astonished English readers to see, as we saw, in the newspaper, the language in which our friend the judge had spoken at a previous meeting of his antagonist. We found Judge Tatten to be a gentleman with very strong powers of oratory and a great flow of language. He was a little too angular in his motions, reminding one somewhat of the picture of Mr. Stiggins, in 'Pickwick,' before he found his head in the water trough. We listened to him with no inconsiderable pleasure for upwards of an hour, but as he then began to deal with allegations against himself, as to his mode of dealing with certain patents and titles, the matter got beyond our interest, and we came out. There was a man posted outside with a good-sized cannon, and every time when at the conclusion of the judge's sentences there appeared in the inside to be applause of the audience, the cannon man gave further point to it by putting his match to the touch hole and giving an additional éclat by the discharge of his piece. Many speeches were made in the streets, both with and without audiences; among the most inflammatory of these addresses being those by a man with a wooden leg, who seemed generally known as "Peg-leg"; the last I saw of the result of his speeches was an engagement between him and a carter, in which his attack had degenerated into actual stone throwing.

Tuesday morning—Everybody agog in election matters. Carriage of voters not being as yet prohibited in this country, several brakes and bands, and all the accompaniments of an election in the olden time, were well afoot in Benton, and last, not least, it was very soon apparent that not only on the previous evening, but all through the day, no small amount of whisky was in circulation, the rule in favour of shutting the outside doors of drinking shops on election days being satisfactorily evaded by allowing everybody to pass from the interior of the house into the bar. Poor Joseph had fallen a victim to this election liberality on the night previous, and on my arriving at our hotel I found him lying against the wall, and I had very considerable difficulty, with the assistance of two waiters, in carrying him up and putting him on his own bed; at this, however, with his tendencies, where drink was so easily to be procured, I was not very much surprised. Having got all our things together we packed them upon our wagons, and started with our two wagons, a span of horses in each, along the trail for the southeast. We crossed the Missouri on the ferry boat, worked across by an overhead chain and the stream acting on the rudder; we had a steep pull up through the clay bluffs on the other side to the prairie level. We crossed the Missouri at about half-past one, and intended to get to the ranch of a Mr. Kingsbury that night, but took a trail to the right, and found ourselves going up some steep hills which we made out to be the High Wood Mountains. It had been blowing hard during the day, and came on cold at night, and so we were anxious to find a comfortable place to camp. As it was clear that the trail that we were taking was one which led up into the hills for the purpose of getting logs, we turned back again and descended to where we found the remains of an old log hut, and made our camp close to it, having driven about 21 miles.

Waking in the morning, we found that our camp was very prettily situated, with wooded hills on the right hand and some curious rocky land before us. We killed in the morning a pretty little rat with a tail like a squirrel, which we had found busily at work devouring one of our worsted stockings. Starting off early, to try and find the ranch, the first part of our road lay through some rocks, which give a special character to this part of the country. The appearance of them is as of gigantic walls which originally stretched across from one side of the valley to the other, but which have been broken through either by the passage of a glacier or some such destructive agency. They rise on either hand from 30 to 80 feet, with a width of about 4 feet, and have exactly the appearance of a constructed wall. We found these through the whole of this part of the territory as far as Arrow Creek. On turning the corner of the prairie we came to a fine grassy plateau dotted over with mounds, on almost each of which were sitting the pretty little prairie dogs, that bolted away and got under ground as they sighted us coming. Passing over this prairie and crossing two or three clear little streams, we reached Mr. Kingsbury's ranch. He has dug a ditch along the hillside to carry the water from the High Wood Mountains for the purpose of irrigating the prairie, and if it is completed there will be here one of the most valuable farms in Montana. My manager had had an offer from him of his cattle early in the summer, and I was in hopes I might have dealt with him upon the footing then offered. I found, however, that the price of the cattle had advanced so largely that the figure that was now put upon them was not one which I could accept. We had, however, dinner with him, although I cannot say a comfortable one, for he was altering his log hut, and had the one side out of it to windward; it was blowing a regular hurricane, and very cold, so that sitting in the house was by no means attended with pleasure or comfort. After dinner, about three o'clock, we drove off, and passed over an undulating prairie till we reached some steep hills in the neighbourhood of the Arrow River. I was driving the two broncos, and rather amusing myself by putting them on at a good gallop down the hill, and watching the extreme anxiety of my companion. Henry and Joseph were driving before us. Turning one of the sharp corners I had a most narrow escape of capsizing; on coming up with the first wagon, I found that what had so nearly happened to me had happened to them, and that they had had a regular turnover. However, as is usual on the prairie, no harm had been done, and the wagon had been put on its wheels again, the goods reloaded, and the passengers on board and well under way in a very few minutes. The last piece of drive down to the Arrow River was across a piece of land studded with bushes of the same prickly bush which we had seen to the east of Fort Walsh. Arriving near the stream, at the end of a day's drive of 28 miles, we found a settler's hut, with a good fold-yard, and some stacks and ricks in it and a stable for our horses. We made a comfortable camp, cooking our dinner and baking our bread in the settler's hut. The "boss" was of French extraction, and had with him a rather nice half-breed squaw who spoke English. She had come from the Blackfoots above Fort McLeod, and upon being asked with reference to those whom she had known as a child among the whisky traders she recognized our friend Kounts under his Blood name of "Stomak," a word signifying "lone bull," as Kounts had always lived by himself and traded with the Indians in a solitary style, without having any partner or companion.

On his way back Mr. Craig had found that an incident had happened here a little characteristic of the life of this country. About two nights after we left one of the men connected with the establishment had returned, wishing to have a talk with the lady of the house. The lady professed to believe that he was some road agent intending an attack upon the establishment, and as he knocked at the door she gave him the benefit of a discharge from a pistol. The bullet came through the door and entered into his groin, and when Mr. Craig got there he found him sitting— having extracted the bullet—keeping the wound open with a sharp stick, and remarking there was not much the matter, and that within about 10 days it would be all right and he should be able to proceed on his journey. He apparently did not bear the slightest malice or ill-feeling toward the lady who caused the injury. The way in which, in this climate, a gunshot wound, or any other flesh injury, heals, is truly astonishing. Of course a good deal is owing to the abstemious and healthy life which the people live, but something is no doubt also due to the excellence of the air and the dryness of the atmosphere; in fact, it is to this that we may in a similar way attribute the excellent state of preservation in which meat will keep in this climate for almost any length of time. Even in hot weather I have carried beef with me for three weeks in the wagon, which has been as good at the end of the time as it was in the beginning, and so long as it is kept out of the way of flies no change seems to take place in its quality.

Thursday—We left Arrow River before breakfast at six o'clock. Crossing the stream, we found in front of us the most tremendous hill that I ever ascended with a wagon in my life; in places it was only a narrow edge with a steep drop on each side, and zigzagged up at angles of almost incredible acuteness. After ascending to the top of the hill to the prairie level, the air was so intensely cold that we found our mitts absolutely necessary. As we drove along I noticed about a quarter of a mile ahead of us two huge birds as large as turkeys—Joseph and Guillaume called them "faisans de Missouri." I got off my wagon, and thought that I could get near enough with my gun, stalking on my hands and knees. I succeeded in getting within about 80 yards when the birds both rose. Had I taken my rifle with me instead of my gun, I could have scarcely failed to have got one of them. I believe it was the bird which I became acquainted with afterwards as the sage hen, a very handsome bird, but of which I have not been able to obtain any exact description. After crossing a wide extent of prairie, we came to a creek, and stopped and dined, and as there was no brush by the side of the stream, we had to make our fire of buffalo chips, which gave a great heat, and which are quite equal to wood, and of these there was a plentiful supply in the neighbourhood of the water. After dinner we drove along down to the Judith Basin—one of the finest of the grazing tracts in this country. Here we came upon a settlement of four or five log huts, and selecting the largest with the most commodious corral behind it, we found that the place had been christened "Garden Land," and we put up our tent under a stack, and our horses in the stable, and went into the house, where we had our tea. It was intensely cold during the afternoon, and a very droll thing it was on arriving in the settlement, to see not only those who were with us, but everybody else there, with their handkerchiefs tied round their faces under their hats, as though all were suffering from severe toothache. It was very necessary, however, as the thermometer was very many degrees below zero, and our ears required protection; we were very comfortable with our tent pitched under the lee of the stack. I had made up my mind to make a very early start indeed, and for this purpose to get off before breakfast, and to stop for breakfast on our road; I relented, however, on hearing that there were some excellent elk steaks being prepared for us in the house, and so we went in, and a most cheerful host with a bright little wife made us very comfortable. I noticed through this country, that where the wife was of a hearty and cheery disposition, everything seemed to be going prosperously, but where the mistress of the house was discontented with her lot, nothing seemed to prosper. The appearance of everything around Garden Land was of a highly prosperous character, and the children and a friend and the friend's baby all of them seemed to be enjoying life—looking forward even to the severe winter with the prospect of considerable happiness. I was rather amused at finding that the friend with the baby being considerably under 21 years of age, was returned in the table of those for whom education grant was made by the Government.

Friday, November 5th—Drove across the stream, and passed up to the high prairie with a cold bitter wind. A band of horses came galloping up to have a look at us, and did not seem to have at all suffered, so far, from the storm. From here we turned round to the Judith Gap, an opening between a belt of the Belt range and the Big Snowy Mountains. We left this to our right and turned along in the direction of a settlement called Ubet, to which we had been directed. The Judith Gap is a narrow gorge, and a guard is kept there to prevent the cattle of the Teton range and the other ranges to the north passing through before a storm; as soon as the storm comes on the guard turns out and heads back all the cattle, there being no other pass through which they can cross over into the southern country. As we were going along through the snow, after crossing a small creek, I turned round, and saw that an accident had happened to the wagon upon which Henry and Guillaume were being driven by Joseph. They had come down a little too suddenly upon the frozen waters of the creek and the ice had given way under the wheels. So smart a jerk had been given to the wagon that Guillaume and Henry had been tipped off on their backs, and were lying there with their seat on the top of them; they appeared to be lying quite still. I was not a little frightened, of course, jumped down and rushed toward them; they got up, however, having had scarcely more than a severe shake, Henry's very thick buffalo coat having saved him from what would otherwise have been a very serious difficulty, and Guillaume, having had the good fortune to have fallen lightly, had escaped with nothing more than bruises from the very hard ground. The cold was so intense that it was almost impossible for me to use my fingers for the purpose of rearranging the seat, and Henry's buffalo coat was immediately after coming up from the stream, where it had got wet, frozen as hard as a board. We at last got "straightened up," and the snow came on with a heavy wind, but most fortunately it was behind us, so we kept before the storm, and reached, in the course of another two miles, the settlement of Ubet, having driven about 18 miles from Garden Land. Here we found a comfortable house and good stables. Shortly after our arrival we were joined by the mail with several passengers, who, like ourselves, were glad to find shelter from the storm. The snow came on very deep indeed, and we were very glad to be under cover, and especially that our horses should be in a stable and not on the prairie.

The name of Ubet had been selected for the settlement from the slang phrase so laconically expressive of "you may be pretty sure I will."

Laconic expressions are pretty much the order of the day in the North-West. A night marauder took advantage of a good moon to place a ladder against a window, hoping to secure to himself the property of the gentleman asleep in the chamber. As he lifted the window and put his head in, the gentleman woke up, and with great promptness presented his six-shooter, shouting out, "You get." With equal promptness the detected thief exclaimed, "You bet," slid down the ladder, "et procul in tenuem ex oculis evanuit aurarn."

We had been told by our friends at Garden Land that at this place we should find every convenience, and that the lady of the establishment prided herself upon putting things on the table in the way in which they would be done in one of the most eastern hotels. We certainly found a nice comfortable house, with a sitting room and dining room and bed-rooms over it—the proprietor being one of the delegates to Congress from the territory—and the stables, corrals, and outhouses, were of the best description. Two or three other settlers had established stores and small farms in the neighbourhood, in short, there seems every probability of Ubet, if it keeps its name, carrying down to posterity this favourite phrase of the early North-West days. We had an excellent dinner, and shortly after we had sat down the stage arrived with two passengers, one of them an American surveyor, and the other a well-known English writer, Mr. Baillie Grohman; he had been shooting in Idaho, and we had a very pleasant evening in discussing the future of some irrigation works in British Columbia, and the mining prospects of that country. After tea, and some pipes, it was time to turn in, and our friends took the beds upstairs, Henry and I preferring a comfortable roll up in our rugs in the corners of the sitting room.

Saturday, November 6th—Up early, and found the snow deep outside the house, but a bright morning, and as there was every probability that the zone of snow did not extend far to the southeast, the direction in which we were to proceed, we obtained careful directions from our host as to our route: he seemed to have rather a desire that we should not take the course through the Judith Pass, but proceed rather to the east of it. So we hitched up and proceeded through the Judith Basin toward Martinsdale. What little of the direct trail there might have been was entirely obliterated by the snow. At the end of some six or seven miles along the course of the stream, we turned up a sharp hill, but found none of the landmarks by which we had been directed to steer our course. I thought, however, that we could scarcely be doing wrong in keeping a due southeast course, avoiding the trails which seemed to lead up the hills and into the woods, and driving over the prairie, which was good firm ground for our wheels. After some seven or eight miles further we came to a nicely placed settlement by the side of a creek, and found a sheep ranch that had been started by a Mr. Moule. Here we arrived after about four hours' drive at one o'clock. The settler and his young wife had not been there long, and the lady did not appear to enjoy the country in which she had been located, which she found very dull and very cold. They gave us a good dinner, and about three o'clock, as there seemed to be an end of the snow, we decided to continue our drive. We passed along over an undulating prairie, putting up two or three bands of antelope, which I endeavoured to stalk in vain; the wary animals taking care not to choose any part of the prairie where there was the slightest cover afforded for an approaching enemy. After about 8 or 10 miles we became a little anxious, on finding that we were getting into the snow again, and as we had been told that there was only one creek on which there was timber and which must have been still 4 or 5 miles off, we pushed our tired horses on as quickly as we could so as to arrive at it before dark, and Joseph and Guillauml had to run on ahead through the snow to endeavour to keep the trail as far as it could be ascertained, and no eyes but those of a half-breed could have discerned it through the snow; at last even they were both at fault, and we were in a very hopeless condition for the night's camp. A cheery shout from Joseph encouraged us to drive on a little further, and we found ourselves descending into a coulée, and at the side of the only cotton tree that there was in the neighbourhood. We made up our minds that this must be our camp, and getting as well as we could through the half-frozen stream, we pitched our tent under a bit of a cutbank, and very soon the one fork of the cotton tree fell beneath the axe to make our fire, the camp was pitched, and preparations made for tea. It came on very cold indeed, and the creek, which we recognized as Swimming Woman River, was as desolate a place for camping as could have been well imagined. We had no cloths, unfortunately, for our poor horses, and they must have felt much the cold that night. We, however, rolled ourselves up after tea, leaving not a single bit of the body or head or face exposed, but all well rolled up under our blankets and buffalo robes. I set the thermometers as usual, having taken care to adjust them and to see that they worked together correctly, and I placed them in the usual position upon the seat of the wagon.

Sunday—A clear morning, but a little inclined to snow, and we grieved to find that the wind was again springing up, fortunately however still behind us, so that we could well drive before it. On looking at the thermometers we found that they marked 29° below zero, or 61 degrees of frost, being about as intense a cold as one could imagine endurable for sleeping with nothing but a linen tent over you. An observation that is commonly made, that we do not feel the cold out in Canada to the extent that the same amount of cold would be felt here, is undoubtedly true. In the dry air there is none of that shivering feeling that a very considerably less degree of lowness of temperature would produce here; none of that creeping feeling down the back, or absolutely uncomfortable condition that we have here; but it must be remembered, that none the less, but rather still more, is it necessary to protect yourself against an extreme degree of cold. How severe the cold was upon this occasion may be judged from the statement that after about a minute from drawing my hands out of my mittens they became quite incapable of doing any work or handling any thing. I did indeed manage to screw my lens together and take a photograph of the old horse "Charley," as he was standing in a most comical attitude with his head over the fire, trying to thaw the icicles that were closing up his mouth. It was impossible to touch metal, and it was necessary to warm the bits in the fire before putting them into the horses' mouths, as otherwise the iron would have taken the skin off their tongues; still there is very little pain with this extreme cold.

The horses did not look very much the worse for their cold night, but undoubtedly it told upon them, and considerably reduced their strength. We got under way, and after a few hours' drive got again out of the snow, and came upon by far the most beautiful piece of prairie that we had seen. We drove through a rugged ledge of sandy ground hanging over a stream, on either hand the ground rising in knolls upon which stood fine black pine or Scotch fir, with large breadths of prairie between them, the land very sandy and thoroughly dry and bearing every indication of deficiency of rainfall. Passing from this we reached a more level piece of upland entirely covered with sage bush and wild lavender, from among which we startled several antelope, and descending what looked like the wooded approach to a beautiful park we came down a rather steep incline upon the main stream of the Musselshell River. Here we found a tolerably good settlement, to which his name of Olden had been given by the previous settler. It is situated by the side of the stream at the end of a considerable extent of good pasture ground, and no doubt the stream may be turned so as to irrigate a very large quantity of land which would become excellent for purposes of agriculture. It is the point where all the streams running down from the Big Snowy Mountains to the north and the Martinsdale Hills to the west, being in fact the easternmost spurs of this portion of the Rocky Mountains, run down into the Musselshell River, which after a run of 100 miles to the northeast and a further course of about 50 miles due north runs into the Missouri at Musselshell City, about the 108th meridian. Having dined well at Olden, and given our horses a feed of oats, we drove on in the direction of the Bull Mountain. It was a long drive, and up some very steep hills, and although our whole day's drive had not been much more than 20 miles, our poor beasts were thoroughly done by the time we reached a settlement on the mountain. The settler had placed his hut in a most picturesque position, with capital timber studded all about, and most excellent grass fields with plenty of water from the streams that were running down from the hills. The Bull Mountain extends from northeast to southwest, and rises in several circular hills of no great height; they extend for only a few miles from the northeast to southwest, their greatest length being from northwest to southeast. We heard of a good band of elk upon the hills, and I very much regretted that I had not the opportunity of staying a couple of days there, when our host assured us that he could have got me within shot of one or two good heads. He had made for himself a comfortable house, but they had been there only since the May preceding, and the wife seemed to regret the home she had left somewhere further south. So pretty was the place and so great an opportunity did there seem to be for farming here to advantage, that I wondered to hear any grumbling till I found that there was indeed very good cause for it. On looking at a large stack of hay, I asked the host with reference to his getting it, and he told me that every bit of that hay had been cut and got between sunset and sunrise, as the bulldog-fly was so bad there that it was utterly impossible for either man or horse to live outside during the months of July or August between sunrise and sunset. He was obliged to put his horses in a dark stable and himself and his wife to sit indoors in darkened rooms. Upon our talking about game, I further asked him how it was that with so much game in the neighbourhood the grass had been allowed to grow so that he had got such an excellent cut.

"Waal," said he, "I guess that them flies will shepherd any game. There is no game, nor nothing else, could live outside here during the time that grass was growing."

The cause of the flies being so bad about here was undoubtedly to be found in the existence of two small hollows; here the snow lay deep during the winter, and as it thawed there would be produced a moist muddy surface, a grand breeding ground for the fly. The bulldog-fly is one of the worst scourges of this country; I don't know that they can be said to be absolutely fatal to man or horse, but at any rate, when a certain number of them attack a horse, the effect not only from the loss of blood, but from the terrible irritation is so great that the animal becomes frenzied and in a very few hours utterly incapable of work. The flies, however, do not come far from the bush, and it is on this account that you generally see on the prairie the settler's house planted in what a casual observer would think to be a most ugly and uncomfortable spot, and you would say to him, "Why do you not place your house in that pretty little hollow?" and he will tell you at once that to be near the bush is to be in a situation in the summer months where life is almost unbearable, and that the only refuge from the fly is to get well away from the trees and out on the prairie.

Monday—Our horses being nearly done up, we found that it was impossible to get more than one team together, and so leaving one wagon on the Bull Mountain, Henry and Joseph took a portion of the luggage on a wagon with a man who was going down to Billings to bring up his wife and family, and Guillaume and I managed with the other pair, and the third horse tied on for an emergency, to drive on our journey toward Billings. We drove over a very bleak country of the same character as that which has been so often described in the Yellowstone National Park— the prairie land, with broad valleys, and curious yellow rocks standing up in all sorts of shapes, to which they had been undoubtedly worn by the passing of glaciers down the valleys. Most frequently they assumed, amongst those we passed, the appearance of a huge flowerpot, with possibly a small tree growing from it, and here again are occasionally seen protruding from each side of the valley the yellow sandstone walls broken through in their stretch across the valley in the way in which I have described in the country near the Arrow River. We came down at dinnertime to a settlement where there were congregated a considerable number of wagons and horses on their way up from or on their way down to Billings, from two or three trails which met there. Hay was a scarce commodity, and the person to whom the establishment belonged absolutely refused to let us have any for our horses. We managed, however, to find a bit of grazing ground, where we turned them out while we had our own dinner. After dinner Guillaume and I had a cold bleak drive over some high land, Henry and Joseph having stowed themselves comfortably away in the covered wagon; as it got toward dark we descended to a stream, where the snowdrifts were again pretty deep, and where we had very great difficulty in finding our way down and up the opposite bank. It was quite dark when we sighted the lights of the town to which we were making, and driving round a basin we at last came across a settler, who told us the way that we might take to get to the lights, and so we came to what Joseph called "the place where are the cars," and found ourselves in the city of Billings, the point to which at that time the "North Pacific" was finished. A comfortable hotel in this newly erected town and a good stable for our poor horses, were things by no means to be despised; but as there was very little indeed to be seen in the town, we made up our minds that Henry and I and Joseph and Guillaume would leave our friend Craig to arrange as to his return journey, and get off by the train eastward the first thing next morning. I had heard of Billings as a most lawless place, and one of the worst of the new camp cities. On discussing this matter with the proprietor of the hotel, he said it was a calumny, for there had not been above three men shot since the city was founded. On my asking for the date of the founding of the city, I discovered that he fixed it at 10 weeks previously; however, I must say that everything we saw of Billings was as of a quiet and well-ordered town. The next morning we were up at daylight and tied up our traps, and I purchased a large pair of elk horns, which added to no small extent to our luggage. We had great difficulty in getting our traps into the freight car to take us on in the direction of Chicago. It was a little amusing to see the mode in which, where there is no great supervision, railway matters are taken in hand by the officials. They refused to allow me to take my elk horns amongst the luggage, as they said they were not allowed to be answerable for them, and that the only way in which they could be taken was by my paying the guard, and so two dollars were paid to that guard, and when we got to the end of his line a couple of dollars more to another man, and so my horns cost me a pretty considerable sum of money by the time I got them safely to Chicago; how far the railway company were benefited by the transaction it is not for me to guess. The stable charges at Billings were of the most extravagant character;

five dollars, or one a day for each horse, defended only by the statement that they had such a very long way to bring in their hay and their oats; but, even under these circumstances, I think we must consider that a stable bill of seven per horse per week was something outrageous. The train started off at half-past seven, and we passed along the Yellowstone valley, the stream running along on our left hand and a broad extent of prairie up to the base of the hills which bounded it to the north. There were at this time plans for the irrigation of this ground by carrying a long ditch of some 40 or 50 miles from one of the principal bends of the river, and this work, I believe, has been since very satisfactorily carried out, and I hear that the land is extremely valuable. After a run of about a hundred miles we stopped at Forsyth for 20 minutes to dinner, and keeping still to the left bank of the stream, ran long through what will be eventually, no doubt, some good farm country, until we came to the crossing of the Powder River, which runs into the Yellowstone from the south. At a distance of about a hundred miles further to the east we stopped 20 minutes for tea, and night came on, and as there was no "sleeper" we had to make ourselves as comfortable, or rather about as uncomfortable, as we could be in a carriage in which every seat was full. During the night we passed through the Bad Lands, or to use the full expression of the old voyageurs from which this name is derived, "Mauvaises terres a traverser," so called from the fact that you are no sooner up at the top of a steep bank than, after a few steps along a bit of a level at the top, you have to descend again, and so on up and down, and very little of your journey is accomplished in the day. From the little that we saw of it in the late evening and in the early morning when we arrived at Bismarck, it appeared to be a most picturesque country. At Glendive we had left the Yellowstone, and shortly after that we passed out of Montana into Dakota, through which we ran to Bismarck, the capital of the territory on the Missouri River, which the line crosses here, and we stopped to breakfast. The bridge over the river is a very fine structure, the river being nearly a mile in width. Bismarck itself has all the appearance of a flourishing town; it is in the middle of a good agricultural district, and after leaving it we passed through farm lands of Dakota, of which so much has written that I need not here enlarge upon them further than to say that it seems to me to be of a very excellent character. Passing through James Town, where the line crosses the "Jim" River, as it is called, to distinguish it from other James rivers, a stream which runs parallel to the Missouri, into which it enters at Yankton on the frontier of Nebraska, we came on to Glyndon, where the change is made for the passengers to Winnipeg. Glyndon is situated at the edge of Minnesota, and on the bank of the Red River of the north. Here our good friends Guillaume and Joseph left us, as they had to return to Winnipeg, and we were to proceed on our journey to St. Paul. Many shakings of the hands, and much proof of kind feeling toward us was shown by the dear boys as they left us, and we looked forward to the day when we might again have some repetition of our pleasant camping together. Little did we think that one of the youngest and strongest of the party, my dear old guide Guillaume, would never join us again. The poor dear fellow went off to a farm of his father's, having made up his mind to settle down, and being engaged to be married; and shortly after the following Christmas he took up a good farm with his new wife, and away they went for a few days for their wedding tour. During those few days that terrible scourge of the Indians, smallpox, took hold of him, and in a few hours the poor fellow was no more. I did not hear of his death until, in the following year, I had sent up to Winnipeg to know whether he would be able again to join me on my excursion of 1883. A more sterling good fellow, and one with whom I could more entirely trust myself and all that was dear to me, ready in any emergency, looking first to the safety of those who had been entrusted to him, no man ever had the companionship of. If Guillaume had been the only one of the race whom I had known, I had seen quite enough of him to assure me that the Metis of the North-West have much of those excellent characteristics which have ensured their commendation from one who knows them so well, the Archbishop of St. Boniface, against detractions which come often with a bad grace from those who are most responsible for what there may be of evil in their character.

During the night our train ran on. Henry and I had dropped off to sleep, as, indeed, had almost everybody in the car, and some thoughtless fellow, feeling it cold—all the doors and windows being shut—had piled up the stove to such an extent that, waking about two o'clock,

I felt almost suffocated. The heat was tremendous, the stove was red hot, and there was not a bit of fresh air in the carriage. About the same time that I woke up, another man sitting near me woke up too, and we rushed and opened the doors, and saved the party, I believe, from no small danger of suffocation.

Wednesday—Arrived at St. Paul about 9:00 a.m. We were tolerably tired with sitting up for two days and two nights, and were by no means sorry leave the railway cars and betake ourselves to the Metropolitan Hotel, where we had a good clean up and a most excellent breakfast. I have described St. Paul in my previous journey, and we thought it no less beautiful than I had found it then. Having had a pleasant walk round the town and a good dinner, we started off by the 4:30 train for Chicago, and arrived there at nine the next morning. After all our care at Billings with reference to our luggage, it appeared not to have been registered correctly, and as the competing lines were now working at cut rates—the fare from Billings to Chicago being, I think, only a few cents more than to St. Paul—we found that while we had come on by one line our luggage must have gone on by another. I got a sort of costermonger's cart, which they called an express wagon, and drove about the town from station to station endeavouring to find it; at length, after a long search, we found it at a station at the other end of the city. By this time we had missed our train to Toronto, and so wasted a day. We breakfasted at the "Union Pacific," and, as Henry had not been there before, I rather devoted myself in visiting again the stockyards, where we heard and witnessed the usual amount of pig killing, and started off for Toronto at 5:15 p.m.

Saturday—We woke in the morning in passing the Customs at Port Huron, and crossing the St. Clair River got to Hamilton at eleven. I wished to show Henry the Falls, so we turned off at Hamilton by the branch line, had a good breakfast on the train, and ran on to Niagara, where we spent a pleasant three or four hours looking at the wonders of the falls and the whirlpool. We were especially interested in our view of the latter in consequence of the recent sad death of poor Webb, and we came to the conclusion—the only one, indeed, that anyone could arrive at—that the attempt made by him was absolute suicide. Our luggage had been sent on to Ottawa, but we went to the "Queen's" at Toronto and stopped a night and got a few Canadian letters, and hoped for some from home. These had been sent to Government House, and very sad indeed it was that on this late day in November I found that in consequence of an announcement in the papers that we had sailed for Europe in the *Sarmatian*, our good friends had reposted all our letters to England.

Sunday—Went to the Cathedral in the morning, and spent the afternoon with our friend Colonel Gzowski, and had a pleasant evening at Government House.

Monday—Having transacted my own business, and given some little information to our friends of the newspapers, who had duly interviewed me on the subject of the North-West, we left for Ottawa at five in the afternoon, and arrived there at seven the next morning. A little business in Parliament House, and a talk with some of our friends and a second lament over those of our letters which had been sent to Ottawa, and which also for the same cause our friends had two or three days previously reposted to England, concluded our day.

Wednesday—A pleasant stroll over the library and Houses of Parliament, and a drive about eight miles out with our friends Mr. and Mrs. Lindsay Russell to a lake, and a most pleasant evening spent at the house of the Prime Minister, brought our day to its close.

Thursday—We left early for Montreal, arriving there at noon, and went up to the "Windsor," intending to go off to Quebec at night. I found, however, a telegram informing me that a gentleman was coming down from Winnipeg to see me on some business, and we decided to stop over another day, and on Friday, having settled all my affairs and seen my friend from Manitoba, we started off to Quebec about 2:00 p.m. along the "North Shore" line, and arrived there about eight in the evening. Here we found a considerable depth of snow and all the traffic going on runners. Very lovely indeed the old city looked in its white raiment, fringed as it were with tinkling sleigh bells. We took one of these little sleighs up to the Russell Hotel and had supper, and turned in about ten, to be ready for our start on the following morning.

Saturday—Up by daylight, and got everything ready to go on board the boat, and having found at last a letter or two at the post office which most fortunately had not been reforwarded to England, we drove to the boat at eleven and got on board the "Peruvian," and sailed at twelve o'clock. A very uncomfortable commencement of our voyage we had down the river and into the gulf. As it was still snowing, the decks and the rigging were one mass of ice, and it came on to blow hard; however, our Captain Ritchie was a pleasant fellow, and we sat next him at dinner, and although there was only a very small party on board we managed to make ourselves very comfortable and very happy.

Sunday—Snowing all day and very cold; the same on Monday, while we were still in the gulf. It was of course too late in the year to take the northern passage through Belle Isle, and so we proceeded on the southern course after leaving Cape Gaspéand away past the Bird rocks to Cape Ray, and from thence round Cape Race into the Atlantic. We were the last boat out from Quebec for the season, and a very rough run we had of it, keeping, however well ahead of a heavy sea, but rolling a good deal.

On Saturday it came on a little calmer, and we made a good run.

On Sunday, after a curious service by a dissenting minister on board, a small vessel ran under our bows, wanting to know her longitude. This was the only sail we saw on that voyage.

On Monday we arrived at Moville at seven o'clock. Here our good friend Sam McCanless, so well known to all passengers by the Allan Line, brought us a telegram from home, and having returned the little complimentary message, we started off again for Liverpool at eight. Arrived outside the bar, had to wait some time for the tide. As we were coming down the channel the night previous, the moaning of the engines interested me, and I called to Henry to come and hear what they were saying. "Does it not sound like 'Poor Peruvian,' 'Poor Peruvian'?" I said laughingly, and why should she be grumbling in that way, for she has had nothing to grumble about on this journey? The moan seemed almost like a little prophecy; for about five o'clock on the next morning, Tuesday, December 5th, as I lay in my bunk, watching the lights on the Birkenhead coast, as we were turning round to go into the docks, I felt a tremendous thump. Being pretty well used, professionally, to the account of collisions, it struck me that this was such a severe bang that it was as well to get up and see what it was, as I thought that she had come into contact with the dock wall. I had scarcely got my trousers on when the order came down the cabin stairs, "Hurry up passengers: ship's sinking!"

I woke up Henry pretty sharp, and rattled away at the door of the cabin opposite to bring out a young man and his wife who were there with their child, and we hurried up on deck as quickly as we could. I found that in turning round the vessel, our pilot, who had been introduced to me the night before as the best pilot on the river, had not taken quite sufficient consideration of the force of the tide, and the stream catching our boat, had carried her broadside on against the bows of a vessel at anchor, and had cut us through just against the engine room, down to below the waterline, staving in the bows of the vessel against which we came and sending her adrift. Our captain of course gave the order for the boats to be lowered, but, in the condition in which the ship was, with all the luggage and goods moved out of the holds ready to run into dock, there was no time to shut the watertight compartments, or to do much in the way of getting down the boats. We were in water about a hundred feet deep, with a very strong tide running, on a very dark morning, and if we had gone down, there would have been but little chance for most of us. The water rushed in and our fires were out in less than five minutes, but most fortunately during that short interval our pilot was able to drop us down upon the Crosby Bank, and we lay there in safety till some tugs came up and took us off.

I must narrate here a little story which has amused one or two of my friends.

In the bad weather, coming across, I used to take the opportunity of letting Henry get up first, and then, as there was nothing particular to be done during the day, I took things very easy, ordered a nice little breakfast, and took my time over my toilette. The lady who lived in the adjoining cabin, and who had got through her own breakfast, used to seat herself behind me and take the opportunity of undressing and redressing her baby of a few months old, an operation which did not improve my comfort at breakfast, as I could see the whole thing every moment I looked up in the glass opposite me. I think at last she found that it put me out, and for a little malice carried on the operation every morning in spite of my black looks reflected from the glass. Well, on this last morning, when we rushed on deck, I found on board the tug the husband with the little baby. "Where's my wife?" said he. "Oh," said I, "she's just putting on her hat downstairs. I asked her to hurry up, but she did not seem sufficiently frightened to trouble herself much about it." "Hold the baby," said he, and before I could say anything, I found this object of all my bad temper at breakfast reposing in a shawl in my arms. As I am not aware that I ever before had a child in my arms, I cannot say that I made either a happy or a pleasant nurse. At the end of a few minutes, however, a dear old cheery fellow traveller, a Jersey man, engaged in some fisheries on the Labrador and Cape Breton coast, came up to me and said, "Oh, Mr. Staveley Hill, who's child is that. Give it me; I am very fond of children." "For goodness' sake take it, then!" said I, and handing it to him, felt myself happily relieved of an unpleasant responsibility.

The Custom House people most unkindly kept us—the poor shipwrecked passengers—waiting for a very long time, until it suited them to come down and open the Custom House, but at length the trouble was over, and we got to the North-Western Hotel to breakfast. We were, soon after arriving, joined by my wife, who had come to Liverpool to welcome back to England those of whose safety many bad reports had been circulated freely during the time that we were completely shut out from the world.

I think I must add, in justice to Captain Ritchie, that in the trial that took place afterwards, with reference to this collision, he was entirely acquitted from all blame, a result at which we were much rejoiced, as he certainly had shown himself a most careful and competent captain throughout the whole of a somewhat difficult voyage.

CHAPTER VI

~

THE YEAR 1883 PROMISED to be a stirring year for the North-West. In addition to other visitors, the Directors of the Canadian Pacific had invited several friends to run down the line in company with their enterprising President to view their attack on the Rocky Mountains. I had a further object for a visit in a desire to see the ranch and the general progress of the country, and if possible to cross the mountains and to see their western slopes, and I hoped to reach the Pacific and Vancouver Island.

Having arranged with my partner, the Earl of Lathom, to meet at Montreal, whence the Canadian Pacific party was to start, I sailed with my wife and my niece on the 9th of August from Liverpool on board the steamship *Sarmatian*, or rather I should say the ladies started from Liverpool by themselves, I being detained on Circuit; and I was obliged to take a later train, and crossing the channel to Dublin, rush across Ireland to meet the boat at Moville; and starting thence on August 10th, we had our usual pleasant Atlantic voyage, and arrived off Point Levis on the morning of Saturday the 18th.

As we wanted a day in Quebec we drove up to the hotel, and stopped the night there, having arranged to drive out to Silleri to breakfast on the following day. The morning, however, was so wet that we were not able to keep our appointment, but it cleared up in the forenoon and we drove out, and I made the excursion to the locality of the little chapel which I have already described in my account of the Jesuit Mission. Returning to

Quebec in the afternoon, and having paid my respects to the Governor General and the Princess Louise at the fortress, we left by the 4:00 p.m. train, and had the long slow drive of 158 miles along the north shore; the scenery was interesting during the remaining hours of daylight. We got to Montreal at 10:45, and after much difficulty in getting a cab, we reached the "Windsor," and got to bed at 1:00 a.m. The following day I had an early breakfast, and drove to the station to spend a business day Ottawa, and leaving Montreal at 8:30, arrived Ottawa at 11:45. I found, however, that the great part of the officials in the departments were away on their holiday. I managed, however, to arrange a few matters of business, and returned to Montreal by dinnertime.

I found the Russell House at Ottawa very much improved as an hotel, with a fine building and excellent rooms, and used as a residence by many Members of the Dominion Parliament during the session.

Eight-thirty p.m. of August 21 saw a party of about 40 English, Germans, Canadians, and Americans assembled in the hall of the Windsor, with a varied assortment of portmanteaus, bags, and cases, guns, rods, and saddlebags, ready for the Canadian Pacific trip. With the usual fuss of such a departure, and with many a goodbye and *glücklichen Reisen* from our ladies and friends, we stowed ourselves away in many omnibuses, and were off to the station. Here we found provided for our conveyance two private pars, three sleeping cars, a dining room, a kitchen, and a large baggage car; the latter, however, not containing luggage in the ordinary meaning of the term, but every eatable and drinkable that a most excellent butler and first-rate chef could provide the table at the hours of breakfast, lunch, dinner, and tea. The cars were the best that the American continent could provide, and as each of these cars is 60 feet long and weighs about 36 tons, it will be seen that the "motor" had behind it when the train was loaded up the gross weight of some 300 tons.

At 9:30 p.m. our train moved out of the Montreal station, and as all had had a busy day in the city, the beds were soon got ready, and an early hour found, I think, most of us comfortably asleep as we passed along the Grand Trunk for Toronto. Some disarrangement of the coupling, or some little trouble of that sort, which did not appear much to affect the sleepers delayed us for some two or three hours during the night, and the consequence was that we were still many miles from Toronto when we were summoned to an excellent breakfast, which with a morning smoke and the view of the Lake Ontario as we passed its many bays, filled up the time till our arrival at Toronto a little before noon. Here those of us who were not connected with the business matters of the railway, which summoned its directors to certain meetings, passed the time very agreeably in this pleasant city, and there was very little difficulty in filling up the time that intervened before lunch awaited us at the club.

The journey to Chicago along the Credit Valley did not present any objects of striking interest beyond the remark of a good road and a good run. In crossing the St. Clair River, the outfall from Lake Huron into Lake Erie, our train was divided into two blocks, and was with an additional passenger train taken on one of the huge ferry boats, the rails of which are adapted so neatly to the permanent way both of the departure and arrival platforms that no more jerk is felt than is experienced when running over a turntable, and we found ourselves landed on the other side of the water with great comfort, in the United States. How one wishes that there was somewhat more of this practical energy in our country and France, and that, failing this tunnel scheme, we might at least have a decent ferry communication to take the place of those wretched channel boats, which are a disgrace to the locomotive facilities of the day.

A little difficulty occurred here in the Customs, as our cellar contained no small store of champagne and other beverages adapted to the emergencies of the dust, whose irritating particles no dust-screen could keep out, and of a thermometer rising to nearly 90 in the shade.

"Well," said a very good-humoured Custom House officer, "I am very sorry for it, but I must obey the law, and I must just put a lock and seal on; and these things must remain in bond till you get again across the Canadian boundary at St. Vincent."

"Then I will tell you what it is," answered our most intelligent manager, "I shall just have 40 dead men in these cars"; and so to prevent the possibility of so dreadful an occurrence it was at length most diplomatically arranged that an inspector should accompany the party to the boundary, to see that no breach of the Customs law occurred, and we started again on our journey. It is wonderful with how little friction and with what excellent common sense the Customs duties are levied both in Canada and in the States. Everybody seems to recognize the necessity and utility of this mode of taxation, and to conform to it with the utmost readiness.

On finding ourselves thus safely on the soil of the Great Republic, we, with the exception of a few for whom whist or poker had superior charms, betook ourselves to our beds, and ran into the Chicago station shortly after eight o'clock the next morning.

Again on this journey about three in the morning I was awoke by an odour—the source of which my prairie life had made me acquainted with; it roused me from sleep, as though a pistol shot had been fired in my ear. We had run over a skunk, and the dreadful stink—the only one, I take it, capable of awaking any man from deep sleep—struck me like an electric shock, notwithstanding that the doors and windows were closed, and it rendered further slumber for some time impossible.

Arrived at Chicago we were carried away to the Grand Pacific Hotel, where we found an excellent breakfast and rooms provided for us, and where good baths and a change from our bigger boxes made us comfortable and fit to enjoy the day. As our President and directors had railway meetings and other business awaiting them, it was arranged that we should lie over till the following morning and their guests had therefore the whole day devote to sightseeing in this wonderful town, would indeed believe that only 12 years this town was entirely consumed by fire. Street after street of magnificent buildings cover ground which, not many years ago, was but a swamp at the head of Lake Michigan.

A great number of our friends devoted themselves of course to the sight of the stockyards and slaughterhouses, which I have already described; but as my two previous visits had given me quite enough of that, I devoted my morning to an inspection of the new law courts. These are not only remarkable buildings outside, but are most useful and admirably arranged inside, and much indeed did I wish that the designer of our own new courts in London (which I venture to think would be far better adapted for a home for "the bishops and clergy of all denominations" than for the purposes for which they were provided) had taken this building as his model. If Mr. Street had but had the American architect at his elbow to remind him that he was engaged on a building where utility should have the paramount claim, a different result might have been brought about, and another magnificent facade fit to stand by Somerset House might have been added to the beauties of our river embankment instead of this Gothic jumble in a back street.

The courts at Chicago are well arranged internally, and the approaches are of the most simple character, without any of that indulgence in labyrinthine passages which distinguish our new law courts, and though placed on the third and fourth floors no inconvenience whatever arises therefrom, as four large lifts in the centre of the building, accommodating each from 10 to 20 persons, are continually on the move for the use of judges, jurymen, counsel, parties, and the public.

A pleasant stroll along the beautiful new parade, where a park is being laid out by the side of the lake, prepared us for the banquet at the hotel, and a pleasant chat over the events of the day filled up the short remaining hours, when I tumbled inside my mosquito curtains to be ready for an early start the next day.

In the morning we were called at five o'clock to a hot cup of coffee, which having swallowed, we started comfortably on our journey.

As the prominent members of the party, and especially those of us who belonged to the English Legislature, had been interviewed by many newspaper correspondents on the subject of our views in general, not forgetting Ireland in particular, no little amusement was afforded by reading the report which the energetic assistants of the *Chicago Times* and *Inter-Ocean* and other papers had provided for the benefit and amusement of their readers; more especially the description of the personal appearance of many of us made the word painting quite as interesting as though they had been illustrated sketches from *Vanity Fair*.

Our journey from Chicago to St. Paul was most interesting. Fairly fertile farms cover the land till we reach Lacrosse, where the Chicago, Milwaukie, and St. Paul Railway crosses the Mississippi, and where our train had to await the passing through the open bridge of two huge lumber rafts steered by steamers with a paddlewheel astern, so lightly touching the stream as to recall the saying of the Yankee builder with reference to his boat, that she could make her way over a damp plank. From the crossing of the river the line keeps the right bank; the river here being in its babyhood, only about a mile and a half to two miles wide. The line rises to the prairie level shortly before the approach to St. Paul, and then descends again to the river level at its terminus. The excellence of this line may well be inferred from our day's run, for in spite of the long delay of 20 minutes at the bridge and a shorter one for heated axles, we covered the 409 miles in 11 hours and 20 minutes.

A few minutes' delay at St. Paul, and then on through Minneapolis to Minnetonka, a run of some 18 miles, where it had been arranged for us to stay the night at the new hotel, and to give us a glimpse of the beautiful lake scenery. The Hotel Lafayette is one of the wonders of rapid construction. Capable of accommodating some 800 persons, it was built, furnished, and opened in 102 days. It stands on a knoll in the peninsula of the Lake Minnetonka—"wide water"—a lake which though only 15 miles long, is said to have 104 miles of shore, breaking into numberless bays, with sandy beaches, fringed by graceful shrubs and trees. The lake is full of pike, and in one of its little skiff's pleasant days may be passed, either camping out for the night, or quartered at one of its very comfortable hotels. I will not quite say with the guidebook that "he who has not. passed a summer at Minnetonka has missed a golden thread from the strand of life," but certainly a more charming place to idle away a week or 10 days could scarcely be found; and perhaps its highest praise may be found in the words of a Scotch gentleman of our party, who admitted that it only wanted Ben Lomond in the distance to equal that beautiful loch. A good dinner, followed by songs and speeches, brought our evening to its close.

Saturday, 25th—Our kind entertainers allowed us till nine for breakfast and to prepare for our return to St. Paul, giving us an hour in Minneapolis to inspect the mills there. The united efforts of these mills, taking advantage of the water power, turn out 26,000 barrels of flour per week. We walked over the handsome stone bridge which the St. Paul, Minneapolis, and Manitoba Railway Company are constructing over the stream below the falls. Standing there we saw also another great work by which the Government have protected the falls from the very rapid decay and detrition caused by the swift flow of the water over the soft rock, under which influence they would rapidly recede, to prevent which they have under-built and faced the fall along their entire breadth.

A stay of four hours in St. Paul enabled our directors to attend to some important railway business, and we utilized the delay by purchasing a tent, excellent tea, and some other stores for camping. At 3:00 p.m. our train moved out of St. Paul on its way for Winnipeg. It was a very hot afternoon, with the thermometer in the carriage at 87°F, and a dusty road, though pleasantly varied by the pretty lakes which lie along the line as far as the Feargus Falls, which I have already described in my previous journey.

By this time we had done justice to the dinner provided by our excellent chef, and as the cooler evening set in many rubbers of whist carried us on to a late bedtime, from which I was woke up a little before eight the next morning by the announcement that we were approaching Winnipeg, and our train shortly afterwards pulled up, having accomplished the 458 miles in 17 hours.

We breakfasted at the newly erected station room, which had sprung into existence since my last visit. We had but a short half hour to inspect the progress of this young capital of the North-West, which has sprung up to 25,000 inhabitants from the few shanties that surrounded the Fort Garry of only half-a-dozen years ago.

Ten o'clock found our train on its westward journey, and the rapid progress in settlements that has been made since my visit last year leads one to feel, with something of regret, that the time is fast approaching when there will be no further western land to explore.

In passing along to Portage la Prairie we saw good crops, but rather lighter than those we had seen in Illinois and Minnesota, and it was quite clear that if nights of frost came early the result would be somewhat disastrous to the yield. This, unfortunately, did in fact take place, and the late sowing and early frosts of 1883 resulted in a disastrous harvest for Manitoba as well as Minnesota.

As we got further west to the neighbourhood of the Grand Valley about Brandon, we found the harvest in progress. I had previously thought the farm land about Portage the most eligible of the North-West, and with its excellent roads and good situation, Brandon, which is 168 miles from Winnipeg, promises to secure for the very good land in its neighbourhood up to Oak Lake a very large proportion of the early settlers.

After Oak Lake the land immediately along the line is by no means of the same quality. Of the land near Regina, which the line reaches at a distance of 356 miles from Winnipeg, I have already spoken. West of this it has yet to be proved what are its capabilities for grain growing. It must be admitted that strong opinions in its favour have been given by those who have spent this last year there. There is no one, however, who will not regret that Qu'Appelle was not selected as the site for the capital.

An unfortunate delay of some two hours during the night found us at breakfast time still a long way from the crossing of the Saskatchewan at Medicine Hat, which we reached at a distance of 660 miles; from Winnipeg, and it was consequently late in the evening when we reached Calgary, making a total distance from Toronto of 2,040 miles. Along this last piece of the line to Medicine Hat the land had been much burnt up under the broiling sun, but still even in its sandiest parts the growth of oats springing from the casual grains dropped from the feeding of horses and mules during the construction of the line, showed that there was even here no inconsiderable producing power in the soil.

This is, however, in my judgement, the least eligible land of the whole through which the line passes; but in answer to the criticism that the line might have been taken through more fertile territory by passing farther north, we must remember that the primary consideration has been to carry out in all good faith the arrangement under which British Columbia joined the Dominion and to secure the shortest inter-ocean route; from this main line, wherever run, branches must be made feeders, stretching away into other and more fertile lands.

Our 840 miles from Winnipeg to Calgary was thus accomplished in 34 hours; and while it has to be admitted that in our journey westward we were pursuing the flying hours, and so on our arrival in Calgary were bound to deduct a considerable number of hours from the time told us by our London watches; still, considering that I had left the shores of England on the 10th, and had spent 24 hours at Quebec, 48 at Montreal, 24 at Chicago, and that we were in sight of the Rockies on the 27th, it ought not in future to be charged on loving relatives as a reason against the more enterprising of the younger branches settling in the North-West, that it is so far from home. In fact, taking out the time that we had lain by, our journey from Liverpool to Calgary had taken but 13 days, and friends in England had heard by cable within a few minutes of our arrival where am how we were; and the energetic and accomplish manager of the Canadian Pacific Railway, Mr. Van Home, assured me that on the 24th of next June he would undertake to run from Winnipeg to Calgary between sunrise and sunset.

The next day a construction train took us on after breakfast to the crossing of the Bow River, where found the boarding cars which had entertained us hospitably at Moose Jaw last summer. The grading had been carried on a very considerable distance further, almost, I believe, to the divide of the main range. Our height above the sea on the bank of the Bow River, marked on the posts as shown to mo by Mr. Langdon, the contractor, a little below the crossing, is 3,466.49 feet.

I spent an hour or two fishing in the Bow River, and caught some nice trout, grieving much, however, at the same time to see the vast numbers of dead bodies of the unfortunate cattle that I had seen being driven up just before the snowstorm last year.

L. and I had arranged to meet our manager and wagons to take us to our ranch, and after dinner Mr. Craig came up with his outfit, consisting of one four-horse wagon, one pair-horse wagon, one heavy four-horse wagon for lumber, and a saddle horse. We got our packs off the train and made camp down near the river.

The site of Calgary is well adapted for a town, but the country is too far north, I am afraid, to be suited for cattle in the winter.

We found a comfortable little dining place kept by a Mr. Dunn, who with his neat little wife had stayed the night before the storm last year at Oxley, and having had a good tea there, we passed an excellent night in our canvas home, not sorry to be free from the jolting of the train.

August 29th—Breakfasted at Dunn's, and after breakfast with two of our friends, who were going up into the mountains, we got our things together. I had a great alarm with respect to my big deal box, in which were stowed all my most desired effects, and which not finding with our other traps, I feared had been taken back by our friends in the train to Winnipeg. I found it, however, standing by itself by the railway at the bifurcation of the rails, a spot which I found to be dignified by the title of the depot. About eleven we hitched up and started on our journey. A young friend who had come to spend a few days at Oxley and to see what ranch life was, rode the saddle horse. Tom, one of our boys, drove one of the four-horse wagons with our packs and tent, and four of us were mounted in the pair-horse wagon. At the end of about 10 miles we came to a creek, where we found a farm that has been cultivated for some two or three years by a Mr. Glen, and which has been a good deal put forward as illustrating the capabilities of this land for farm and garden produce. There was a very large field of potatoes, some poor barley, fair oats, turnips, and some excellent cabbages; Glen was using the water of the creek to irrigate for this last and for a part of his potato land. The articles grown were indeed of a very fair quality, but I cannot say that the experiment has satisfied me as affording any security for corn growing with profit at so high a level above the sea in this latitude.

We went on across Tongue Creek and the High Wood River, called by the Indians Aspasquehow, and met some cattle going up to Calgary for the Mounted Police. The cattle were rather a rough, poor lot. We got to High River at dark and camped there. The Bishop of Saskatchewan was camping there, on his way to Calgary, and a most pleasant little chat we had by the campfire. He has been many years in the North-West, and is a very excellent and energetic worker for the Church.

August 30th—The air was so full of smoke from forest fires that there was no view to be obtained of the hills, which we cannot yet be said to have seen. I went to have a talk with a rancher named Quirk, and we were much interested in inspecting a feature of this locality which we had often discussed with Kounts last year. He had amused us by declaring that by cutting through a few yards of land at this point he could take steamers up the Little Bow River, which we had found so absolutely dry in the year preceding. Well, I don't know about steamers, but it is quite true that there is only a small interval of about 200 yards dividing the High River from the springs of the Little Bow, and that these last are at a lower level, and undoubtedly by cutting through this space the whole of the water of the High River above this point would be sent down the Little Bow, which there seems very little doubt has at one time, and probably not long ago, been its course.

We hitched up about nine, and crossed one or two creeks and coulées, and made dinner camp at Mosquito Creek, and then on quickly to Oxley, where we arrived about four. We found all well there, and the house much improved by the addition of a piece at each end, at the northernmost of which we had assisted last fall on our return from Snowy Camp; the other addition was a very convenient room for stores, saddles, etc., and I had a good walk round the property. Our young friend, who had not been riding lately, was rather glad of a rest. After dinner and a good chat with the men, we turned in between our buffaloes in our tent, which we had pitched down by the Willow Creek, and where L. and I and my young friend, and our good dog "Boxer"—a most intelligent black retriever whom I had brought with me from England—made ourselves very comfortable.

August 31st—Up about five, and after breakfast we had some rifle practice and a stroll round with our guns, when L. shot a prairie chicken and two teal; after dinner we rode up to the big canyon to look at some cattle belonging to an adjoining rancher. It was a beautiful sight as they all lay, with the hills around and the lake in the background, comfortably enjoying themselves in the deep grass, and in a thoroughly natural condition. We got off our horses and drew as near as we could without disturbing them, and after a long rest and many pipes we rode home past our corral which we had newly put up, and finding the mail in we devoted our time to writing letters, the mail wagon from Fort McLeod to Calgary still stopping for the night at Oxley as it did last year, making the journey of 70 miles from Fort McLeod to Calgary in three days.

Saturday, September 1st—A mizzly morning. We prepared for a start through the rain. Craig had had some good saddle horses broken for us. I rode a pretty chestnut mare, which I christened "Winona," L. rode a grey, and we started for our cattle camp. On our way we caught sight of several of the bands of horses which I had bought last year. They were looking very well, although there has not been, of course, any great crop of foals in this their first year on the range. We also came across about 2,000 head of our cattle, all looking well. One of our cowboys followed with a buckboard, L., Craig, A. and I riding. We dined at our cattle camp, and after dinner rode with two of our cowboys to look more closely at the cattle. They looked very well, and riding on, we camped on a knoll above the north fork of the Willow Creek, at a place which, from our finding a very old gunstock that had belonged to some Indian, we christened "Gunstock Camp."

September 2nd—Thermometer 22°F. Off at nine; rode east by north to the forks in Willow Creek, arriving there at one o'clock. We had a beautiful ride looking over land which I had seen last year. At 3:30, having had dinner, we saddled and rode west, and as I was riding along I seemed to recognize the country, though it appeared now under a very different aspect; and catching sight of a wood on the right hand, and hills rising on the left, I said to Craig that I thought we were near our first camp after Snowy Camp. He seemed to think that we were still many miles from the camp, and I, of course, bowed to his opinion; though like most others who "comply against their will," I also was "of the same opinion still"; and cantering on I came to the spot where we had shovelled away the snow, and where the log still remained on which last year we had sat to dry our clothes. Close by was the thicket where I had shot at the wolf; and there were the remains of our fire just as we had left it. So we camped on the very spot where we had camped last year, and L., without knowing the name which we had given it and which I did not remember at the moment, suggested the very name by which we had called it, "the Camp of Happy Return."

September 3rd—We rode along through land through which we passed on our return last year from Snowy Camp, but very different in its aspect to that which it bore when under its sheet of snow. After about four miles, instead of bearing to the left as we should have done to reach Snowy Camp, we kept straight on in a westerly course. We first visited the Lakes Henry, and found that the first lake, which is about a mile and a half long, emptied itself into the Willow Creek. There were but few ducks on the water, it being too early for the great migration of these birds, and looked quite deserted when we compared its surface with the appearance it presented last year, when it was literally covered. We had indeed some difficulty in getting near them; my young friend A. having gone along a little too far ahead of us, the birds had risen. I went up to the second lake, and very difficult work it was jumping from point to point of the swampy land, shot some teal, and as I was calling "Boxer" to fetch them out of the water, a falcon made a swoop at one of them. I shot him, but not being quite dead he made a strike at "Boxer," who had come up, and went to retrieve him. After this "Boxer" prudently declined to have anything more to do with a bird whose beak and claws showed that he was not the sort of game he was used to. I fished him out with a fishing rod, intending to stuff him, as he was a fine specimen of a young bird; but I unfortunately lost him out of the wagon. We then rode up the hill, the west side of the lake, and regaled ourselves plentifully with serviceberries and gooseberries. Arrived at the high ground we got a good general view. There appeared to be four lakes; the three upper not so large as the lowest, and I am inclined to think, as indeed it appeared to me last year, that the most northern drains toward the High River; the big coulée in which it lay trending clearly in that direction. We were a month too early for shooting on this lake. Assuming the latitude to be not too far north for it, some wild rice might well be sown here, and these lakes would make a splendid duck preserve; all that would be required would be a good duck punt, and the duck shooter would get every variety of waterfowl at the proper season.

We camped in a beautiful park-like ground which I had selected last year when riding with Kounts, and had christened Lathom Park. There is an old whisky trader's shanty there, and the creek is very pretty, with plenty of fish in it, and on the south side a few big cottonwood trees are dotted about the park-like enclosure. We skinned and plucked our ducks and some chickens, and had a capital camp.

September 4th—Thermometer 22°F. Up early; after breakfast we rode west, rising the hills. About eleven we got well into the hills, and turned to the left in order to work round to the south fork. The country consisted of beautiful wooded knolls with a good deal of brush, and was certainly the most beautiful land that I had seen in the west. We put up some blue grouse, which, however, did not fall, as I had hoped they would have done, to the gun of my friend A. They rose sharply and flew quickly, and are better sport than the other birds, flying more like the blue rock. The scenery was lovely. We lunched by the side of a stream, using some tins, given me by Mr. Silver, of Cornhill, heated by self-contained fire, and a most excellent invention we agreed that it was, and one which I can thoroughly recommend as likely to be very useful for cover shooting in England, enabling anyone to select what he wishes for his meal—whether turtle soup, or mock turtle, or Irish stew, or anything else. All that has to be done is to place the tin on two stones, strike a match and light the wick, when in three minutes the contents of the tin are hot, and a basin of soup is ready for you.

I was feeling a little bit seedy, but I stuck to it, as I knew how soon this grand air would put me all right. I could not help thinking that our luxurious life in the train had rather told upon both of us, and that a little abstinence with a wholesome diet of bacon, biscuit, game and tea would bring us back into our best form.

Riding along after lunch we came to a splendid piece of prairie encircled by rising grounds and brush, with plenty of water, and well sheltered by wooded knolls. Here we came down again on the stream, and though we were approaching from the west I seemed to recognize the bearings of the land. I put my horse across the stream, and found myself on the bank where we had last year so anxiously waded through the deep snow, and face to face with the blaze on the tree that we had made last year, and the inscription which I had written when I scarcely knew whether it might not rather prove our epitaph. There it was; hardly a letter effaced, and upon looking at it I could not but thank God that I had lived to see it again, and to know that all who had left it on that morning were alive and well. The grass had grown between the logs and where our tents had stood. All else was much I the same. We found that Charlie, our teamster, with our buckboard, had done all that was required, and had well worked the course we had given him, though he had never been there before. We had sent him off in the morning, with full instructions how to find and where to strike the stream, and he had carefully carried out my directions. He had pitched our tent on the bank above the little hollow where Snowy Camp was; and as we sat round our fire to dinner, many were the reminiscences and tales of the snowed-up travellers.

September 5th—It had been a warmer night, and we started off about nine, taking for about a quarter of a mile our old course across the little plateau. Then steering nearly due east, or perhaps a little to the southeast, we came on to Kounts' hut, the locality of which we had so often discussed in the previous year. It was most curiously concealed in a little hollow, and close by it our men had been camping this summer while cutting logs, and we saw the remains of a fire which had broken out after a dinner camp, had burnt up their camp and tools, and had nearly set them afoot. We made our dinner camp at the forks. "Boxer" was very lame, his feet having been a good deal cut by the sharp grass, and was very glad to jump up on the buckboard. We had a pretty ride, keeping quite to the south of the course which we had previously taken, and arrived at Oxley a little after dusk, and camped on our usual spot by the Willow Creek.

September 6th—Many things to be done, and much luggage to be got together for a journey with pack train across the Rockies, and a great deal business to be transacted, as we could not afford a much longer stay at our ranche; we arranged to go for a short ride, and L. and I and Craig started off about eleven, in order to have a look the other parts of the range, with a view to the consideration of the requirements and the necessities of the coming winter. Wishing, however, to see all we could of the cattle and the horses, we made a very long ride of it. We went to the top of a steepish hill, which has a rising of some 200 or 300 feet from the prairie, and which we named "the flat-headed butte." The smoke or haze from the forest fires still prevented any extensive view. After a long canter we arrived home about four in the afternoon, having ridden some 25 miles. We had our usual meal in the house. I can't use the word "comfortable," for the swarms of flies prevented anything like comfort while we were inside.

September 7th—We left Oxley at 10:30. L. and A. with Charlie in the four-horse wagon, Dan on the saddle horse, driving six others for our use in the mountains, and C. and I following a little later on the buckboard. We had a good deal of luggage, as we required to take with us stores to last us for some four weeks. We got to Fort McLeod, 30 miles, about 3:30. We dined at Kamoose's, and looked over this not very interesting town, including in our survey a small house which we had recently purchased for our men to stay at on their way through to Standoff. We got together the remainder of our stores, hitched up at 5:30, and reached Standoff, a distance of 19 miles, at 7:45.

I found my old friend Cottingham of last year, who had now the management of this farm, all right. He had just finished getting in the oats, with a very fair crop. Having had our tea, we turned in, making up our beds on the floor of the old shop, where Dutch Fred's counter stood when I was here last year.

Saturday, 8th—Up at six, and after a bit of a walk to freshen me up, we breakfasted at 7:30. The air was still so full of smoke that we got no view of the hills. After breakfast we had a good long turn over the ground, examining especially with a view to an irrigating ditch from one of the rivers, and to what extent squatters were encroaching on this lease; during last autumn we had obtained an assignment of Fred Wachter's claims, and everything that he had there, as I had come to the conclusion that it would make an excellent breeding farm for high-class cattle, bounded as it is on each side by the two rivers, and requiring only a fence at a narrow point, about four miles from their confluence, where they again approach, to make it a complete enclosure. After dinner we rode off across the river to the Blood Reserve, taking especial notice of the dead lodges, placed as I have before described, not only in trees, but on scaffolds; and some of them very elaborately prepared. We noticed one in a tree with a full-grown person below, and a child above in a box on an upper stage, with all kinds of trinkets round the bodies. There were children's playthings around them, and among others a little cart, by the side of the small box in which the child had been placed. The poor Indian who put these boxes there little understood that one was branded as a prize soap and another as Zoedone or some other drink, while one poor little brat had for its epitaph "2 doz. Epernay." Another erection, a recent one, contained a young son of "Little Spotted Dog," the present head of the tribe. In this case the body had been placed on the ground with a mound of earth over it, and a log hut built round it, and the top covered over with straw and calico. Other bodies were placed along the side of the hill on trestles. A few were buried in the earth. These were baptized Indians who had been buried by the Missionary. We went into the school kept by Mrs. Bourne, the wife of the Missionary—a quick little woman, who had come through in the storm of last fall, and had been at our ranch on the night preceding, and had taken a great interest in the account which she had heard of our being snowed up in the hills. We had much talk with her about the Indians and about their peculiar mode of disposing of their dead, and she told us that their reason for opposing burial in the earth is because the spirit of the departed cannot then come from and go back to the body, which it loves to visit for many months after it has parted from it; and such is the force of their belief in that respect, that even those who profess Christianity, when they do bury in the earth, keep open a small hole at the corner of the grave down to the body, so that the intercourse between the corporate and incorporate may still be continued. She told us, when on this subject, how the squaws meet round the dead lodges and sit there howling at each new moon, and it was a common practice for them to cut off a finger on the death of one they loved, thinking that the pain from the wound might overcome and drive away the grief for the other loss. I had more than once noticed squaws who had lost a finger, but had not guessed the cause, and a few months after this the squaw of the chief who had died came into our camp with the stump of her finger, which she had cut off in her grief, only then healing. She had found herself, I fancy, in poorish circumstances, as she was offering a daughter for sale for five dollars.

We had a long talk with Mr. McCorb, the Indian agent, and some others round his agency office. A hairless old Indian, I think it was "Spotted Dog," examining us closely, as he looked at L. and Craig and myself, remarked, "What a lot of grey beards." The Indian himself allows no hair to grow on his face, and his principal occupation as he sits and talks with you is in going over his face and chin with his little brass tweezers, to remove any hair which may accidentally be found. We cantered home across the river, over the prairie as the sun went down, and a beautiful sunset—a charming ride over that firm green sward. McCorb had been clearing out the Crowsnest Pass, in pursuance of an order from the Government, made on a representation by me last year to the Prime Minister on behalf of those interested in bringing in horses and cattle from British Columbia. After a comfortable tea and a cheery talk, with a short stroll out into a beautiful night, we turned in between our blankets and soon dozed off.

Sunday, 9th—Up at six, both of us beginning to feel all the better for prairie life and its quiet enjoyments and healthy living. We had left instructions at Fort McLeod for the post, which was due shortly before we left, to be sent off to us to Standoff; and as we were both anxious for letters from home, we waited till after dinner, having spent the morning in going again over the land, writing letters, and giving directions as to the mode in which the farm should be conducted. We arranged with our manager that he would meet us at Helena, driving thither, after a visit to Oxley, by the direct southern road, while we took a route across the mountains, to see as much as we could of British Columbia, and then striking the "North Pacific," to join him at Helena, in Montana territory, on the eastern slopes of the Rockies, on October 5th.

I had during our journey taken what, as I had hoped, were six valuable photographs: two on the Atlantic of icebergs, two of the ranch, and two of the crossing of the Mississippi in our railway trip. The great difficulty which I had always found in photographing had been in the changing of the plates. Fortunately at Standoff we had a good root cellar, which was made, as is necessary in this country of severe frosts, well under ground; and so having taken my little ruby lamp into the cellar and having the cellar lid put on and all light carefully excluded by robes and blankets thrown on the top of it, I proceeded to change my plates. My annoyance may be guessed at finding that the arrangers of my photographic apparatus before leaving England had omitted to put any plates in the slides which I had been using, so that these six endeavours, though carried out with the greatest pains, had been productive of no results. Having now put the plates in the slides, I took two photographs: one of the log hut and stables at Standoff, with our wagon and horses ready for the start, L. on the grey horse which carried him through our long rides, and own pretty little sorrel mare, "Winona," saddled and ready for the start. The other photograph was taken, turning my lens and looking exactly in the opposite direction, toward the Belly River, at a point a little above where we crossed it toward the Blood Reserve. Some Indians were coming across, and upon seeing my lens pointed toward them, stood still and concealed their faces, so as to prevent their portraits being taken.

Having got under way, as we rode off in the direction of the mountains and in an almost due westerly course, we were met by Mr. Cochrane's manager, who was looking after the range which Senator Cochrane has taken, and which extends from our boundary right up to the Kootenai Lakes, at the foot of the hills. It is an excellent range; I have seen scarcely anything better in the North-West. We had a useful discussion with the agent as to sales and prices; and then drove on about 20 miles to a hay camp, where some of Cochrane's men were putting up hay for the ensuing winter. We arrived at the camp about six, and found that the men had already put up three large ricks of hay. Many geese flew over our heads, but they are far too wary for anyone to be able to approach them on these pools, round the margins of which there is no cover.

We turned in about nine o'clock, being very well satisfied with what we had seen of our range, and certainly the whole of this ground, from the junction of the two rivers to the lakes, is as good a grass country and with as excellent bottoms in it as can be well imagined.

Monday, 10th—Up at six. Packed up as quickly as we could and got under way by 8:15; L. and I with Charlie in the four-horse wagon. We pulled up at two or three of the little lakes, of which there are many on each side of the trail, of an extent from about half an acre to four acres. We got as much duck and teal as we wanted for dinner, and could in fact have shot almost any number that we required.

Early in the afternoon we arrived in sight of the house of Kootenai Brown, an old settler who has been there for many years, and who in the autumn previous had been recommended to me as a man who could show me and tell me all about sport in that part of the mountains; we had a little difficulty in getting across the stream, as this eastern end of the lake meanders about, and no direct trail was visible. But everything is known in the North-West, and the proprietor had heard of our probable visit to him, and sighted us from the hill, and came down and guided us in. He was a wild Indian-looking fellow, in a slouch hat and curiously constructed garments and moccasins. He told us that he had come across, 18 years ago from British Columbia to hunt buffalo, and after wandering about for some years had settled in this place, where he has been for the last four years. We calculated that it was as near as possible 40 miles from Standoff to the Kootenai Lakes. Brown was occupier of the log hut belonging to Kanouse, in which he lived with a rather delicate wife and some little children. He had seen something of service in the British army, but with his long dark hair and moccasins had not much of a European remaining about his appearance. The view here of the hills is indeed magnificent, rising as they do on each side from the level of the lakes. We strolled about and for the first time this year got a view of the Rockies, though with some difficulty, in consequence of the smoke, which interfered with the distant view; we had a pleasant tea and talk with Brown over the campfire, and arranged for his assistance at the rate of five dollars a day for himself and his horse, to go with us about the mountains for two days and take us for a day's fishing if the weather was calm enough to allow of a very rickety boat venturing out on the lake; and after this that he should set us on our way into the Kootenai Pass and see us on the right trail for one day's journey. We made a comfortable camp by the lake.

Tuesday, 11th—Up at six o'clock, and off at 8:30 to drive round Sheep Mountain, the hill on the left-hand side as we were looking west. Their name had been given to them from the numbers of "bighorn" or mountain sheep which formerly abounded there. We went up along the south side, and rose the hill through brushwood, looking for bear among the berries, which are very numerous. We were not, however, fortunate in discovering any sign, and reached the snow at the height of about 2,000 feet above the lakes. Having scrambled up to this, I made a snowball, and brought it down to my companions, who had remained a few feet lower down. I found a pretty little parsley fern growing up at the edge of the snow. Thence we wandered away round the hill, and rose again to the ledge, from which peaks stand up against an escarpment of the hill, reminding one, by their shape, of the Needles off the Isle of Wight. There was no sign of game except a few prairie chickens, and so we turned back through the woods, and across piles of dead trees, and down the hill home. I made the Kootenai Lake level to be about 5,400 feet above the sea, taking Standoff as about the same level as the crossing of the Bow by the Canadian Pacific Railway.

Wednesday, 12th—Thermometer 28°F. Started off on horseback again about the same time with Kootenai Brown for a ride up the Goat Mountain, on the other side of the river, to see if we could come across any track of bear, as he told us that one had been seen a few days before near to his hut on that side. It was much wilder country than that through which we had ridden yesterday, running up into the hills, where Brown said there were plenty of goats. We were not, however, fortunate enough to see any. A storm came on, so we got off our horses and got under some brush and ate our lunch, and began to get rather low spirited as to our prospect of big game. The only thing that we came across was a jackass rabbit, which Brown shot with his rifle, and a chicken. I had a long stalk after some sandhill cranes, a beautiful large white bird. I had seen them first on the other side of a deep stream, and leaving my companions I went down on the marshy ground by the side of the stream till I got close up to the place where I thought I heard them. But after the manner of the corncrake, they had quite as much ventriloquistic power as a professed ventriloquist, and their cry appeared to come from the brush which was but a few yards from me. As I could not get across the stream to it, I kept throwing stones into the brush, and at last I felt so certain that they were there, that I fired my first barrel into it. They rose up, however, at a spot some 300 yards off, and settled down again, but I could not get near them. L. found a beautiful autumn crocus of a mauve colour, with a peculiar woolly centre. He came up to show it to me, and we agreed that it would make a beautiful addition to our garden flowers. We hunted long for the bulb of the pretty crocus, but the only guide had been plucked, the world-old simile came to mind, "as if the wind had gone over it, it was gone, and the place thereof knew it no more." It is, I think, from his observation of the death and reproduction of the flowers of the prairie, their absolute deadness in winter and the fresh outburst of life in spring, when beyond all apparent hope the lost is found again, that the Indian has learned so firm an assurance of a future life. The Greek idyllist had the same facts before him, but they led him only to complain when his loved friend died—may I translate his lines—it was but a thought on the prairie—

"Ah woe! the mallows and the parsley green,
And rank-grown anise bright with emerald sheen,
Lost to the garden in the autumn sere,
Live yet again and greet a coming year;
But we the great, the mighty and the wise,

The lords of earth, the men of high emprise,
When first we die, unheard in earth's deep womb
Sleep the long sleep where morrow's ray breaks not night's
    endless gloom."

But the Indian holds not this view; for him beyond the grave the Great Spirit will find a home, and, if he has been a good Indian, a keeper of his word, a true hunter, and an unyielding enemy, his spirit will revisit this old body for a few moons, but then, when all has been prepared, he will find plenty buffalo to hunt, and squaws to work for him, plenty hunting grounds untrespassed on by hostile tribes, or by the white man, and all the beasts and flowers of his prairie in its brightest beauty, when, as in Hood's pretty lines—

"Roses shall be where roses were,
    Not shadows but reality;
As though they never perished here,
    But bloomed in immortality."

The Indian would in his death song chant forth his faith as confidently as did Socrates when he welcomed his executioner; he would tell you in his many-worded language, "Παρ' ανδρας ελπζω αφιζεσθαι αγαθους και παρα θεους δεσποτας πανυ αγαθους"; but his ανδρες αγαθοι would be good Indians, like himself, and his θεοι πανυ αγαθοι will be no δεσποται, for he has no word to express it, and knows not its meaning, and can understand no happiness under control; but there will be a good and generous Manitou, a supernatural Being who will see that he is well and amply cared for and rewarded.

Thursday, 13th—It was blowing too hard for us to think of Kootenai Brown's cranky little boat as of any use for fishing on the big lake, even if we could have got it up there, so L. and I and he started off on horseback about nine o'clock for the upper lakes. We took our rods and guns and camera. On arriving at the top of the middle lake, we had a lovely view of the hills and of the wild lake that stretches away to the international boundary. I had to send Brown back for the keys of my camera case, which had been left in camp, and meanwhile, L. and I having picketed our horses, went for a stroll. I shot a duck, which Brown's dog brought out in a most gallant style, and when Brown came back, I got a photograph of the lake taken looking toward the southwest; beyond is the furthest lake, across which runs the boundary line of Canada and the States. We went on to the falls, and passing a corner of the lake, saw some stages and rails, on which Brown had been drying some of the huge trout which he told us he got out of the lake, of 30 or 40 pounds weight, and riding on along the edge we came to the falls. The stream from an upper fall is carried inside a trough of rock, breaking through which, it comes down into the pool. It was one of the prettiest waterfalls I have ever seen. The stream is not a large one, but from the size of its now dry bed, it must be a torrent in June and July, as it brings down the melting snow. We had no sport fishing; it was too late for the trout in these cold clear streams. L. caught one small one, and we had a pleasant ride back. With the exception of a coyote which the dog chased, as we were riding out, we did not see a head of big game during our stay at Kootenai, and I doubt if there is any to be found here, with the exception, perhaps, of a stray bear or sheep in winter. Bathing in the lake in the evening, as I was dressing by the shore I saw in the dusk what looked to be a pretty bright-coloured flower, and gathering two or three of them, I put them in my buttonhole; as I walked along, I found from the smell of my fingers that it was a wild onion. Turning back, L. and I got a good large bunch of this excellent vegetable, which added no little to the flavour of our soup that evening. The wild onion grows in very considerable abundance, as I found afterwards, all about this part of the slopes of the Rockies.

Chapter VII

~

There are two passes from this part of the country across the mountains, both of which are known by the name of Kootenai; one is, however, now better known as the Boundary Pass. The northern has its eastern opening almost adjoining that of the Crowsnest Pass, the southern or Boundary Pass starts at its eastern end from the Kootenai Lakes. We originally intended to find our way into British Columbia either by the Crowsnest Pass or by the pass adjoining it, but as we had now spent so much time at the lakes, and it would have taken us two or three days more to strike the northern pass, we determined to try the Boundary Pass. I had some hope that we should find that the north and the south Kootenai tracks met after separately crossing the Main Range and were united in a joint pass through the Selkirk Range. We had no maps with us, and perhaps a more careful recollection of what I had seen last year should have told me that those hills left no road to the south, and that it was in that direction that the Boundary Pass trended. We made up our minds, however, to try the Boundary Pass and to see where it would take us, and so all being ready on Friday, 14th, we started at 10:30; five pack horses, four saddle horses, and Brown on his cayeuse. After a ride of two miles, when we had attained a height of 250 feet above the lake, we struck the base of the mountains. After this our track was wild and rough. I wanted to push on as far as we could. The packing, which is always a matter of very considerable anxiety, had been done with much skill, and the packs travelled fairly well for the first day. The horses were a little awkward, but Dan and Charlie were good tempered with them; there were some delays of course. Kootenai Brown came out very strong on the subject of packing, and was learned in the various kinds of knots, and in his criticism of inferior artists and in all matters of packing straps and cinches he was clearly a connoisseur. The poor brutes did not bear the compression of stomach with much equanimity; had they spent a few months under the charge of a European dressmaker, they would no doubt have understood it better. We found some good grass at the foot of what was obviously about to be a steep climb, and as Brown seemed anxious not to go for more than one day's ride from home, we camped there at the edge of a wood of burnt spruce, with a good view of the hills and some snow. I took a photograph of the hill at the back of the camp: it was of a perfectly pyramidal form, but my camera got a little moved over to the left as I was taking the view, so that the hill did not show so completely pyramidal as it is in reality. We christened this camp "Pyramid Hill Camp"; height above sea level, 6,300 feet.

Saturday, 15th—Thermometer 23°F. The horses had wandered far back along the trail, and we were rather alarmed at Dan's long absence in search of them, fearing lest they might have made back for Standoff. He brought them back after a long ride, and with a farewell to Brown we started at 10:15 up a steep hill and through some thickly growing spruce at first of a good size, but smaller as we got up to the top of the hill. At 12:30 we arrived at the divide at 1,100 feet from our morning's observations, and took two photographs; one looking back to the east, from which we had come, and the other along our forward road to the west, with the Selkirk Range in front of us. This was a most interesting and characteristic view, the sides of the hills both before us and behind clothed nearly to the top, except where there had been fires, with almost impassable wood. On the rocks we found a saxifrage and other plants of an alpine character; that which I have called saxifrage was a grey plant, with small pointed leaves and long spreading roots running amongst weathered rock; it had small round pinkish flowers on stems of two or three inches long. We each of us brought a plant home, and mine put out one shoot during the next winter; but it was its last effort, and it died shortly after. The summit of the pass here is just below the snow level, and from thence we descended through a thick sprucewood, the trees changing very considerably in character, with a greater variety of berries and brush.

We descended for 500 feet without a level bit, through pinewoods of fairly good poles; it was, however, *tenuis semita*, and required a careful regard for the knees against the fir trees. At this elevation we came to a little spring, the first water that we had seen running to the west; thence, after a further descent of nearly 1,000 feet almost without any break, to springs that looked like the rise of a river in a bit of swampy ground which we had remarked from the summit. We found that we had come down 400 feet more than we had gone up. The horses were getting tired and a little footsore. I had been riding the sorrel mare "Winona," and L. the old grey; my mare was not shod, and I should certainly advise always to have the riding and pack horses shod before taking them over these stony passes; unless shod they become footsore, and to a considerable extent useless, after the second or third day.

One of the prettiest and certainly most useful bushes in the mountains is the Canadian raspberry, a bush with broad palm-like leaves; I have it in my garden in England, but it does not fruit there. The fruit is of the colour and character of the English raspberry, but is much more flat, and in shape does not so well bear out the name of thimbleberry, by which very descriptive title this fruit is known in. Canada. Black currants there were in abundance, serviceberries in millions, and a small berry like the bilberry, but which I believe was a box. We made camp a little before four o'clock by the side of a beautiful stream, which L. and I tried for fish, but could not see a fish in it; plenty of fly on the water, but nothing more. A beautiful site for a camp, and we recognized it as very kind of the paternal Government of the Dominion thus to provide, free of rent and taxes, plenty of fuel and drink, and lots of bedsteads on both sides of the trail. It was a glorious day, with scarcely a cloud in the sky, and we found, as soon as we got over the ridge on the western slopes, a warm balmy air filled with the odour of pines, and very different to anything we had felt on the eastern side.

In calculating the heights, and taking Standoff and Oxley as the same height as the crossing of the Bow River above Calgary, viz., 3,600 feet,

Kootenai Lake would be at a level of 5,400, "Pyramid Hill Camp" 6,300, and this summit 7,400 feet above the sea. These being barometrical observations, the height is of course only approximate, but I don't think it will be found very far wrong.

We camped in a large meadow, with what we believed to be the headwaters of either the Flathead River or of the Tobacco River—a large tributary of the Flathead River—on our left hand, barish hills rising on the right, the great hills from which we had come down with their shoulders interlocking, so that the question arose down which of the slopes behind us our road had lain, in front a continuation of the wood; we christened this "Flathead Springs Camp." This stream may be one of the headwaters of the Columbian Kootenai River, as it was only by following it down that we could say for certain into which of these big loops it runs, but both the Kootenai and the Flathead, under the name of Clarke's Fork, join about the 49th parallel and the 117th meridian, and form the Columbia River.

September 16th—Thermometer 18°F. Up at 5:45. Had had a good night, but very cold, and I made a mental memorandum to put more clothes on for the night following. Just before starting I wandered off to take a photograph of a beaver dam which L. had noticed in process of construction on the night previously. It is a most interesting photograph, as I doubt if one has ever been taken before, of the work of these little animals while in process of construction. I found three or four very good dams, but it was difficult to get my camera in position to take them. I had a heavy drag through the wood down the hillside, in which I planted my lens opposite the only part that was attainable for a view. The work of these little animals is indeed wonderful. I saw one tree that they had attacked in the previous night, and which was partly bitten through—it was from 18 inches to 24 inches in diameter, and the chips that had been bitten out, of which I have one before me as I write, were about four inches long and one inch wide. The end of one log is of a big tree of about 15 inches diameter, which they had felled the night previously, and were about to bite up into logs, and no doubt a boss beaver had stood by and had taken care that the tree should be bitten through so as to give the least trouble when fallen. The poor little fellows had not a long life before them, and they would be polished off as soon as the fur was good enough for Brown or the Kootenai Indians, who were hunting in these woods, and all their summer's night ingenuity will have been wasted. Let us hope, however, that they had been happy in their industry. After photographing I rejoined camp, and we rode for miles through the forest, under white pine of about 20 to 25 years' growth, very tall larch or tamarack, poles 90 feet high, like long whips, and towering up among them old trees 150 to 200 feet high, showing traces of a big fire which they had survived. After a fire the same growth of trees never follows; thus, black pine is succeeded by tamarack, or white pine, or spruce; it is Nature's own rotation of crops. After about five miles we came down to the river level at a descent of about 200 feet, and after about four or five miles further ride through the wood—the last part of which was mostly tamarack—we descended again to the river level, crossed the stream, and as our horses were footsore, and we had heard that beyond this point we should find no grass or camping ground for nearly a day's journey, we made camp at 1:45. It was a blazing hot sun; the mountains had died away, and there remained only what looked like a low range in front of us. As soon as we had made camp and driven our horses into a very good meadow, L. started off with his rifle to look after big game; he saw tracks of deer, but got nothing except a rather bad tumble in the brush. The woods were very thick, in fact impassable, the hills rising behind us all wooded. I went off with my "fishing pole," and saw four or five large trout together, the only fish which we had seen in these western waters. I threw my bait close to them and tried grasshopper and fly, but could not touch them. It appeared to me that all the fish had gone down the stream, and that possibly earlier in the year good sport may be found in all these waters; at this time of year, however, there is clearly no fishing to be done. Having to change my photograph plates I determined upon utilizing the Indian sweat bath. These constructions are found at nearly all camping grounds—a few wickers bent over in the form of an arch, just large enough for a man to sit under, with a small hole at his feet, into which red-hot stones, heated at a fire close outside, are thrown, and the wickers being covered with skins, and water poured over the stones, a complete vapour bath is obtained, which is to the wild man the cure for every complaint. He generally takes a dip in the stream afterwards, and sometimes, like a Russian Moujik, a roll in the snow. This is, as I have said, the Indian panacea; but his adoption of it, as he always does, when attacked by smallpox, is certainly one of the causes of the universally fatal results of this disease amongst the Indians. So I squatted under the wickers and lighted my little ruby lamp between my feet and arranged my plates so as to change them easily, and then got Dan to come up and cover me most completely with blanket and buffalo robes, and I found that I had a perfect dark chamber, the only trouble being the dustiness of the ground and the almost suffocating heat. As Dan observed, if an Indian had come up he would have been frightened out of his wits, thinking that the white man was making some dreadful "medicine against him." L. and I had a grand washing up of clothes, which the sun quickly dried for us—ironing was dispensed with. We named this "Wash-up Camp."

No game, no fish, and our grub getting low; but we had pretty well of flour, and Charlie began to bake fairly well, and his cakes went excellently with our marmalade and jam.

September 11th. In saddle at 9:30. After rising a slight hill, we came down through a beautiful wood till, at 11:30, we struck a stream running from right to left at a descent from our former camp of 500 feet. We had passed through a good deal of fallen rock on our left, a profusion of berries of all sorts, and wherever the rock had fallen the raspberry growing from the debris was our English variety. I saw one plant of *Osmunda regalis* and one *Pteris aquilina*, the only ferns that I had seen since Kootenai. My aneroid at starting this morning stood at 24° 50'. Many of the trees through which we passed were about 150 feet high, and 10 feet in girth at about 5 feet from the ground. About this time we thought we must have crossed the boundary, and that we were either in British Columbia or in Montana. Unfortunately, however, as our maps had been left behind, we were much in the dark as to our whereabouts, and in our uncertainty as to our then domicile we named our camp "Doubting Camp."

September 18th—Very cold during the night, thermometer registering 17°F. We had slept well and were up at six, when we found the ground white with frost, but the sun rising over the mountain at seven cleared all this away, and we were saddled up and off at 9:45. We had a most beautiful ride all day through forest. The damming of a stream by the beavers had created a beaver meadow extending over many hundred acres. The fallen timber, of which we had a great quantity to get through on that day, and which made our progress slow, gives the effect of posts and rails, and adds more completely to the home-like look of a piece of land in reality so wild that in all probability no foot of white man had ever trod it. Nor indeed do I believe that any Indian ever ventures many yards from the trail, as he has a great dread of the hidden dangers of the wood. We had a little rain, and after skirting a lake on our left hand we turned round into a gloomy defile with huge rocks tossed about, amongst which our trail wound, the detritus from the hills having formed a deep soil from which sprang a luxuriant vegetation. Above all the berries attracted our earnest attention, and L. and I gathered a handkerchief full of serviceberries and currants, as he was bent upon trying his hand upon a fruit pie. There were all the indications of swollen and big streams running through these gorges on the snow melting, but at this period of the year they were reduced to very small runners. About half-past four we came to a beautiful little opening in the wood, and we unpacked and camped. Here L. began his pie, and having secured the lid of the kettle for a baking dish, and duly lined it with the paste and filled with fruit and sugar and covered it with an upper crust, a good deal of burning of fingers had to be submitted to in order to save the great culinary effort from extinction in the flames; but the result was very satisfactory, and it received high praise from those who sat round the supper fire at "Pie Camp."

September 19th—Up at six; thermometer 15°F; altitude 6,175 feet. There was a good deal of rime—it was a charming little oval piece of prairie surrounded by tall spruce and silver firs, but so buried in the hills that the sun did not reach us till nearly eight.

We started at 9:30 and rode all day through forest with magnificent timber. One of the tamaracks we passed was an enormous tree; I did not measure it, but we calculated the height to be over 200 feet. There was a profusion of wild fruit and many traces of bear, and we met a party of three trappers going up into the north fork of the Flathead. We had a long day's ride, as there was no camping ground; the pretty little chipmunks and other varieties of squirrel running along the fallen trees were the only living things. We had some bad places to get through, but our packs held on well in spite of several severe squeezes and bumpings against the trees, in one of which L. smashed the stock of his gun, but made a neat splice of it with some whipcord, and we got yesterday and today a good supply of that most excellent bird the tree grouse or "fool hen." At length we found a good place for camp at seven o'clock in a pretty bit of prairie with single trees dotted about it. It was a beautiful starlight night, but very cold, and we calculated our altitude as 4,125 feet.

September 20th—Thermometer 15°F. Up at 6:20, and struggled through the thick brush to the stream for a wash. A bright sun took away the feeling of cold. It was a fine rushing stream, too cold and shallow for one to get into it, but I rolled a big log to the edge of the water and it made an excellent tubbing apparatus, and I amused myself with the idea of my beautiful bath and dressing room, about 100 feet square, curtained round with high brush, water laid on so lavishly that it would have satisfied Mr. Dobbs, the furniture of birch and pine and the walls of hills all decorated with wood scenery, the heating apparatus consisting of the sun's open fireplace; the approach to the room, it is true, a little troublesome, as a good deal of the said birch and pine furniture had been tumbled about rather promiscuously, not to say carelessly, but the carpenter and joiner must put this to rights.

Got back to breakfast, and saddled up and off at 9:45. As we went along the appearance of fungus on the trees showed the moisture of the climate that we were then in. Not a sound as we rode along through these woods, excepting only the weird sound that comes from the scolding of the jays and the groaning of the trees as they grind against one another in supporting a fallen sister in her decay. From the hills, following the stream, we debouched upon the prairie, with occasional glimpses of Scotch pine, and reached the Tobacco Plains. These plains are said to have received their name from the attempts of the Jesuits to grow tobacco there; we had not, however, come across any of the narcotic. Many of the big trees are destroyed by the fires made against them, and they gradually get burnt out and killed. I could not make out how it was that so many of the fireplaces appeared to be two feet from the ground, until the suggestion arose that these fires are made principally in the winter, when the snow puts everybody at that level above the root of the tree. The worst of it is that it is always the finest trees that fall victims. The firs here are indeed singularly beautiful, and standing singly or in groups of three or four, have had room for their boughs to extend. During our journey we had from the first, on the instructions of Kootenai Brown, been looking forward to "Sophy's" as the place on the western side of the mountains where we should get stores and directions, and generally should be set on our road. Soon after leaving the mountains, or rather shortly after we left camp, we had entered upon rolling downs, with a growth of bunch grass and clumps of Scotch fir trees, clothed with that beautiful red bark which contrasts so well with their dark green foliage. The trail here ran along a stream on the left hand some 80 feet below us, and at one point white clay bluffs washed away into needle-peaks skirted the stream; after that the lands got more open, and we rode along the edge of a lake in which I could see some trout; it was so transparent that a small bough lying on its surface looked as if suspended in the air—the bottom of the lake being so clearly seen through the water. We came across some cattle and horses which belonged to the Indians—as was apparent from some of them being unbranded, others with only an earmark—amongst which I noticed one cow with a cross of buffalo. We came to a single log hut and saw there a settler, with whom we had a little talk. He told us his name, and that his comrade had gone down to Missoula to buy stores, as he was about to open a store for sale to the Indians; there being a settlement of Kootenai Indians, under Chief Edwards, close to him. These Indians seemed to be doing work and to be well off; they claim to be British Indians, but the resurvey, which has placed the boundary line some eight miles further north, has shown this land to be in the States. They have endeavoured to put a stop to any squatting on their beautiful park-like land, and the settler, who seemed to be in considerable anxiety with regard to them, told us that they took his goods by boring under his lowest logs and letting in their coyote dogs to steal his grub. His pal had been away and he had been alone for 40 days, and when he saw us coming toward him had been in great hopes that we were going to camp near him, so that he might have a big talk with us. We left him, however, after a short conversation, as it was very hot; and I fear that the anxieties of his solitude were too much for him, as I heard in the year following that when his companion did return he found that his mind had given way. After two or three miles further we saw two or three log huts and Indian teepees on a knoll; Dan rode up and found it to be "Sophy's." He inquired of an old woman in green spectacles, who answered his inquiry with, "Me Sophy." So we rode up, and found that she had plenty of stores. We bought half a sack of flour, some rice, 10 pound of venison, and some butter, which last was very rancid and uneatable. We made a capital supper on the venison and rice, and tinned peaches, and turned in about nine o'clock. Very cold night.

Friday, 21st—Thermometer 17°F. Up about six. Having breakfasted, made up our minds for a rest day. This is a very pretty place for a settlement, the log hut and the stores and the teepees of some Kootenai Indians who were settled near, and were employed in making Indian work, mats, and generally in hunting and making themselves useful to Sophy. Sophy is a person of very considerable energy—had three parties out prospecting mines, and possessed a good herd of cattle. I went off to fish, but found no water in the small stream which runs down at the distance of about a quarter of a mile from the settlement; we were told that there had been no rain here for at least 18 months. Going further down, I struck the Kootenai fork of the Columbia River, a very large and rapid stream, about 80 yards wide. I bathed and came back, when I took a photograph of "Sophy's" and some Indian teepees.

These Indians were very suspicious, and averse to having their likenesses taken. They were Nezperces, or, as they call themselves, Santon. They were under an impression that I was "a Boston man," meaning a United States citizen as distinguished from a "King George's man," and that I had come to take their pictures, that I might hand them over to the Government and have them sent back to their reserves. These are the people who, under Chief Joseph, gave so much trouble to, and killed so many of, the United States soldiers in 1878. A Kootenai man who had lost his squaw was working for Sophy, looking after her horses and cattle, and supporting by his wages his three little children. He was a much sharper-looking fellow than any Indian I have seen before. On my return to camp, I found L. with some 12 trout he had caught in the river. Charlie had been away at Sophy's, baking the bread in her oven, and a confounded Indian dog had taken advantage of our deserted camp to run off with half our bacon and all our venison, and Sophy had most kindly given him a fowl to replace our loss. The distances given to us for our next journey were: Sophy's to the Flathead Lake, 94 miles; Flathead Lake to Dayton Creek, 22 miles; Dayton Creek to Horse Plains, 45 miles; total, 161 miles.

Mr. Bovaris, who at that time occupied the position of husband to Sophy, had a talk to me about the Indians and their fight with the Boston men under Howard in 1878. The Nezperces under Chief Joseph who had turned out on the warpath consisted of only part of the tribe. The tribe were settled on their reserve in the States, and of these, one half were Catholics and the other half still held on to their Indian faith; the Indians turned out, the Catholics remaining on their reserve. He told me that Captain Howard had admitted that if the Indians had had as many men as he had they would have beaten him. Chief Joseph prided himself upon conducting the war upon the principles of civilized nations, and announced that he made no war upon citizens or women or children, and did not kill any but soldiers. His men shot much better than the United States soldiers; they said: "We shoot kill soldiers, why not soldiers shoot kill us?" Then showed in their sham fight how they, riding back, hung on by one leg, shooting from under their horses' necks, or jumping off, availed themselves of any cover, and thus lost but few men, while they killed a great many soldiers. Bovaris thought that they were very hardly used by the Americans. The Government gave enough, but it did not reach the Indians, and he quite acquiesced in my suggestion, that if an Indian agent or two had been hanged for thieving, the life of many a soldier, not to speak of the lives of the Indians, would have been saved. Our worthy friend Sophy treated our men to a good deal of whisky, and we began to feel the disadvantage of being a mile over the frontier and in the United States, where intoxicants are permitted. Charlie's head was strong enough to resist the influence, but poor Dan, who turned in without coming to the campfire or having his tea, looked very muzzy in the morning. Poor Bovaris! on my visit in this fall of 1884 I found that he had fallen a victim to the six-shooter of Sophy's brother in a quarrel, when too much whisky had been drunk.

September 22nd. Thermometer 20°F.; estimated height above the sea level, 3,675 feet. After getting our things together, and purchasing a good little horse from Sophy for 50 dollars for me to ride, as "Old Pal" was too idle, and "Winona" too footsore, and having arranged to leave these animals behind us to be picked up by the men on their return, we pushed on with the others. Sophy gave L. and myself a special bottle of whisky for ourselves. We bought some martins' skins, and some small ermine, and some buckskins for shirts, and a few Indian things at her store. I had a pair of moccasins and deerskin gloves from a Kootenai squaw, who had barely finished them for me in time for my departure. Then wishing everybody a most hearty goodbye, we travelled off along the plain. We went for 12 miles along our back trail as far as a tree where we had noticed a huge wasp's nest hanging, and it became a good landmark as "The Wasp's Nest Tree." Thence we took a right-hand trail for about four miles, where we found some Indians camped. I was ahead, leading my horse, looking out for a good place to camp, when I came upon four Indians, the best grown fellows I had seen, young fellows—I fancy they were Nezperces. The best-looking buck of the lot, a roughish fellow, called out, "You one man?" "No," said I, guessing pretty easily the object of the question, and holding up four fingers. "We four." I called to L. to show my friend that if he meant going in for trying to take my horse, or any game of that sort, he had more than one to tackle. Looking at my gun, which was in its case, "Winthorsty?" said he. "No," said I, seeing that he wished to know if he was in the neighbourhood of a Winchester repeating rifle; "Martini Henry," which, as he could have never heard the name, had somewhat the effect upon him of the celebrated reply to the Billingsgate fishwife. I am afraid that upon this occasion I was led to deviate from the truth, in giving so murderous a character to my modest fowling piece: but the address of the noble savage made me think it prudent to suppress the fact that my only arm was an unloaded gun. It must be remembered that we were in the States, and amongst somewhat hostile, or at any rate very doubtful Indians, and they all insisted in believing I was a "Boston" man. By this time, however, our men were coming up, and we turned off to select with them a place for the camp, which we made in a little wood in a hollow by a stream, and the Indians went back to their own teepees. This was the only time I ever saw any Indians whom I mistrusted; I may have been wrong, but I think if I had been alone my horse would have been taken, and I should have been set afoot. They had with them about 60 horses, some branded "H" on the left shoulder and flank. Poor Dan was very seedy, and could not take supper, and L. exhausted the pharmacopoeia of his neat little medicine case, but as Dan got rid of the physic pretty well before he had swallowed it, I don't know that it did him much harm. He was, however, very much pleased with L.'s attention to his distress, and we christened the camp "Medicine Camp."

Sunday, 23rd—Up at 6:30. Washed in the creek; very cold, thermometer 12°F. The Indians went off with all their horses, seated on their horses—they were smart-looking fellows—four men with squaws, and the horses, some of them, very good. Charlie quite thinks that the band have been out horse stealing. Seeing the bad effect of the drink, we made up our minds to point the moral, and L. bringing out solemnly our whisky bottle, poured it all away on the ground as a libation to Sir Wilfrid Lawson; our poor fellows looked upon it as an act of sinful waste. Poor Dan had been very sick all night, but made up his mind to drink no more whisky, and we wondered how long "the devil a saint would be."

After skirting for some distance low, swampy ground, we passed through a grove of high tamaracks, pine, and balsam spruce. At the end of this we came to some curious rocks, and through a small glen to alkaline lakes, where we dismounted to get a shot at the ducks floating on them. We could not manage to get near them, and, after a couple of miles' further ride, found ourselves at our stream again, with some good grass, the best we had seen on this side of the mountain, and we camped about 4:00 p.m. I went for a stroll with my gun, as we heard geese go over our heads. I found that in the piece of meadow on the edge of which we were, the flood water had been over many acres of what was beaver meadow; but the dam had been broken through, though it had been deeply flooded some 10 weeks before. I saw plenty of sign of deer, but nothing within shot except two spruce partridges; I picked up a shed horn, skinned a bird which L. had killed, had tea, and to bed at eight.

Monday—Up about five. Thermometer 13°F; height, 4,425 feet. I took Charlie, with a gun and my rifle, to a little alkaline pool, where there were marks of duck and geese, but nothing on the water; had a long beat over and round the meadow, but found nothing. It was quite clear that game in abundance had been here at no great distance of time, but I think it was pretty clear also that there had been a hunting party over the ground. Breakfast at seven, for an early start, and we saddled and got off at 8:30. We rode through woods much the same as yesterday— no sound, except the hawks, jays, and crows. Fine bold rocks to the left side of the valley through which we rode by the side of a river, spreading out occasionally into lakes, where it has met some natural obstacle, or has been dammed by the beavers. We found one or two lodges of dirty-looking Indians close by the side of the trail, and met a squaw and two children who were gathering roots. At eleven we came to the first lake, on which we saw some duck, but not within shot. The water is beautifully clear but shallow, and the trail runs close by the side of it, up and down banks beautifully timbered, but there was too much smoky haze to see the hills beyond. Where the first lake runs into the second we saw an Indian fly-fishing; he was the first whom I had ever seen engaged upon such an occupation. I went up to him, and saw that he had a rough pole and a big hook and thick line, but he was handling it very dexterously, and had landed some beautiful trout on the bank, of about four pounds weight each. We left him, thinking we should find another fishing place, but did not. If ever I find myself in that country again, I will not, if I know it, pass that spot without becoming better acquainted with the fish, as the stream running down from the upper into the lower lake made exactly the water where big trout might be expected to lie. A great quantity of pine and tall dead poles, the remains of a fire. Getting to the top of a knoll, after scrambling across an awkward gully, L. and I sat down for a smoke, and waited for the pack train. After they came up we mounted again, and had a long ride, and got into drier ground, having left the stream far away to the right. We began to be anxious about a camping ground for the night. Riding on a long way ahead, I found nothing I much liked for camping, and so turned back; but L. coming up, we halted on a little spring by the edge of the wood and camped, after a very long day's ride. We named this camp "Spring Creek Camp." I felt sure I heard water falling at no great distance, but we did not like to venture further. It turned out that the river was but a very little way from us. We had a very cold night, though the thermometer only went down to 18°F. We made a huge fire in a big fallen Scotch fir, and I tried to take a photograph of this the most picturesque scene we had on our ride, but without much belief in the possibility of its success—a want of belief which has been fully justified by the event, as no photograph appears of this lovely night view.

Tuesday, 25th—Up at six; started at 8:45. In about 20 minutes sighted a pretty lake, into which we had heard the water falling during the previous evening, and which we should have much liked to have reached for camp. As I rode along the lake I was indeed struck with its beauty in spite of the haze, a lovely triplet of islands running down the centre, the bush glowing with autumnal tints. We rode through woods of big tamarack all day, of which during the last part of our ride we noticed a different variety; it was a larch, with rough bark more like our English tree, and more branchy than those we had hitherto seen, in which there were few branches except at the top. This variety lasted for a few miles, and then we got back into the same sort of tamarack we had seen along the rest of the route. About 3:30 we came to a large grass plain, but no water; I rode on through a little belt of trees to a second smaller prairie, and after that to a third, with a slough at the nearest end; the pack train coming up, we camped there. A big dead tree had been barked for pine gum, which the Indians and trappers take from the trees, and, baking in the bark over the fire, use largely for chewing. On a part of this tree, which had been barked, was a rude sketch, which I gather to have indicated that the sportsman, whether Indian or trapper, had secured by his skill some deer and beaver; two animals of one kind, and five of another, and probably the mark indicated to him the whereabouts of his cache. We had a very comfortable camp here, and the grass was splendid for our horses.

Wednesday, 26th—Up at six. Thermometer 20°F. Very foggy, with smoke, so that Dan had a long walk after the horses, having passed them in the fog. This is a large grass plain, with islands of Scotch firs about 130 feet high, and 10 feet in the girth at 5 feet from the ground. It must be a desperately bad place for fly in the summer, and I much doubt whether at an earlier period of the fall the flies and mosquitos would not have made camping here impossible. Every indication of game; plenty of geese passed over us out of sight. L. had carefully plucked a chicken overnight to be ready for breakfast in the morning, and deposited it at the root of the fir which stood close by our tent. On going for it in the morning, he found that it had been eaten by an owl which had been whistling in the tree during the night, and the India rubber tube of my filter had been gnawed by a rat, and was thus put *hors de combat*. Off at 9:30; I rode ahead of the pack for about five miles through wood, and after that about four miles through a piece of prairie land. It was still so hazy that we could not see what the country was on either left or right, but some trees on the left seemed to indicate the course of a stream, and after about nine miles we came to the river, running very slowly to the southeast at the bottom of a cutbank of white clay. I got down and picketed my horse to a big stone and waited for L. After he came up I rigged out a fishing pole, and with a bit of string and a hook, with some cake and a fly, tried for fish in the sluggish creek; nothing to be got. Rode on to the crossing of the creek, where there had been a bridge made for driving cattle, but it had been washed away, so we had to flounder through the muddy bottom. We came to a settlement where a Mr. Moore had, by an irrigating ditch, got some capital oats. He said that he should have 100 bushels to about two and a half acres, and he had also a good crop of turnips, and the best potatoes, according to Dan, that he had ever seen. We then rode on about three and a half miles further to Sweeney's store and had a talk with a Mrs. Foy, who had come up from Galatin Valley, which she had left on account of the June frosts. Sweeney, who has been here three years, reports well of the settlement, and altogether Flathead Settlement promises well. About 4:30 I took Dan to find my way across the creek to the river, and after some difficulty in wading the creek, a walk of about two and a half miles across a bushy plain brought us to a broad sluggish stream, some eighty to a hundred yards wide, running between sandy banks. Walking by the side of the river my feet sank so deep into the muddy sand as to show that the crossing of it with animals was impossible. We found a series of meadows with a good deal of scrub, and by the side of the river, in a little hollow, there was laid up a dilapidated bark canoe—interesting to me as the first which I had come in sight of. No fish to be got, and it was clearly too late in the year for them in this water. Back to tea, and afterwards had

219

a long talk with Mr. Sweeney, who brought us a paper with an account of the driving the golden spike on the completion of the North Pacific Railway, and with it a map of the country, which was very useful, and told us more of the land through which we had traversed than we had been able to make out before. We made up our minds to strike south for the Pend d'Oreille River at Batiste's ferry, and thence to make for Ravalli, on the North Pacific Railroad. It had been getting so cold the last few nights, that L. and I made up our minds that we would each have a roll in a separate buffalo, and we found the comfort of doing so on this occasion; each of us taking one to himself, got well rolled up, and found it much warmer. We heard that the settlement that we were at was known by the Indian name of "Selish."

Thursday, 27th—Up at 6:30. Thermometer 21°F. Off at 9:30. Rode along a slough on the right hand to get a shot at the ducks, but could not get near them, though they were very plentiful. I shot one snipe and L. a duck, but in the absence of "Boxer" we could not retrieve them. After five miles, passing through some settlements, we came to the Great Flathead Lake, but there was so much haze and smoke that we could not see the opposite bank, and this we regretted the more, as I believe it to be one of the most magnificent views in this western country, a statement entirely borne out by the report to me by our men after their return. We went on for about 18 miles through a wood, approaching and leaving the lakes at intervals; about 10 miles further we met a wagon, the driver of which told us that we should save 2 miles by taking an Indian trail on arriving at a pine about a mile further on. The driver must have been making slow progress, as I arrived by the side of the pine in about five minutes, and from there had the longest and dullest ride of the whole route, at the end of which we came down a very steep pitch and camped among some black pine a little above the lake at 5:30. On our way down we passed a curious rock standing by itself in the wood; this had clearly been consulted by the Indians as a medicine stone, as was apparent from the bits of plate and sticks and other trifles that had been stuck about it, and the great amount of foot tracks round it. I walked down to the lake to have a wash. I put up a couple of fool hens, as the spruce partridge is called, but had not my gun. Tea at 6:30. Our provisions were getting low, so we were reduced to bacon and a small tin of soup, but had a comfortable night.

Friday, 28th—Up at 5:10. Thermometer 28°F. Took my gun and washing things down to the lake and had a bathe, though I found it uncommonly cold dressing, as there was a little bit of a breeze. Saw no birds and got back to breakfast at 6:30. I took an interesting photograph of a Scotch pine, which I measured with my clinometer, and found to 126 feet high: it was 13 feet in girth. We started at 8:45, and leaving the wagon trail, I cantered on between the hills. It was a very bleak piece of country, and reminded me very much of the "Valley of Desolation," near Lynton, in Devonshire. I hunted through the scrub along the bottom of the hills, but found no game, and riding on five miles came to Dayton Creek, where there were plenty of geese, and at a distance of 200 yards from the bank there was a pretty island. Still very hazy, and no view to be seen of the opposite shore of the lake. We had lunch at 12:45, having ridden 12 miles, and I managed during lunch time to get two teal. For the last four miles the prairie was all burned. On our getting to the ferry we found that our men, who had been ahead of us while we were looking after some chicken, had just gone across the river, which runs down from the lake and which here takes the name of the next lake which it falls into, and is called Pend d'Oreille River. It is here about a quarter of a mile wide, and for the greater part of its width is shallow at this time of the year, with about 50 yards of deep rapid water, which has to be swum; our men, however, had crossed in the ferry boat, a luxury not generally availed of by the Indians, which is not surprising, as we found that the fare for carrying across eight horses and four men, necessitating only two journeys across, was six dollars. The ferry boat was a very good conveyance, and on landing I saw that the ferryman's daughter, a half-breed girl, Miss Batiste, had plenty of freshly caught trout, so, as we had no time to fish that evening, after we had made camp, I went up to the hut to buy some. She wanted 50 cents for four trout weighing about one pound each. I grumbled at the price, but the young lady assured me, pointing below the waist, "I stand, so deep, cold water, catch them." So I said no more, but took the fish and paid my money, and very good they turned out to be. There was another girl in the cabin, who had come over with her mother to enjoy some fishing with their friends. She was the daughter of old McDonald, at a place 23 miles off, for which we were bound after leaving the ferry. Having made a supper on the trout, which were excellent, and on our teal, we enjoyed our quiet camp by the side of the beach which fringed the river, and after many pipes we turned in to bed. It was a warm night, the warmest we had had since we left Standoff.

Saturday, 29th—Thermometer 29°F. We made up our minds to give our horses a rest, and to fish and see the falls. After breakfast L. and I walked down the river. Very fine, but a series of rapids rather than falls, with a total descent from the lake down to the first pool of about 60 feet. L. got a little sport shooting, and in the afternoon I went down to the pool, about two miles off. It was a curious walk, the trail leading along a high bank, continued round the bluffs. I had gone by myself, having arranged for Charlie to follow me. I fished in the pool below the rapids, both with fly and grasshopper, but got nothing. There must be some very beautiful scenery below the pool. The pool itself is about half a mile wide, and from its far corner the river again descends; below this there must be rapids and some very fine pools; this part, however, as far as I know, has not been visited. On Charlie coming up to me we scrambled out to a rock in the middle of the stream.

The water was tumbling, as will be seen, around me on all sides, and the noise and rush of it all round the rock was very impressive. After some more equally unsuccessful attempts to lay hold of fish, we worked our way back upstream, and found that L. had caught some good trout with a fly above the falls. As today was Michaelmas Day, I had been particularly anxious to have a regular constitutional dish, but, as no goose had been shot, we were obliged to keep the feast of St. Michael on trout and bacon, and rice and apples. From a hole in the bank near our tent two skunks emerged during the night, and wandered about the camp, seeking what they could steal, but we, having been warned by the owl a few nights ago, had put our grub quite safe out of their reach, and out of the reach of the magpies—"meat-birds," as they are called in the North-West—who are always on the prowl. During the night I caught sight of one of the skunks coming up to the tent, and, clapping my hands, I chivvied him off. In the morning we missed a bag with some biscuits, and after hunting about we found that the skunks had dragged it to the mouth of their hole, but could not get it in, and had not seen their way to get at its contents, so we retrieved it unharmed. The two elderly ladies, Mrs. Batiste and Mrs. McDonald, rode past us on their cayeuses to fish in the river, and there they sat perched on the top of them in the middle of the stream fishing with grasshoppers, and they kept the poor brutes standing up to their bellies in the cold water for three hours. They came back with good bags full of trout. The two daughters had been fishing out of the boat a little nearer the lake with grasshoppers, and seemed to have been almost as successful as their mothers.

Sunday, 30th—Woke up, after a warm night, with the thermometer at 35°F. As our horses were getting very footsore, and Dan's horse had a bad back, we hired a wagon of Batiste at a dollar per day, the men to take it with our horses, and to bring back 40 lbs. of freight for him. We had a long and interesting talk with Batiste of the early days of this country. I learned from him that the word "Selish," the name of the place at which we had camped, is the Indian name for "Flathead." Mrs. McDonald passed us, to have an early fish, as we were hitching up. We left at ten o'clock, L. and I riding as usual, and Charlie with a passenger in the wagon. It was a nice firm turf to ride over, with occasional breaks of trees, but all very dry in this very rainless district. After 12 miles we stopped at the Muddy Creek to lunch. It is a very good stream, the mud being at the bottom and not in the water; it winds through some good prairie land, very well adapted for farms. From there three miles brought us to Crow Creek, and riding on through very similar country for 22 miles, we reached McDonald's at three in the afternoon, and passing his house, we camped within about a quarter of a mile of Hudson Bay Creek. All this country was considered to have been within the Hudson Bay Territory, and the settlers there still look upon themselves as Hudson Bay men. We found, as before, that the fish had all gone from the creek, and that Mrs. McDonald and her daughter had done quite right in leaving this, their home, to go up and catch, with their neighbours, some of the fish that were passing down from the lake. A more likely looking stream for fish it would be difficult to find, and the fishing poles lying about showed that much work had been done there. After tea McDonald came and sat by our campfire.

He is an old Hudson Bay man, who had come over from Scotland in the year 1838, had been in London, and liked to hear of it, and in return gave us many tales of the old time and old-timers; of his journeys up the Columbia River, through the Rockies, between Mount Brown and Mount Hooker, and from that point down the Athabasca, and so on to Churchill, on the Hudson Bay, and back, doing the round trip between April and December. This had been his regular work in the Hudson Bay Company's service for many years. He had come out in 1838, and had married his Flathead wife, by whom he had several children. He was a remarkably fine-looking old fellow, about 70, with a touch of the military about him; a good tall figure, bronzed face, and grey hair. He was above all things taken with my Norfolk jacket, and said, "I should like to see you at the Horse Guards in your helmet and cuirasse." I informed him that was not my dress, and that a horsehair wig and silk gown was the dress in which he would be more likely to find me; but he had an idea that tall men like L. and myself must be soldiers. He sent us down some beef, which was excellent. A heavy rain came on during the night, and it was very wet in the morning, and everything on the low ground on which we had pitched our tent was very soppy. It cleared a little before starting, and then settled into a drizzle.

Monday, October 1st—A ride over prairie, with an occasional farm, for about five miles, brought us to the Jesuit Mission of St. Ignatius. It is quite a neat little village, with a nice church, and a comfortable little priest's house, and a house for the Sisters. They are building an academy, and are planting fruit trees. The Mission is on the Flathead Reserve, and is now under the charge of Father van Gorff. I believe that they receive some payment from the United States Government, and most certainly they deserve it, as they are doing really good work. It is the only Indian place I have seen in these wild countries which seems really flourishing and successful. The stream has been turned to work a sawmill and to irrigate some land. We looked into the church; on all the chairs and desks and benches, was the Catechism of Religion in the Flathead, called by the French "Pend d'Oreille," and in the native "Kulli-Spelm." The letter "i" signifies the root "camus," "kull" meaning "eater," and "spelm" is translated "plain"; it is also said to signify peoples or tribes, and thus Kulli-Spelm means either, the plain of the root-eaters, or the root-eating tribes. McDonald told me that the number of edible roots which the Indians have is very considerable. Camus is a root of a plant like an onion, with green leaves, and a flower like a lily. They boil it and dry it and prepare it with great care. Kous is a sweet root, and sklocum a much-prized vegetable, with a taste like peppermint. After leaving St. Ignatius, we passed first through some land, which will make magnificent farm or garden land, when watered from the ditch which the Fathers are training round it. After that the trail wound down among some hills, where we lamented more than ever the smoke which obscured the view. In about four miles from the Mission we reached Ravalli, on the North Pacific Railway, and our pleasant ride was at an end.

Ravalli is named after a Jesuit missionary priest, and here we found a store and restaurant kept by Duncan McDonald, a son of our friend of the night previous. Ryan, the passenger whom we had brought with us from Batiste's ferry, invited us to dine with him, an invitation which rather to our loss we accepted. They had told us that the train would not come in till six, but just after dinner, and before we could get our traps, it ran in, and we found ourselves fixtures by the banks of the Jocko, the stream which runs down past Ravalli, till the next afternoon. We made the best of it, and camped by the line, near the teepees of some Nezperces, and then went for a walk up the line toward the east. We found many signs in the empty boxes of provisions and empty champagne cases of the enormous Villard picnic that had spent some hours here a few days before. The three trains that had conveyed the guests to the Pacific had stopped here with their burden of German, Yankee, and English notabilities. During their stop, an excursion had been made to the Butte Macdonald, to enable some of the excursionists to see a bear's winter cave. Our informant gave us many amusing accounts of the party.

"They seemed to think they were roughing it," said he; "but they had got as much to eat and drink as they could put away, and more than was good for them; they had good beds to sleep in. They were the most helpless set of men I ever saw: they could not ride, and they were too fat to walk."

I hope, however, that none of this description had any application to any of our English friends who may read this book.

"What were they talking about?" said we.

"Well, they were mostly standing about together and talking about London. There was one very jolly-looking old chap with grey whiskers, who did not say much himself, but was always laughing at the others."

The great practical joke, however, seemed to have been, that young Duncan taking the party up to the bear's cave, going on ahead himself, wrapped himself in a buffalo, and when the party arrived at the hole of the cave, in a breathless condition, he gave a growling grunt, at which the visitors took to their heels (as well they might), remembering (to use a North-West phrase) "that they had not left anything behind them."

After we had gone to bed we found ourselves disturbed by the noise in an Indian tent; they were playing their favourite gambling game. The game is of a most simple character, and is played by two rows of men sitting opposite one another, to one of whom is handed, on behalf of his side, two small pieces of wood—one marked by being bound round or stained in the middle of a different colour, and the other left plain. The player who receives the two sticks on behalf of his side takes one in each hand, and throwing up his arms and, ejaculating, shows them, and putting his hands behind his back, changes them quickly from one hand to the other; the whole of his side shouting and crying and singing, so as to distract if possible the attention of their opponents, and prevent the eye watching the movements of the player. At last, when his hands are still and held behind his hack, the bets are made, small bundles of sticks or "chips" indicating the amount that is wagered by the one side against the other, the side on which the player sits backing him, the opposite side laying against him. A certain number of these sticks counts for a blanket, so many more for a cayeuse, which has been named by the party wagering. When the bets have been arranged, the man with the pieces of wood produces his hands from behind him, and if the parties wagering against him have been successful in naming the hand in which the marked stick is, the stakes are handed over to them. This game began about ten o'clock at night, and having been kept awake by the yells and shouting until nearly midnight, I got up and went out to look through the tent at the scene that was going on; but I soon returned to bed, and the game and shouting continued till late on into morning. Some of the

Indians were pretty well cleaned out, and we noticed next morning one Indian who was pointed out as having lost everything that he possessed; a more wretched-looking played-out gambler I don't think I ever saw, as he stood by a bush with no blanket and very little clothes, looking thoroughly chapfallen, twiddling his fingers, whittling a bit of stick, and utterly miserable. I succeeded in getting a photograph of the tents, and then turned my camera round to take an Indian and squaw who had wandered up to have a look at my operations. There was still the same belief that I was a "Boston man," and was after no good; the buck rolled his face up in his blanket to prevent his likeness being taken; the little squaw, however, by his side, with a woman's curiosity, could not help looking over her blanket and laughing. These Nezperces are a very fine set of men, but are entirely given to gambling and horse stealing, and are, I believe, as worthless a set of fellows as is to be found in the North-West. About noon we prepared for our departure by train, sitting down by the side of the line, and at 1:45 it rolled in, and we got all our goods on board, said goodbye to our friends Dan and Charlie, not forgetting a kindly pat for the animals that had carried us so well, and with a wave of the hand steamed away up the slope of the mountains.

We soon began to ascend, and rose 1,100 feet in the short piece up to the Agency, going up the zigzags. The wood was not unlike much that we had driven through in the Rockies. About the summit and on the descent we crossed several canyons on high trestles, one being as high as 225 feet, very well and solidly built of wood. On our way down we seemed in several places to be almost doubling back, and reached a good grassy plain sloping to the south. We arrived at Missoula, a dull-looking town at the very end of a valley, having descended 700 feet. Thence we went up the Missoula valley, the water for the first time being muddy in colour. Many Chinamen's camps along the road; the men not very strong in physique, but looking clean, and every tent having a stove. The day was closing in as we left Missoula about 5:15, and it was late in the evening when we arrived at Helena, the mining capital of Montana, and being met by some friends, soon found ourselves in a tolerably comfortable hotel.

The town of Helena is situated in a gulch on the southeastern side of the spur of the Rocky Mountains. At its back are the high hills, and in front, to the northeast, a broad plain extending away in the direction of the Prickly Pear Canyon. It was founded by a party of miners about the year 1862. They had been prospecting for many months, and had nearly come to the end of their stores, but made up their minds that they would have one more fling, and arriving here, christened it "Last Chance Gulch," and began to wash for gold. It turned out to be the richest of all the washings that they had undertaken and the minerals extended up into the hills and away into the gulches lying to the north and west. So rich, indeed, were these washings, that, after an interval of some years, it is well worth while to rewash the remains, and excellent wages are being made. The water had been brought by a ditch from the hills many miles distant, and yields an excellent water power, and every convenience for bringing out the gold. It was in those days one of the most lawless of camps, and was one of the scenes of the wild tales of the "Vigilante Committees." It is now a thriving town, with good stores, and some pretty houses in the neighbourhood, not least the house of the Governor of Montana, who has found a quiet home here after many years' pleasant residence as ambassador in Turin. Our hotel was, of course, in the unfinished condition which is pretty well the characteristic of all places of this sort in the Territories and in the North-West.

We spent our first morning in going over the Assay Office, where the Government business is conducted by a Pole, and certainly it would be difficult to find any place where information is more prompt and more accurate. The accurate work of the analysis interested us very much. The afternoon of our first day we spent in driving round the neighbourhood of the city, and the next day we prepared to go up to see some mines that had been discovered by a hardworking man in the neighbourhood, better known to his friends as Tommy Cruise: the mines have now been sold by him to an English company. On arriving there, after a drive of some 12 or 15 miles, we found the mines in complete process of development; the superintendent was ill, however, and we were not able to go into the drift. I obtained some specimens from the output, and we heard very golden accounts of the mine itself, and no doubt, from what we saw, if properly and carefully managed, it will turn out a valuable property. A great amount of machinery was apparently being put up for milling the ore; the only doubt that seemed to be entertained was as to whether it would be necessary, in order to make it a complete success, to smelt rather than to break up. We had a pleasant drive home, heightened only by the excitement of a runaway animal, which necessitated my taking refuge in the carriage of a friend, who was passing us on the way down from the mines. Toward the close of the evening I lamented the absence of my gun, as I came within shot of one or two sage hens, a bird which I had only seen once near to the Missouri in our journey last year. As I had not had the opportunity of going into the mines, and wished very much to see for myself how the lodes lay, I arranged that night, after my return to Helena, for a drive into the hills to the northwest, to see some mines which had been opened there. Early next morning, having obtained a carriage, I started off. At about four miles from Helena, we came to a hot spring— so hot that I could scarcely put my hand into it; there was a very large flow of water, and the sulphur smell indicated it to be a valuable mineral sanitary resource, for which purpose indeed it appeared to be used to some slight extent. A very long drive up a steep hill brought us into the snow and to the edge of the mines, and we found there an old man, to whom they either belonged, or who had a considerable interest in them. I went round with him, and picked up some half-dozen specimens, which I placed in a bag and took back to Helena. It was four o'clock in the evening when I arrived there; taking my specimens with me into the Assay Office, I deposited them, and paid some 12 dollars for the six analyses. Upon my asking how soon they could be ready, I was told by three o'clock the next afternoon. I mention this to show the wonderful promptness with which this business (deemed so vital to the interests of Helena) is attended to at a Government office. As I was leaving the next morning, I left directions that the report should be sent to me in England. I had not communicated to anyone the numbers which I had affixed to my different specimens, so that nobody but myself could appreciate the value to be attached to the different parts of the assay. On receiving the report after my return, I found that the ore which I had taken from a dump outside one of the headings was of very high value in silver, and indeed the whole of these mountains seem to me to contain an enormous mass of wealth, almost if not quite equal to those which had been developed and are being developed with such great success at Butte City. There is a great deal of game in these mountains, and I think, of all the places that I have seen in the North-West, both from its agricultural capabilities, as a centre of a cattle-raising district, and from its mineral resources, Helena has a great future before it.

The next day we took our places in the train, which was tolerably punctual (coming in within three or four hours of its time), and we started off for St. Paul. It was so late in the evening that we soon found ourselves in our beds, and woke up next morning on the Yellowstone River, and so passed along the route which I had travelled last year to St. Paul. After a brief stay here we started for Chicago, where I parted from my most cheery and pleasant companion; as he was to return home via New York, while I went to join my wife at Toronto.

A pleasant day or two in Toronto amongst our old friends, prepared us for our homeward journey, but as I had not yet seen (and we wished to see) New York, we decided, as the weather was very fine, to make a run down to the capital of the States. We took the railway as far as Albany, and there, arriving early in the morning, got on board an excellent steamboat, and had a cold but bright sail down the Hudson River. The beauties of this route have been so often told that I need not take up time in describing it in detail. It is a most lovely trip. In approaching New York, the most notable features on the banks of the river are perhaps the huge Ice Houses, the enormous extent of which tell of the severity of the winter, and the necessities of summer-grilled New York. At New York we found at the "Windsor" as good a hotel as one could desire, so far as cooking goes, and the accommodation of the public rooms; the bedrooms are, for the most part, not up to the mark. Three days at New York passed away rapidly in seeing the shops, purchasing a few of the beautiful productions of Gorham and Tiffany, and a visit to a theatre and to the museum—which is at present in its earliest stage. I made a visit to the stores of some excellent seedsmen, for the purpose of obtaining the seeds of the different deciduous and nondeciduous American trees. The weather not being fine, I had not an opportunity of seeing that which I had specially looked forward to—the exhibition of the trotting of the famous Jay I See. We were very much pleased with the Overhead Railways; their failing is the same as that of our underground lines, viz., the being worked by locomotives. They are very charming in themselves, and the great length of the distances to be traversed makes steam an absolute necessity. They are, however, by no means objects of delight to the foot passengers along the streets, who are liable to receive some dirt from overhead. The absence of cabs in New York is made up for by the universality of the stage or small omnibus and the tramcars, and these, added to the Overhead Railways, make locomotion in New York very convenient. The big bridge uniting Brooklyn and the city is a most wonderful construction. In the afternoon of Sunday, after attending a very good service at the English Church, we took our places on one of the steamboats to see the harbour, and the next day started off after dinner for Albany. Arrived at Albany we found a comfortable hotel and had a good supper. The next morning we started off early by the railway which runs along Lake Champlain to Buffalo. We were more pleased with the lake scenery even than we had anticipated, and certainly these two little journeys on the Hudson River and along the Champlain Lake present scenery as beautiful as anything I have seen in the States. From Buffalo a rapid run brought us to Toronto, where a stay for another day or two prepared us for our homeward journey viâ Montreal and Ottawa. This road had now become to me a well-trodden route, but these two cities never lose in interest. We found ourselves on board the *Sardinian* at Quebec, where in the morning of Saturday, October 27th, the boat was joined by the Governor General and the Princess Louise, on their homeward journey from the land where they had made themselves so useful and so well beloved. A rather rough passage after we had passed through the straits brought us to Liverpool. Our passage was unfortunately varied by a somewhat alarming accident to my wife from her slipping down in a heavy roll of the ship, and considerable alarm was felt that a fracture of the ankle had been the result. A gay sight it was in the Mersey on Monday, November 5th, as we steamed up with the Royal Standard flying at our main, accompanied by three or four of the largest ocean steamers, that had arrived in the Mersey on the same night, and so a conclusion had come to my third pleasant and very interesting journey in the "Western Land."

Chapter VIII

∴

In this concluding chapter I will, if the trial has not already run to too great a length, venture to detain my readers while I sum up the evidence which I have given, with a review of the present condition of the country as the result of the work that has been done during the last four years in the establishment of towns and settlement of the land, with a parting glance at the present condition of the inhabitants, both native and settlers, with some details which the experience of those four years have given us of the land and the climate.

Upon the first point, I think I may say beyond all question that the choice of the sites of these towns do but little credit to the selectors. There is a tale, I think, in Herodotus, of the reputation under which certain colonists had been gibbeted to all time as having selected some particular site for their town to the neglect of a neighbouring site eminently superior, and I should think some future Milesian will hand down under a like malediction the persons who preferred the muddy banks of the confluence of the Assiniboine and the Red River to the superior convenience of Selkirk or the unsurpassed slope at Brandon.

This adoption of Winnipeg, however, may perhaps be excused as the natural successor of Fort Garry, for the choice of which by the Hudson Bay Company in the older days there were sufficiently good reasons, and it is at last emerging from its mud. They seemed to touch the bottom during the September of this last year, when their Main Street was an impassable waste of mud; before October was out they had made a noble advance in wood planting and block pavement, and the streets will for the future, I hope, be rather convenient for than repellent to traffic. No such excuse as to selection can be made for those who preferred the wretched Pile of Bones to the beautiful valley of Qu'Appelle, or for the placing Fort McLeod on the most exposed and inconvenient piece of prairie that could be found, to the neglect of the many excellent sites on the lower benches which the industrious washings and deposits of ages by the Oldman River and the Willow Creek would seem to have elaborated as a site for a future town.

The one well selected town site is that of Calgary, and there is not the slightest reason why the other towns should not have been equally well placed. In this matter, however, the country is young enough to remedy by a process of a survival of the fittest the mischief done by a faulty selection.

In the settlement and development of the land the work that has been done may be mentioned under its two heads, viz.: Agricultural and Ranching or cattle raising. It is perhaps to the former of these that attention would be more popularly directed, although the latter will have greater interest for those who have capital enough to enable them to take up the work.

The bad harvest of 1883 had left Manitoba in a very depressed condition; following, as it did, on a sudden collapse of the inflated prices of the boom of the two preceding years. There were not a few who almost despaired as to the future of the North-West; and if, in the then condition of things, the harvest of 1884 had been equally disastrous with that of 1883, it would have taken many years before Manitoba would have recovered from its depression, and the North-West would probably have shared its adverse fortunes. Fortunately, however, this was not the case, and an experience has been gained enabling us to calculate more nearly the probable average result of a series of good and bad seasons.

The boom which had nearly proved fatal to Manitoba, was the result not only of the very large expenditure upon the railway which had centred there, but also of a desire prematurely to hasten on its development instead of allowing time for the natural spread of population. There has been too much of an attempt to press into the country persons who have not sufficient means of their own, and who are dependent upon borrowed money, and this money has been borrowed at a very high rate of interest—so high, indeed, as to illustrate in its worst feature that "borrowing dulls the edge of industry." However fertile may be the land, however excellent the climate for the production of high class grain, the rent that has had to be paid by many of these Manitoban farmers—in the shape of interest upon the capital which they have had to borrow in order to purchase their implements, stock and seed—has been such as to leave a very small margin for their own sustenance. Let me more fully illustrate what I mean.

A settler has taken up a homestead of 160 acres, 100 acres of which will be as much as he can break up and work by his own unassisted efforts. He has required for the purposes of thus cultivating his farm something like £300, or $1,500, and the cost to him of this money has been at the very least 10 percent. We will suppose that his farm, thus worked, yields to him 20 bushels to the acre, and, although this may seem to many, who have had brought before them highly coloured views of the fertility of the prairie land, to be but in poor contrast to those accounts, I think that anyone who will count the grains of corn upon an average ear will find that 20 bushels to the acre is by no means a low average. The yield, then, of our settler's 100 acres would be 2,000 bushels. He will have to consider his wages, his cost of threshing, and the interest that he has to pay. His wages may be taken to cover all the work that has to be done on the farm during the whole year and the repairs of his implements. If wheat is selling at 50 cents a bushel, the value of his 2,000 bushels, being 20 bushels per acre for 100 acres, will be $1,000, and placing against this the $150 interest on a borrowed capital of $1,500, which will have been sufficient to pay for seed, and $70 for threshing, there will be left to the farmer $780, which gives him $65 per month for his wages and board. I have taken the wheat crop alone as the receipts side of the account, for I am supposing a settler at such a distance from a town as to have practically no market for other commodities. It will be said that the farmer has on his homestead an additional 60 acres, upon which he should do something more than feed his horses; I quite agree that this is so, and that if he has a little more capital to enable him to run a mixed farm he will do much better; but it will never pay him to borrow it at 10 percent.; and what I am rather pressing here is that if this is the state of things which is shown, with low prices I admit, but upon a fair average harvest, and if the misfortune of two or three consecutive bad harvests should fall upon such a man, there would be little, if anything, left to provide for the interest which he has to pay upon the capital borrowed to start his business. With no such load round his neck he may get on fairly well, because things must be very bad indeed if they don't leave a sum sufficient to maintain himself and his family, and he need have no other outlay.

It may be said that a man would fairly expect to have a greater acreage under the plough; this, however, can only be done with a greater expenditure of capital, and a large annual payment for labour—difficult at any time to be obtained, and raising a still greater difficulty in the case of an adverse season. It may be that such seasons will come seldom upon us, and we may eliminate now altogether the great fear which was present to all who were interested in Manitoba in its earliest days, of a plague of grasshoppers. With an increasing settlement any danger on this head may be considered as very largely diminished, if not to be entirely put on one side; but, while I believe that the grain that is raised in Manitoba will grade second to none, I do not think that, under the present circumstances of agriculture there, the yield will ever be proportionate to that which is obtained in our more highly cultivated eastern lands.

I have already in various parts of my book pointed to the extent of agricultural land, and how great an opening there is still for settlers desiring to take advantage of the offers of the Canadian Government. Let us see how the matter stands for such a person. A settler is entitled, as I have said before, to 160 acres of homestead, and 160 more of pre-emption, and all this can be obtained at a cost of about £80. Supposing he has means enough to be able to take up this land, to break it up, and fully develop it, it may be considered as comparable with English land at say 5s. an acre, and we may put the capital value of such land at about 15 years' purchase, or £3 15s. per acre. If this land is in a good situation, where the value is likely to be maintained, and within a reasonable distance of a railway—for it must be borne in mind that unless the grain land is within six miles distance of the railway, it would be very difficult indeed to bring the grain to market at anything like a remunerative price—the total value of such a property would be £3 15s. into 320 or £1200. This then may be considered as the capital value of the property which, at the expenditure of the sum I have mentioned, a person in taking advantage of the offers of the Dominion Government will be able to secure to himself.

Having said so much on the agricultural part of the question, I will now give my experiences of cattle ranching. I have taken for this purpose as the foundation of these remarks an article of mine which appeared in the *National Review* for the month of August, 1883, and from which, by the permission of the Editor of that periodical, I have made a pretty copious extract, qualifying what I have there written by the results of the more complete experience which I have gained in these matters since the date of the article.

The increased demand for animal food, and the consequent increasing price of food-producing animals, is not limited to our own country; and although when I first turned my attention to the cattle growing grounds of the North-West, I did so in the full expectation that the completion of the Canadian Pacific Railway, some improved transit of the lakes, or the opening up of the Hudson Bay route, might, at an early date, enable us to import into England good two-year-old Shorthorns, either as in-calf heifers for the cow house, or as feeding steers, to be fattened into prime beef upon our cheap feeding stuffs, at a price scarcely higher than that which little rubbishy Irish cattle of the same age at present command in Bristol market, I have, after my fourth year's more full and practical acquaintance with the subject, come to the conclusion that for many years the increasing number of the Indians who, under treaty, have to be fed with beef, the crowds of immigrants and of men engaged upon the railway works, and the Mounted Police, coupled with the necessary retention of the females of the herds for breeding and filling up the land, will keep in the North-West for many years to come all the cattle that can be reared there, and will allow of no surplus for export to Europe.

No doubt there may be considerable difference of opinion as to how much of this North-Western country may be considered as really valuable for cattle raising, but as we can only admit as suitable as a breeding district land where the cattle can live through the winter without housing, and for this we can only take such country as will afford shelter in its coulées and riverbeds from the winter storms, we are limited as to the area; and although a very considerable amount of this prairie land has ever been tenanted by the buffalo, and therefore may be considered as valuable for cattle, yet we must remember that the buffalo ranged free, and was enabled, when the storms came on, at once to change his quarters and to work south; but with our own cattle there is not such opportunity of migration, and we are, therefore, more limited as to the area that we may consider available. Guided, therefore, by this principle, we must limit ourselves to the country lying between 49th parallel on the south and the banks of the High River, which is about 50° 30'. This gives us an extent in latitude of about 80 miles, and in longitude we may take from the base of the Rocky Mountains (including in this the foothills and the Porcupines) to such a point to the eastward as will not throw the cattle too far from the streams in summer, or from the shelter in winter, an average distance of some 50 miles, and this gives an area of about 4,000 square miles. We may calculate that this ground will carry cattle at the rate of 10 acres to every head, or 64 head to every square mile. This will give us a probable total for this district of 256,000 head, and taking it that when the country is stocked, one-fifth of them are saleable in each year at an average price of $65 or £13, we get from the whole area an annual yield of about 50,000 head, of the value of $3,250,000, or about £650,000. Undoubtedly, however, by skill and care, this number may be considerably increased. If we take a larger area, extending our limits further to the north and to the east, so as to include about 5,500 square miles, we should have to limit the number of cattle over such area, allotting not less than 15 acres to every head—so that our calculation of the number which the country would carry would be practically the same, as I am crediting the whole of this territory with the capability of holding its cattle in winter. I believe, however, from our experience of the two last winters, that over a great deal of the land of the northern part, it will be found that the snow lies to such an extent as to prevent the possibility of cattle wintering there unless during exceptionally mild years. The cause of this great difference of climate in lands so closely adjoining, is undoubtedly to be found in the "Chinook," the warm wind which comes down in the winter, melts the snow, and displays freshly springing green grass underneath by which the cattle are kept going. I have not in my Journal described the "Chinook." It was as we were coming away from Snowy Camp, and during the time that my eyes were nearly closed when I was suffering from snow-blindness, that I felt a hot breath on my face from the southwest, as if it came from across some heated surface. I at once recognized the wind I had heard described, and turning round, called out to Mr. Craig that it was the "Chinook." But where should this hot wind come from? On the side from which it came towered the high range of the Rockies, and the enormous fringe and deep covering of snow and ice would, one would have thought, have effectually cooled, long before it reached us, any warm breath of air that might pass over. It may be that it comes through the gorges and the breaks of the mountains, but certain it is that after passing through somewhere about the latitude of the Chief Mountain it bends up to the northeast in a course, if I may compare small things with great, parallel to that of the great gulf stream, which stretches across the Atlantic; but in passing over this high plateau, it soon loses the warmth possibly derived from its home in the Pacific, and melting and licking up the snow, it rapidly parts with its heat, and seldom, I believe, will it be found exercising its benign influence further north than the High River, and that country is left, therefore, to endure a winter of far more lasting snow, which, though it disqualifies it as a cattle country, by no means interferes with, but rather raises its value for corn-growing purposes. About this "Chinook," however, we have yet much to learn, and I am cautious in giving my views upon the phenomenon, with which we are not yet acquainted in sufficient detail. In addition to the wind of which I have spoken, there is the cold wind which drives the snow off without melting it, leaving the ground absolutely dry, and which is called "A Lemhi Chinook."

Cattle ranching can, as I have said, only pay when carried on in a country where the cattle can winter out. This on the prairie, with the probability of "blizzards" or high winds, with a low temperature of say 40° below zero F., when even the game goes south or seeks shelter beneath the snow, is obviously impossible. It is the shelter of the hills and woods and coulées in the country I am describing which enables cattle and horses under ordinary circumstances to winter out safely. So long as the snow remains in the condition in which it falls, the animal will manage to get at the grass which still springs green beneath it; the danger is when the snow has been thawed, and a sharp frost setting in again, produces a surface through which neither claw nor hoof can break, and we have to provide against that which would be fatal to the herd. The cattle man must get together in each year a sufficient quantity of hay to meet the emergency when it comes. The hay bottoms are numerous, and will cut as much as two and a half tons to the acre. As no haymaking is required, the grass in this dry air "curing itself," all the labour that is required is to cut and carry; and the prudent cattle man will during each summer and fall put up and fence in as much hay as he can, placing his ricks wherever he can on his winter range; and when the dreaded time comes, out will go his cowboys, break down the fencing round the ricks, round up the bands of horses and cattle, and drive them in the direction of the fodder, and the loss will, it is hoped, be comparatively small.

Up to three years ago the Canadian Government had no idea that there could he any value in the lands on the eastern slopes of the Assini Matchi, or Rocky Mountains; but a report reached Ottawa from the Mounted Police, that this district might not be altogether unsuited for cattle, and one of the officers gave such information as to lead Senator Cochrane to add to his large and well-conducted breeding farm in Ontario, a ranch in the North-West. Others, some simultaneously, some following his example, applied to the Government for lands in this neighbourhood, and Sir John A. Macdonald's Government granted leases in quantities suited for ranges of about 100,000 acres each. The leases are "by and between Her Majesty Queen Victoria, represented therein by the Honourable the Minister of the Interior of Canada," and the lessees, and are a demise of all the lands in the enumerated townships, with the exception of Hudson Bay lands and school lands, which the Government may withdraw from the lease as soon as a survey has been made. The term is for 21 years at a rental of a dollar for every hundred acres, and is subject to a forfeiture in case of assignment without consent. The lessee is bound to have on the ground within three years one head of cattle or horses to every 10 acres of the land leased; he is prohibited from grazing it with sheep, and from cutting down timber trees without leave. This leave is granted by the Mounted Police for all building purposes, for log huts, corrals, &c., and the Government reserve the power to terminate the lease on a two years' notice if the land is required for settlements, the rights of any settlers upon the ground at the date of the lease being protected, but new settlements during the currency of the lease without consent of the lessee being prohibited. The Government also takes power to withdraw any land containing coal or mineral, with any required water power, and to grant timber licenses upon the lands leased, and to withdraw from the lease any lands to which the Canadian Pacific Railway, or any other railway, becomes entitled under their grants or statutory power. I believe that this system of leasing by the Government is the best that can have been adopted for developing this pasture land; let me add a few words upon the system which prevails where the land has not been thus appropriated, but left so long as it is unsettled, as public lands. Free ranging, as this system is called, is producing ruinous consequences in Montana and the other grazing territories and States of the Union. The "Lone Star State" had, however, on joining the Union, obtained a recognition of their then existing rights, under which it continued to act, of selling blocks of land to individuals, and I believe the State of Oregon obtained by cession from the Federal Government their lands; in these States, therefore, lands may still be purchased in large blocks. In all the other States and territories, every precaution is taken against the possibility of any large extent of land accumulating in the hands of one proprietor in the first instance.

A similar state of things exists in British Columbia, and the result of it has been that, there being no proprietary rights over any land, any person possessed of cattle has had the full right to run them wherever he pleased. The payment to the State is a tax on the capital value of his herd, and the only control has been that of the Round-up Association. This is the real governing power, and to see the working of it we must go to an already established cattle country. We find a ready illustration in the neighbouring territory of Montana, south of the boundary line, where we have associations of the cattle men ranging over the basins of the Teton River, the Judith, the Musselshell, and the Yellowstone; in fact, of all the rivers which on the southern side of the Milk River ridge form the headstreams of the Missouri. Men having herds dispersed over this country are united in an association which holds meetings at which are fixed the dates of the two roundups of the year, in summer and in the fall, and rules are framed as to the number of men to be sent in proportion to the head of cattle on the books, the disposal of "mavericks," or calves that have left or lost their mothers, and are therefore unowned, of the disposal and distribution of its funds, and the admission or rejection of any new members. By these means some control is kept over the admission of additional bands of cattle. But subject only to this difficulty, under this system of free ranging every human being has a right to turn upon the lands, not homesteaded, any number of cattle he can bring there. I will take the result upon the territory of Montana. I must premise that the most feeding and valuable wild grasses, the buffalo grass, the blue joint and the bunch grass, do not come again when eaten down too closely. Of the buffalo grass I doubted altogether the seeding, never having seen any seed-bents on the plants until this last fall of 1884. In travelling through Montana from this Milk River ridge, through the basins of and over the divides between the Teton, the Judith, and the Musselshell to the Yellowstone, I passed through what has been some of the finest grazing ground in the territory. The rainfall is very slight, amounting to scarcely more than half an inch; no crops can be raised except by irrigation, and this can only be obtained within a limited distance from the river; and for scores of miles, as I drove over the prairie, have I found the herbage utterly destroyed and the value of the land therefore entirely gone, except on those belts near the rivers where irrigation is possible. If, therefore, our Canadian land is to be rescued from a like fate, I cannot too strongly press it as of the first importance, that leaseholders should be compelled to keep their cattle as much as possible to their own ranges, and should thus have the strongest interest to prevent the destruction of the grasses, and a further incentive will thus be given to protect their property against those fires which are the greatest danger to our lands and our timber in the North-West, and which would "set afoot" the leaseholder on whose land such an event should happen.

Such, then, are the food-producing capabilities of this most interesting and, I may say, most smiling angle of the North-West. It is small in its dimensions as compared with the other regions, but it has qualities which if the Canadian Government continue to carry out the prudent and yet liberal policy which it has inaugurated, by which capital may be brought to bear upon the natural elements of wealth, will make it of a very high value to the Dominion. If men are encouraged to develop, without squandering its resources, this land will long remain the pasture ground, the meat-producing district of the western portion of the Dominion, and the natural complement of the corn-growing districts of Manitoba, Assiniboia, and the Saskatchewan.

And now a few words as to the climate of Canada and the North-West. There is no greater mistake than to crack it up as if it were a very paradise. There are better climates in the south of Europe, but we have nothing so bad as the stink of the coasts of Italy, on the almost tideless Mediterranean, or the blood-curdling tramontanas of Italy and the Savoy. The climate of Canada is not a bit worse than that of England. The Australian colonies or New Zealand may have less or greater severities of winter, but I do not believe that the world will present a zone better adapted than is that of Canada to produce and continue in its vigour the human race. A night in a snowdrift in England would be at the best but a sleepless business, but out in the North-West roll yourself up in a blanket and a buffalo and don't be afraid of getting well into the snow, it will keep you snugly out of the wind, and if you have only a good lining of fat bacon and hot tea, you need not be afraid of anything. You will sleep soundly enough, the snow just crispling and crackling under you as it takes the cast of your body. Cover your head up well, or else if it should come on very very cold you might be led to oversleep yourself. Sometimes such a sad result follows, but I am told that the poor fellow is found with legs gently crossed, hands under the head, and no sign of suffering, and I doubt if you would ever have a chance of going out of this world so comfortably as you would do when rolled up in a buffalo in a snow bed on the prairie. You leave behind you the troubled dreams and waking sorrows of this world for ever—then, if this τέλος be not the end, but, as we hope, the perfecting of our being, awakened from the body's sleep, unwounded in life's worst agony, the soul shall pass within the gates of immortality. And we from among whom he is lost, may not raise too loud a wail of unavailing sorrow; for the enterprising explorer, as for him who feels a pleasure not to be found elsewhere in the exercise of the combination of those vigorous faculties which lures him on in the chase or adapts him for his special work, for the soldier as for the skilled mariner in his struggle against the powers of nature, it is the danger to be avoided, the difficulty to be overcome, that gives the zest without which life would be all too tame and dull; and if the danger turn out too real and the difficulty too great, if on the slippery rock or in the foaming flood the sacrifice of the life shall be demanded, and we feel how that too soon the knell has sounded, we must remember that it was that very brightness and energy, the loss of which we now deplore, which led him to the struggle, and that while he well knew the risks to be encountered, he would have been the first to have smiled at those who would have warned him from his task by fear of danger or possibility of defeat.

In order to give an opportunity of forming a more accurate opinion as to the climate I annex in an appendix tables of the thermometrical observations taken at the ranch of Messrs. Garnett at Pencher Creek on the Oldman River during the winter of 1882–1883, and that kept at New Oxley during the last year.

The subject of ranch life almost invites to something in the nature of a fifth Georgic on the merits and work of the cowboy, did I not fear that my present power of Latin versification would scare Mæcenas; but undoubtedly there is something in the exciting life of the cowboy which would have commanded the attention of Virgil if Augustus had bid him popularize the North-West. Let me, however, attempt a description in more sober prose.

A large share of the working of the cattle business falls to the cowboy, and to his care and industry the rancher must look in no small degree for the success of its results. He has not, it is true, to look after the management of the cattle in the manner in which those duties have to be discharged to our domestic herds, but none the less upon skilful handling at certain periods, and frequently in such critical emergencies as never occur here, depends the well-doing and often the actual safety of the animals. It is said that the cowboy has only to ride about the range, to see that his cattle are safe and undisturbed, and to do a good deal of galloping at rounding-up, and undoubtedly this description applies to a good deal of his time, but let me describe with a little more completeness his actual work. The spring has set in.

Solvitur acris hyems gratâ vice veris et Favoni. The Favonius of the North-West being a roaring Chinook, the grass begins to spring with its brightest green in the treacherous alkali swamps, and the cow, weak from nursing its calf through the stormy days of winter, is tempted to the generous pasture, but the white clay draws her down and the poor beast is helpless; at such a time, unless speedy help is nigh, she is lost; but the watchful cowboy knows where these holes abound, and is ready at hand, his rope is thrown skilfully over her, the end is twisted tight round the horn of his saddle, and adjusting his weight so as to help his little cayeuse, that seems barely as large as the floundering beast, but who strains every muscle in its little body to the effort, the poor muddy cow is by the joint efforts of horse and rider hauled safely to the drier bank. She is scarcely landed when another is sighted in a similar difficulty, and upon the energy of the boy during all the daylight hours of the May and June days the lives of most of these beasts, "mired down" and helpless to save themselves, depend. But the snows have melted on the mountains, the rivers are running down and cease to be roaring torrents, and cattle may be driven up; the roundup has been arranged by the Cattle Association, its captain has fixed the day and the place at which the camp will meet, and in proportion to the number of cattle on his books the stock owner sends his quota of cowboys, allotting to every boy his pick of five saddle horses, and adding to the outfit tents, a four-horse wagon, with a cook and his *batterie de cuisine* in the shape of a handy boilerplate stove as its furniture. The camp is made near some river, water, or lake, and the next day all sally forth under the orders of the captain, who details them in twos or threes to take the whole sweep of the country from this base line to the right and left to scour every coulée, canyon, bench, scrub, and bottom, and drive together to an appointed spot all the cattle that they may find therein. And charming gallops they are over the firm prairie, only spoiled by the too frequent badger holes into one of which even your quick-eyed cayeuse may put his foot as you are "loping" along, and then over you both come, and lucky are you to escape with nothing worse than the wind knocked out of you, or such a shaking as a stretch of a few minutes on the prairie may recover you from and enable you to proceed on your work. I will not trouble my reader with all the details, but I will suppose that we want to cut out the cows with their calves for the spring branding. We have all met again from our morning's ride, and the result is some 1,500 or 2,000 head gathered together of each sex and of all ages. We ride round them and bunch them up in a goodly ring, and the lowing and the bellowing gives a sonorous chorus, and while the three or four boys ride round and keep the cattle together, those who are going to cut out receive their instructions from the boss, who sits book and pencil in hand ready to tally. Presently the cutters-out ride into the ring among the cattle, and two of them have picked out a cow of the brand that is being looked for with her calf; they work them to the edge of the circle, and having got them there a push is made and cow and calf find themselves outside the ring. In vain they strive to double back among their friends; on the right and left they find a nimble cayeuse with its rider to give them a gallop round, a turn, and they find themselves on the prairie; driven off a few hundred yards they are left, the riders return to cut out another, shouting out as they pass the boss who is tallying, the brand of the evicted cow, "Crooked stick," or "OX," or "H," or "Shield," or "Half circle," or "Staple," or whatever else may be the description of the device that marks the hide of the cow; she is quickly joined by another cow with her calf, and the cuttings out become quicker, the galloping more excited, and the labour of the tallyman in entering up more incessant, until, at the end of a few hours, the work flags, there is a check, and it is announced that all the cows are out; it is late in the day, the cows and calves are herded off "over the hills and far away," and the rest of the cattle are marched off so as to be at least "lost to sight," and both parties are jealously watched by the night herders, until the following morning, when cows and calves are brought up to a large stockade fold called a corral, where the wood fire is lighted, the branding irons are heated, and not without considerable manoeuvring at length all are run in. Into the corral they are followed by some three or four cowboys on horseback, each calf is roped by the lariat round its heels or its neck, is dragged remorselessly and laid on its back, and the poor little beast, yelling sadly, is branded, earmarked and qualified for its position in the herd; and all being accomplished the corral bars are drawn and the bunch is again driven out upon the range. And now jump on your horse and come back to the rest of the herd, get one of the boys to give you a real good cutter-out, tighten your cinches, and you shall have some sport, for we are going to tally out the heifers, yearlings, and two-year-olds. Come into the ring, and we two will work together. Look out, here's a real bonny heifer, "I" on right hip, fit to go into any show yard in the old country. Hurry up. We've got her to the outside of the ring, drive at her and out she goes. Round the ring she races, but she doesn't intend leaving her friends yet, and is too quick for us this time, and doubles in again, and we miss her; but let her go. Never mind, try another; come, we've got this one away, but she can gallop quicker than we can, and up a knoll and over a runner she goes like a deer; but we have got her far away from the herd, and we can cut her off in her doubles, and she has to settle down to form the nucleus of another bunch that by similar effort is quickly gathered round her by all the cowboys, who, as each heifer is safely separated and deposited with the new bunch, calls out her brand to the tallyman, by whom she is duly numbered on her owner's books. When it comes to cutting out three-year-old steers and bulls, they for the most part, especially the latter, trot out decorously, shaking their fat sides as they rejoin their companions, but the yearlings and two-year-olds give you some fine galloping, which wants but little of the excitement of a burst in the old country.

But the cowboy's work does not end with his roundup. The summer is perhaps his easiest time, and when his cattle are on the range they require only a careful eye to see that there are no poachers, and that nothing is going wrong, and with the end of September his Fall roundup and Fall brandings come on again, and after that, with open weather in November and December, his work is still easy; but the storms have to be looked out for, and with January and February they will assuredly come, and with the thermometer 40° below zero F., out he must go; he must see that the cattle are not too lazily yielding to the numbing influence of the cold, and if the snow has frozen again after a thaw, so that the poor beasts cannot break through it, he must break down the corrals round the hay ricks which the summer foresight has provided, and rustle up his cattle and move them in the direction of the stored up provender; and dreadfully cold work it is, but his wooden stirrups with their leather coverings protect his feet from a cold which would render contact with metal fatal, his chaps protect his legs, and folds of flannel or many socks beneath his boots made large for this purpose effect a sufficient medium between animal heat and atmospheric cold, and mittens and a buckskin shirt keeps out the wind, while fur and Montana broadcloth keep in the heat; and if night sets in, he must trust to the shelter of the brush for the cayeuse, and a hole in the snow for himself; for the cowboy feels as he rolls himself in his blanket and lays his head on his saddle—

"Ours the fresh turf and not the feverish bed,"

and as he takes his time from the stars, he wakes with the earliest streak of dawn, and finds in his round of work health and, I believe, no small amount of happiness.

I should like to stop here. The boys know how well I like them, how happy I have been with them, and that they will have to go far to find a better friend, but this picture of work and health and happiness has its darker side, and nowhere a sadder one than where the wages of perhaps a whole year pass into the hands of a professed gambler, and the hundreds of dollars, which might have been so profitably invested, are squandered in the poor excitement of an evening at euchre, faro, or draw poker; and his ready money gone, he has nothing to live on but "jawbone," i.e. credit, and to "call his jaw" i.e. live on credit, till he has got further employment and more wages. The cowboy is in fact the Mexican vacchero in his dress and his language, having much improved, however, in habit and manner by a residence in a country where order is observed and law is supreme. It has probably not been his lot to mingle much in town life or society, or to become much acquainted or impressed with the external form of religious worship. A droll illustration of this occurred one Sunday at our ranch, when some travelling preacher being stormed up, remarking that it was Sunday, invited the inmates to a service. All duly mustered, and the preacher began a long prayer. One of our neighbours, an Irishman and a Romanist, but too much of a Catholic to allow sectarian differences to keep him away from the service, was on his knees bolt upright, with his hands crossed upon his breast following the minister. The opportunity was too irresistible to the boy sitting near, and putting his foot sharply under the kneeler's toes, he sent him flat on his face. Our friend gathered himself up again and said nothing till the Amen announced the end of the prayer, when he broke out with his fullest powers of malediction, furnishing a most vigorous antidote to the benedictory prayers of the minister. Order was, however, restored, and the minister proposed that all should join in singing. "I shan't sing," said another boy. "Well, but my friend, you will join us, perhaps." "Waal," said the boy, who was clearly under the impression that each one was to take a verse when it came round to his turn, "you can all do as you please, but I just warn you that I never could sing, and I never mean to."

There are many practices of civilized life with which the cowboy does not altogether fall in. A friend tells me that it happened at a ranch that the boss was in the habit of saying grace before meat. Now it is the custom of the North-West, that when you come to a ranch at dinnertime, you tie up your cayeuse or put him in the corral, and walk in, eat your dinner and pay your half dollar or dollar, and a cowboy arriving at dinnertime at the ranch in question, marched in, sat down at the table, and stuck his fork into a piece of beef. "We usually," observed the boss, "say something before we eat." "Waal, you can just say what you like," remarked the boy; "I guess you'll say nothing that'll turn my stomach."

I should perhaps add a few words as to clothing, for the information of any who may be inclined to try this life.

Persons who have travelled both in Russia and in Canada will scarcely fail to notice a point of difference between the two countries in the mode of wearing fur and skin coats. While the Russian wears his coat with the skin outside, and the fur inside, the Canadian always puts the fur outside. For myself I have no doubt as to which is the better. It seems to me that as the fur is the nonconductor, and the skin is most useful in preventing the air passing through, if you put the skin outside, you ensure having a surface as cold as the air can make it, the coldness of which is only prevented by the nonconductiveness of the fur from reaching your own skin; but put the fur outside and you prevent the cold of the air from reaching the skin surface, which thus adapts itself to the warmth of the person inside. Anyhow, there is this to be said in favour of the Canadian plan, that all the animals whose clothes we thus appropriate wear them with the fur outside; at least, I have never known one that adopted the opposite practice.

This may perhaps remind us of the argument which was addressed by an old stockman at a meeting of his cattle association. There had been a discussion as to the best bulls to be kept on the range, and an enthusiastic admirer of roans and "coloury" cattle moved a resolution "that this association deprecates the keeping of white bulls as tending to perpetuate a breed not sufficiently adapted to the rigour of our winters," upon which the old stockman rose to his legs: "I suppose, then, Sir, you think that the Almighty made a mistake when He put the white bears in the Arctic Circle."

I scarcely know what is to take the place of the buffalo robe, now that that most useful animal is passing away, unless indeed we import some long-haired kiloes as his natural successors; so long as they are to be had, I strongly advise every one to procure as good a skin as he can get, and if it is within his means a buffalo coat. Your hat will be a flabby felt hat in summer, and a fur cap in winter; a buckskin shirt is the only thing which will keep out the wind, and I have always found coat, waistcoat, and trousers made of the thick, closely woven blue pilot cloth, such as my friends Messrs. Silver and Co. will turn out, the most useful garments both in summer and winter; homespuns are of little use in that clear cold air, good cord breeches are very useful on the range, and as you will soon find the convenience and comfort of leather "chaps" or overalls it does not so much matter what the texture of these cords may be. Flannel for underclothing and for shirts is absolutely necessary, and good worsted socks and stockings are best got in England—have them loose, so that you may pull on two pairs in winter; and while for spring, summer, and fall high boots are the best, you will in winter have to take to felt boots and moccasins and any other possible contrivance for keeping the cold from your toes, and good buckskin gloves and mittens are an absolute necessity. A belt, to which will be attached your knife and your match box, is most necessary, as these two articles, upon which so much sometimes depends, are continually liable to part company with their master, as he rolls about on the prairie, and if you have lent one of them to a friend, the empty chain warns you to call in the loan before you part company. A six-shooter is, I am happy to say, no necessity with us, and is, I believe, anywhere more of an inducement to mischief than it is of a protection, and can only be very occasionally wanted to get a crack at a wolf, or, though rarely, at some large game. One last word for my cowboy. I have had it said to me when an adventurous lad is bent upon the North-West, "Isn't it a pity that with his education, money spent at schools and college, he should take to such a life as that?" "No, sir, not a bit of it; the better his education, the more knowledge he has in his head, not only of practical science, but of real book learning, the better calculated he is to enjoy and appreciate a life where the old world reading will constantly suggest in his frequent hours of solitude, pleasant trains of thought. I was lying on a hillside miles away from a human being, watching with interest the cattle grazing. Look at that young steer; that which was a patch of green when I lay down has been shorn by his rough tongue, and is now as brown as the adjoining. How exactly the same circumstance must in the days of old have been present to the mind of the cattle king, Moab, when he addressed the Senate of Midian and pointed out to them that the onpouring hosts of Israel would destroy their people "as the young ox thoroughly licketh the green things from the prairie"—and who shall tell me that the remembrance of this little bit of septuagint Greek did not give a pleasure to my leisure hour of contemplation which would otherwise have been absent. No, you will find in the North-West men perhaps your superiors in practical knowledge, and if you can bring into the common store even a little love for higher learning you will never find it superfluous or out of place.

With regard to our native races a question arises, of no little interest, as to their increase or decrease. I know of no matter connected with Canada which makes me more regret that my work there did not begin years ago than the loss of this opportunity of having seen those tribes in their better times, when big game, and the means of subsistence arising there from, was plentiful. I am now, at the end of these journeyings, which I have recorded, more than ever of opinion that as they have very little of the past to record, so they have no future before them. They may perhaps in the intermingling of their blood with the white man still be found even centuries hence to have left the mark of an old established family, and to have given some special character to an on-coming race; something perhaps of their sharpness of national sense may still be found in their descendants, but no chance could have ever advanced them to the position of a dominant race. As to what their numbers in the North-West were even a century or half a century ago we have no opportunity of calculating, and even prior to 1870 there is no reliable information. So far as I can learn from my friends still living there, who were amongst the whisky traders of 1872, there was about the headstreams of the South Saskatchewan scarcely a larger population than there is now; but it is fair to suppose that they were more numerous to the extent probably of 25 or 50 percent. At the Treaty payments last fall at Fort McLeod there was paid to the—

Bloods	. . . .	for 2,000 persons.
Peigans	. . . .	" 800 "
Blackfoot	. . . .	" 1,300 "
Sarcees	. . . .	" 800 "
and to these may be added—		
Stonies	. . . .	" 800 "
Total	. . . .	" 5,700 "

These people occupy the land between the Bow River and the 49th parallel, and by comparing the figures with my calculation given above of the size of this country, a pretty fair estimate of the former population of this, the best part of the Territory, may be obtained; of course no such population occupied the prairies to the east. During this last year there was undoubtedly a good deal of smallpox on the Blood Reserve, and there was a very large mortality; but there was an influx from the States, which made up for this decrease of population, and the last year's account may, I think, be taken as fairly indicating their numbers. Under our present system the Indians are undoubtedly increasing upon us; but I am, after some experience, still strong in my opinion that with proper management, they may be made useful for agricultural and probably for ranching work. I found this last year at our farm at Standoff, that some three or four had been working well in harvesting and potato-getting, and as they came in to their tea, and sat down to enjoy a good square meal, they reminded me much of the farm boys in the days almost gone by, while their absence of observance of those precepts of the Church Catechism which inculcate good manners, would give hopes for their future to the President of the Board of Trade. As an illustration of their ways I may mention an occurrence of the last morning I was at Standoff. A calf had been stolen and killed, and a reward of 100 dollars offered by bill on the wall to anyone who would give information. We are close to the Blood Reserve, and as soon as the bill was out "Marque-o-pis-toke"—*Wolf-cropped-ear*—a young Indian belonging to "White-calf's" band, came and gave information against a friend which led to his conviction. "Wolf-cropped-ear" had not received his reward, and came to complain to me about it. We had no language in common, but he soon made me understand his claim. He kept writing with his forefinger on the palm of his left hand till I understood he was alluding to a dollar bill, and then he pointed to the wall till I understood the allusion to the reward, and then with his hand to his pouch and a look of enquiry at the same time, he made me know that he was asking for his 100 dollars. I gave orders that the money should be paid, and although I believe that my good-looking young friend was a rank thief, and that he and his companion had agreed as to how they should spend the 100 dollars when the imprisoned one had served his six months, it was clear that we must keep our promise. "Marque-o-pis-toke's" parent was an example of the fatal effects of grasping after wealth; he had rejoiced in the name of "Minne-stokes"—*Father of many children*—but coveting after some Indian cayeuse, he had, after the Indian fashion, sold his name to a younger man, and had to be content for the rest of his life with the name of "Kippa-takke," or *Old woman*. This practice of selling a good name is generally attended with bad results. I know of one very fine old fellow down in Montana who sold his name, about the best which an Indian could have, and had for the rest of his life to put up with a nickname so bad that it could not be mentioned. Well, our Indians are very comfortable now. I had intended, but that my book has run on to too great a length already, to have said something of the Cree and Blood languages; but one observation I must make on this head. I should very much like, before it is too late, that the Kootenai language should be examined by some person acquainted with Japanese. This Indian language differs, as I have said, wholly in sound from any other Indian language, and the idea is strongly impressed upon my mind that this tribe had its origin in Japan, and that after drifting across the Pacific it was driven into the mountains by the wild tribes on the western seaboard of America, and that they have there remained, with perhaps some traceable remains of the language of the inhabitants of the Seven Valleys. The identity of the name of this Japanese district familiar to all lovers of Eastern porcelain was not, however, present to my mind when the idea of the similarity of the two races first occurred to me.

I may not close without a word of the tribute of praise to that fine force which made for us this country. The North West Mounted Police have been thus spoken of by an American in drawing the comparison between the two systems of the management of the Indians by the United States and by Canada.

"And now to speak of the fear some may entertain of the Indian tribes in these British possessions. In 1872–1873 there was formed what is known as the 'Mounted Police,' stretching their broad arm of protection westward to the Rockies, along the 49th parallel, with well-established stations throughout this broad domain, and we are compelled to state the British management of the Indian question is so far superior to our own, that I can but make the comparison with a feeling of shame.

"A single Mounted Police will ride hundreds of miles into the camps of those who have committed depredations on our side, have a 'talk,' and tell them so-and-so is expected of them; these instructions are known by each man, woman, and child, ere an hour, and are most sacredly kept; woe be to one who breaks it, he is dealt with most severely. That same messenger will return alone, demand the particular evildoer, and, in many cases, where they have had any misdeeds among them, their own men have brought the guilty one to the nearest post.

"What is the meaning of this dread, and the faithful performance of the laws? It can be accounted for but in one way: when the Indian enters their borders, he is told what is expected of him, and in return for faithful performance, he is provided for. The law is most rigidly carried out on both sides; the promises are always kept. The evildoer knows what to expect, and he receives it.

"A white man is as safe within the entire boundaries, let him go where he will and when he will, as he would be at his own fireside, so far as any Indians are concerned.

"Why cannot our Government handle them in the same manner? We do not live up to our promises to them, and they do not receive the one-half that the Government allows them: 'it passes too many hands.' Can they be expected to keep the peace under these circumstances? Here are 400 Mounted Police who do the work that 15,000 of ours cannot, or, at least, do not, do.

"There is a great defect somewhere. It is not our desire to find fault, but let anyone live but a short time near the boundary line, and these facts will be presented to him so strongly he cannot help but remark it, and this very improper handling of this question is what is, and has, kept back for so long a time the settlement of the finest lands our Government is in possession of."

I have only to add to this quotation the expression of a hope that the system that has been thus adopted may long continue, that no party political influence may lead to the appointment of men less qualified for this work than those to whom it has hitherto been committed. If on a large scale a system of this sort had been adopted in Southern Africa, how different would have been the state of things past and present in that Colony! And while their work has been so well done by the Mounted Police in securing the advance of the Dominion, allegiance to their Sovereign Mistress has held full sway, and the Indian has learnt to love the great white Mother as the embodiment of that true justice and respect for right which can be found only under a stable and solid Government. Thus have they helped to bind us all together as England and her Colonies should ever be bound, and to maintain the spirit in which she and her children should ever be united, however great the distance from Home to Home.

NOTE

An unfortunate accident to my minimum registering thermometer has prevented my verifying the daily observations at New Oxley, and I am therefore unable to add the table which I promised.

Endnotes

:~

1   The word Manitoba is shortened, as I learn from Archbishop Taché, from the Indian word Manitowapaw, meaning the abode of the Manitou, the unseen spirit or supernatural, the province taking its name from the lake.

2   "Old Pal," as I found out long afterwards that the old horse was named, was about the best known horse in the North-West; he had been sold and traded oftener than any other, and wherever we went he was recognized. He is a sagacious but wilful old gentleman, thoroughly to be relied on in swimming a stream, or in other dangerous places. I have ridden him many weary miles, till my legs ached in trying to urge him to a better pace; but take him after a band of horses and you'll find him a "real dandy horse."

3   I wrote this before leaving England this year, and having often warned my men on this subject, I little thought what a narrow escape I should have myself. The streams, as I have said, rise in June, and such a thing in the fall of the year has never been known by the oldest timer. On the morning of October 11, in the fall of 1884, I was coming back to Oxley from Stand-off with Craig in our light buggy. We were both clothed in all our thick clothes, and our horses had just got into the water of the Kootenai when an Indian called out to us. We pulled up, and he pointed to the high state of the river; and putting his hands on our horses' quarters and on the splashboard of the

wagon, gave us to understand that the river was "swimming." We wanted him to take one of his horses and go in for us to see, but he properly enough declined thus to corroborate his own evidence, and putting two of his fingers astride of his other hand intimated that if we would go across we had better swim our horses, and as I was quite convinced that he was right we determined to go back to the ranch to get one of our men to ride down with a saddle horse to try the depth. An American buggy is not to be turned on a short pivot, and as we advanced a little into the stream to get room to turn, the look and attitude of the Indian as he sat on the bank in a most composed manner, and rested his chin on his hand, seemed to say, "Well, if you are such idiots as to go on after what I've told you, it's your own lookout." Such, however, was by no means our intention, and, having got our man down we found that the horse was swimming before he was half way over, and so we worked our way upstream and across a longer ford. The river was coming down with very great strength, and if it had not been for that Indian to warn us, we should have got into the stream, our buggy would have certainly been turned over, and we should have both gone down.

4   I find that in 1884 the Old Agency has become the town of Choteau, and is, I am told, a most flourishing place, with two hotels, three stores, six whiskey shops, two billiard rooms, and a gambling saloon.